Content Area Reading, Writing, and Storytelling

Celebrate the Story!

[signature]

Content Area Reading, Writing, and Storytelling

A Dynamic Tool for Improving Reading and Writing Across the Curriculum through Oral Language Development

Brian "Fox" Ellis

Teacher Ideas Press

An imprint of Libraries Unlimited
Westport, Connecticut • London

Library of Congress Cataloging-in-Publication Data

Ellis, Brian, 1962–
Content area reading, writing, and storytelling : a dynamic tool for improving reading and writing
    across the curriculum through oral language development / Brian "Fox" Ellis.
        p. cm.
    Includes bibliographical references and index.
    ISBN 978-1-59158-701-9 (alk. paper)
    1. Storytelling—Study and teaching. 2. Content area reading. 3. Storytelling ability in
children. I. Title.
    LB1042.C486 2009
    372.67'7—dc22   2008025874

British Library Cataloguing in Publication Data is available.

Library of Congress Catalog Card Number: 2008025874
ISBN: 978-1-59158-701-9

First published in 2009

Libraries Unlimited/Teacher Ideas Press, 88 Post Road West, Westport, CT 06881
A Member of the Greenwood Publishing Group, Inc.
www.lu.com

Printed in the United States of America

The paper used in this book complies with the
Permanent Paper Standard issued by the National
Information Standards Organization (Z39.48–1984).

10 9 8 7 6 5 4 3 2 1

CONTENTS

GETTING THE MOST FROM THIS BOOK

There is a growing body of research confirming what storytellers have long known, namely, that the way the brain works, the way people learn, is based on the personal narrative. *Storytelling is the key to great teaching and dynamic learning.* In many cultures, stories are the vessel for conveying important ideas and giving listeners a sense of connection to the world around them.

As modern educators, how do we use storytelling and oral language development to teach reading skills and improve writing? How can we use stories to teach science process skills, social studies concepts, math and problem solving? This book, through a balance of pedagogy and practice, is designed to give you the skills and confidence you need to become a better storyteller. It also includes dozens of great stories and classroom-tested lesson plans to improve students' reading fluency, comprehension, and vocabulary. With better reading skills, students' ability to learn content will improve. By telling their own stories, students will also learn creative writing strategies.

Most important, *students will find their voice,* and in so doing become empowered as active players in their education!

The preface and introduction explore current research while providing you with the inspiration to learn and tell stories. Each chapter explores one content area: reading and writing, social studies, science, and math. There is also a series of interdisciplinary units near the end of the book. One unique aspect of this book is that each chapter includes several exciting, easy-to-learn stories and black line masters for a ready-to-use handout.

This book draws the map and provides the compass to help in your search for best classroom practices, providing a well-balanced mix of research and application. *Oral language development is the most important step toward better reading and writing.* This is more than a passing trend in education. Storytelling has always been one of the most important tools in a teacher's bag of tricks, and recent research only reinforces this fact.

We all know that most folks skip over the preface to get to the meat of the matter, but in this book, the preface is its beating heart. My first recommendation is that one read the Preface and Introduction to gain a better understanding of the importance of storytelling.

Chapter 1 will give you a solid foundation toward improving your storytelling skills as well as helping your students to develop the skills they need to be better storytellers—thereby improving their reading and writing skills. Take the time to play the theater games with your students; please play along, and everyone will have a better appreciation of the art of storytelling. One of my goals is to create a workbook for teachers who then share their newfound passion for storytelling with their students.

If you frequently use one idea in the whole book, it should be the section on storytelling as a prewriting and rewriting strategy in Chapter 2, pages 71–74.

Almost every lesson comes with a story. The stories in this book are written to be told. Read them over a few times, practice with friends or family, and then tell a few tales of your own. If at first this feels like too big a challenge, the stories are also written to be read aloud. As you read the story a few class periods in a row, feel encouraged to act it out, change your voice, step into character, put the book down and TELL the tales! Also know that it is normal to forget parts and make them up as you go!

If you are looking for ideas on a specific subject, jump to the index at the back where lessons are listed by content. Whereas each lesson plan is written to stand alone and take place within a typical classroom period, there is a scope and sequence within each chapter and an overall flow, tying the chapters together. This is not a linear sequence but, more like the World Wide Web, there are links back and forth between sections, so if you are looking for a follow-up lesson or a way to take the idea a step further, you will often find a link in parentheses.

Chapter 6 not only provides several interdisciplinary units that use stories to tie the curriculum together, but also provides a model, a format for creating your own lessons based on the stories you like to tell.

Chapter 7 provides information for building an integrated community of learners through storytelling. Invite your janitor, lunch lady, principals, and parents to tell stories to your class. Organize a storytelling festival in your school where students from each grade level perform for other classes. Invite a professional storyteller to help train students, teachers, and parents, and get everyone excited about storytelling! Help your students apply for the National Youth Storytelling Showcase where they can win a vacation, cash prizes, and, most important, the confidence to speak their minds—articulately.

It is vitally important that you put the book down and tell a story, but the most important thing to do is to create space for your students to stand up and be heard!

The format of each lesson is written to make it easy to learn quickly and use. Lessons begin with both the **STORY TITLE** and **LESSON TITLE** in large, bold type to provide a quick headline encompassing the main topic.

The Story: Every story is written to be told! I have worked hard to create text that leans toward the oral tradition, rather than the flowery, literary text of most collections of folktales. The illustrations provide a storyboard to help you remember the key elements of character, setting, plot, beginning, middle, and end. The stories are also formatted so that it is easy to copy the two or three pages of text so your students can learn and tell these tales. But in a pinch, don't be shy about reading aloud with dramatic effect!

Grade Levels: The most appropriate **Grade Levels** are listed, but most lessons are easily adapted up or down, and all of the stories can be told to almost any age level.

Time Estimate: Knowing the reality of timed, belled periods, I have worked hard to format most lessons so they can be accomplished in the 48.53 minutes of a belled period.

Objectives: These are standards-based goals for each lesson; they provide a quick assessment of whether this is the right lesson for your class during your unit of study.

National Standards: Storytelling is clearly much more than fluff. Instead of saying this is one more thing that teachers must do, the most important objective of this book is to demonstrate that by telling stories, you are accomplishing many of the national standards. With most schools working toward a national standard of education, I have included references to the national standards as published by the various teachers associations, including the National Council of Teachers of English, the National Academy of Science, National Council for the Social Studies, and the National Council of Teachers of Mathematics.

Background Information: Prior knowledge is the key to success. In this section, you will find the facts you need as well as some tips for telling the story.

Materials: The most important ingredient is an active imagination! Other than that, paper and pencil will often suffice. If additional materials are needed, the emphasis is on common items that every student should have or books and Web pages found for free in any public library.

Instructional Procedures: There are many similar but different formats for writing lesson plans. I strive for something easy to follow with flexibility built into the design. There is an **Introduction** written for the instructor as well as background information for the students. The **Activity** is spelled out in step-by-step directions. There are suggestions for grading and evaluating student success in the **Assessment** section. And I always include **Follow-up Activities** that include links to other lesson plans within this book.

Comments: Because all of these lesson plans were classroom tested while I was teaching or presenting an artist-in-residence program, I wanted to share with readers some additional thoughts about adapting the lessons to unique situations. Here you will find tips for getting the most out of the experience. And because I love success stories, I often share an anecdote about when this particular lesson went well and what I learned from my students. If you have a comment about a lesson, please send an e-mail, and I will gladly post it on my Web page for other educators to share in your success!

I would love to hear how the ideas in this book have been useful to you, and if you send me a lesson plan, I will post it on my web page for others to share. Enjoy the adventure and share your stories along the way. I look forward to hearing from you!

Sincerely,
Brian "Fox" Ellis
www.foxtalesint.com

PREFACE

WHY TELL STORIES?

Why is storytelling one of the most important things you can do in your classroom?

Anyone who has been teaching more than a few months knows that teachers are being asked to do more and more with each passing year. Over the past twenty years, educators have seen a constant onslaught of state-mandated curriculums, underfunded federal initiatives, administrative directives, and parent committee requests.

Instead of telling you that this is one more thing you need to add to the long list of duties and responsibilities of a classroom teacher, what I am saying is that simply by telling stories, you are accomplishing many of the demands put upon modern educators by parents, principals, and state and federal legislators. Simply telling stories, and allowing your students to tell their tales accomplishes most of these state and federally mandated goals!

- *Storytelling* is the perfect embodiment of whole-language pedagogy while encompassing phonemic awareness.

- *Storytelling* is interdisciplinary, integrating language arts, math, science and social studies.

- *Storytelling* teaches higher-level thinking skills.

- *Storytelling* addresses the needs of students who have different learning styles.

- *Storytelling* provides opportunity for cooperative learning and building social skills.

- And most important, *Storytelling* builds intrinsic motivation and self-esteem, even in students who are labeled as hard to reach.

As professional educators, it is important that we understand the pedagogical implications of our work. The following essay provides the theoretical basis for the use of storytelling in the classroom. The aim is to lift storytelling out of the fluff of something offered as a reward for good behavior and to place it firmly at the core of the curriculum where it rightfully belongs. My hope is that storytellers and teachers will clip this article and make copies for the next time someone questions the need for spending more money on storytelling programs or the next time someone says, "Oh, she was just telling stories."

Why Tell Stories?

I. Storytelling is the embodiment of whole language and phonemic awareness.

In every storytelling experience, there is speaking and listening and motivation for reading and writing. A good story, well told, embodies phonemic awareness in a whole language context. Through storytelling, students are actively involved in developing the skills necessary for effective public speaking. Namely, students learn the importance of clear articulation and dramatic interpretation. They gain firsthand experience in the performing arts and an opportunity to enhance their self-esteem.

No other medium develops listening skills as effectively as storytelling. Stories stretch the audience's attention span and imagination. Storytellers teach the audience etiquette and the important concept of knowing when to listen quietly and when to listen actively by joining in. Listening to stories also improves vocabulary, which in turn improves sight reading.

Any storyteller or librarian will attest to the fact that stories stir a student's intrinsic motivation to read more books. A story performed for the class will be checked out of the library for months to come. Also, reading aloud is an important step in learning a story for the telling. Comprehension improves, as evidenced by their retelling and interpreting the story. And in a storytelling classroom, students read each other's writing, so writing is given more purpose.

Writing for a specific audience is a dynamic way to inspire, inform, and motivate better writing. Students can write their own versions of a wide variety of tales, using basic folklore as a template for learning story form and story grammar. Through reading and listening, students are exposed to the joy and rhythm of language, which directly translates into clearer, more fluid prose. Through performances, they get immediate feedback on their writing, which improves editing skills. As a storyteller in residence, the comment I hear most frequently is that storytelling not only inspired students to write more, but that it also gave them the skills they needed to become better writers.

These four aspects of language development improve simultaneously: As students are involved in storytelling (or listening or reading or writing), they gain language experience and develop skills that in turn help them in the other three areas. Storytelling, more than any other medium, exemplifies this process and leads to a measurable improvement in the ability to communicate effectively.

Within the context of stories, lessons on grammar, phonics, spelling, point of view, plot, setting, characters, and many of the practical applications of language skills are given depth and perspective. You can meet different learning styles by moving back and forth from the whole to the parts. The debate between whole language and phonics is an unnecessary argument between extremists. Teachers working in the classroom know that different students need different types of instruction, but storytelling provides the best context for these varying strategies.

II. Storytelling is interdisciplinary and the perfect thread for tying the curriculum together!

Storytelling can enliven most any topic. Within every story are many **language arts** lessons and opportunities for reading and writing skill development as outlined above. Events from **history** come to life in a story. Within every tale is information about the culture where the story began and opportunities for exploring cross-**cultural bio-geography**, or for looking at the ways in which a culture relates to its ecosystem using folklore as the lens. Embedded in the story is a wide array of facts and information about the cultures' relationships to their environment and their applied **sciences** such as agriculture, fishing and hunting, herbal remedies, and architecture. Stories contain conflicts and hurdles to overcome: an opportunity to teach problem solving and applied **mathematics.** Within every tale there is an **art**istic mural waiting to be painted, a **dance** waiting to be choreographed, and **music**al ballads, chants, and songs in **foreign languages** waiting to be sung.

If you would like to study another culture, one of the best ways to gain an understanding of its values, beliefs, and way of life is through its stories. Through its folktales and mythology, you can see a group of people as they see themselves. A careful reading of the tale will answer a variety of questions about a culture's political system, religious beliefs, economics, and market systems; its relationship to the environment; and its family and social structures, as well as what types of food, shelter, and clothing are used. Ways in which we are different and alike can also be highlighted to build a bridge between cultures. Not every story will answer every question, but it is amazing how much we can learn from a single story. For example, in *Jack and the Bean Stalk,* we know they are farmers because they have a cow. They drink milk and eat bread and beans, which is a balanced vegetarian protein source. We also know that some people are poor like Jack and his mom, and some are rich like the Giant, so they are class-conscious. A single mother raised Jack. They believe in magic, the beans, and the supernatural—the Giant. In some versions of the story, they talk about the king, so we know their political system was a monarchy.

Other branches sprouting from that vine include a math lesson in which you can calculate the value of the cow versus the bags of gold, the golden harp, plus the golden eggs. Was there a profit? For science you can study domestic animals, milk and egg production, measure the rates of fast-growing beans, and explore the smells of "English Men" and olfactory sensitivity. You can decide as a class if Jack was guilty as a thief. You can hold a court case with students serving as judge, jury, defense attorney, prosecution, witnesses, and court reporters. In language arts you can teach phonics, vowel sounds, and rhyming patterns by writing your own rhyming verse like fe, fi, fo, fum. You can write songs and translate the story into a musical production. Students can make a quilt of Jack Tales with each square representing one of his adventures. There are limitless interdisciplinary lessons waiting to be discovered in every story!

If I were in charge of a school that used an interdisciplinary, theme-based approach to education, I would begin each year with a unit on storytelling. Each grade level would focus on a different type of story: fables, myths, legends, fairy tales, historical fiction, tall tales, and the like. This would ensure variety for the children as they progressed through the grades. Following this unit, every other theme-based unit throughout the year would include an element of storytelling!

Stories can be used to introduce a concept or explain important theories. They can add depth and authenticity in the middle of a lesson. Students' stories are a clear indication of their ability to process the information and a valuable assessment tool at the end of a unit. Stories can become the warp upon which a teacher weaves the threads of the various content areas. Most importantly, storytelling and creative writing can tie the curriculum together and integrate ideas.

III. Storytelling is a perfect tool for meeting different learning styles.

A well-balanced performance includes the spoken word and vivid descriptions for the **auditory learner.** It includes clear imagery, pantomime, and the possibility of props for the **visual learner.** Stories contain emotional depth, conflict, and strong feelings for the **affective learner.** There is also an opportunity to participate, sing along, or act it out for the **kinesthetic learner.** And by including a good balance of each learning style, the storyteller is also challenging the audience to interact with the material using the other modes of learning and thereby stretching the learning skills of each audience member.

IV. Storytelling is a dynamic way to teach higher-level thinking skills.

Before, during, or after a story, the listeners and teller can **recall** basic facts, names, places, and the order of events; **summarize** the story, explain the main idea behind the story, or **interpret** the moral of the story; **predict** the end of the story having heard only the first half or brainstorm and problem solve ways to get the main character out of crisis; **compare** and **contrast** various characters in the story, different versions of the same story, different but similar stories; **classify** the story by type, the characters as good or evil, or the settings by geographical region; **judge** the villain in a mock trial; **evaluate** the teller by a predetermined scale that looks at technique, audience response, and interpretation of the material; **observe** the main character in a new, imaginary setting, make **inferences** about his behavior based on what you know; and **apply** the information learned in a story to the creation of a new story.

With the popularity of retelling classic tales from other points of view, there is a delightful opportunity to teach higher-level thinking. Students can listen to or read the traditional story of the three pigs first and then the modern story from the point of view of the big bad wolf. They can make a Venn diagram to compare and contrast these stories. They can find three different classic versions of the story and evaluate each of these for ease of reading and enjoyment. The class can hold a mock trial to judge the wolf. Students not on the jury can predict his guilt and give three reasons why they hold that opinion; collect and discuss these papers at the end of the trial. Students can also rewrite another traditional tale from a different point of view.

This is just a partial list of possibilities—things that all children do naturally when given the opportunity. Using both critical and creative thinking skills is a natural part of the complex cognitive processing going on in the mind of a child during any storytelling experience.

V. Storytelling is cooperative learning.

Storytelling requires a sensitive interdependence between the performer and the audience; it is a duet of well-rehearsed oration and attentive listening. A cooperative audience and a performer who knows how to elicit the imagination of each listener are the key to a successful event. The experience forces the alert storyteller to honor the needs, desires, and constant feedback from the audience. The audience members in turn learn to follow the lead of the performer, to open their minds and hearts to new possibilities.

In a more pragmatic vein, there are ample opportunities in a storytelling lesson to utilize the theory and practice of cooperative lesson planning, namely:

Circular storytelling games are activities in which someone begins a story, develops a plot or introduces the character or setting, and then hands it off to the next person who adds to the story before passing it to the next person, and so on around the circle.

Peer editing is a dynamic way to get feedback from a partner or team. Students read or listen to a partner's story and then help the partner to work out the details of the plot or correct spelling and grammar errors.

Small groups each choose a story and act it out as a skit.

Teams research the history and background of a story. Using the jigsaw strategy, each member of a group becomes an expert on one aspect of the story.

These are just four ways to capitalize on the benefits of cooperative learning in a storytelling unit. What are other ways to build on these models for helping students to learn the social skills and team building strategies so necessary in today's workforce?

Storytelling Is So Much More

Furthermore, research has shown that **storytelling motivates hard-to-reach students;** they participate more and learn more when storytelling is involved in the unit. More times than I can count, I have heard teachers say something along these lines: "DeMarko hates to write. He likes math and numbers, but he usually forgets to put his name on the paper. That is how much he hates writing. But after listening to stories and telling some of his own, he has written a three-page paper!"

Storytelling also elevates self-esteem by giving students a chance to perform—a chance to shine before their peers. Usually it is the class clown (ME!), the one who is always in trouble (again, this sounds familiar), who gives the best performance. These students have not been given a chance to show their strengths in the typical classroom where being quiet and following orders are encouraged. Their spontaneity and sense of humor are constructively channeled by this experience, and they achieve success. Isn't it easier to build success on success? Logic and anecdotal research shows that the communication skills learned in storytelling are carried over into improved test scores in other areas because one must first learn to read and write to comprehend the science or social studies text.

Storytelling teaches coping skills and problem solving by giving listeners role models and alternatives to violence for dealing with life's everyday crises. Stories allow listeners to know that their problems are not so unusual, that there are others with the same problems—others who have survived creatively.

Storytelling develops empathy and cultural tolerance by exposing listeners to other cultures through the universal language of stories. Stories celebrate our differences, affirm our basic humanness, and build bridges of understanding.

Storytelling stimulates creativity by exposing students to a broader range of experiences, lifestyles, and ways of thinking. If creativity is the ability to recycle old ideas into new situations, then the more raw material or life experience, the more potential for creativity. Stories can give students a chance to travel the world, back and forth through time. Listeners can try on different hats and empathetically experience other lifestyles—rich fodder for feeding the imagination.

Storytelling binds listeners to their community by giving them a sense of history and cultural identity. We know that who we are is much more than a skin-encased ego. Who we are is a culmination of decisions made by our forebears and the aspirations of those yet to come. Stories put our small lives in perspective so we grow larger in awareness of I and Thou.

Storytelling can teach moral development and the difference between right and wrong in a nonjudgmental and non-preachy manner. By demonstrating through metaphor the implications of poor choices and the success one finds in correct behavior, stories model appropriate conduct. Fables, parables, Jataka tales, and koans have been passed down for thousands of years as guideposts, as gentle reminders that we are human, we make mistakes, and we can learn from our mistakes and go on. For these reasons and more,

Storytelling is one of the most important tools any educator can use in or out of the classroom!

INTRODUCTION—INSPIRATION

Many years ago, I was a luncheon speaker at the Illinois Conference for the Teachers of English. Sitting next to me at lunch was an African American college professor and one of his students, a sharp young man who was receiving an award for preservice educators. During lunch the three of us fell into a conversation about storytelling and the similarities between the African "Griot" and the American Indian "Carrier of the Talking Stick." A lightbulb came on for me that has been both searchlight and guiding light for much of my work as a storyteller and educator.

The conversation revolved around this idea: Not only are there different learning styles for different students, and most teachers teach to their dominant learning styles, but there are also different cultural norms for teaching and learning. Some of this is so subtle that only an insider would know it, and even then they might not be fully conscious of the dynamics; for them it has always been this way. Yet when a student finds himself in a different cultural setting, he might have trouble adjusting, and neither the teacher nor the student will know why, causing a real conflict to surface. We agreed that more research needs to be done on cultural differences in pedagogy, yet storytelling is a universal mode of teaching and learning.

I reflected on my childhood experiences of learning to hunt, fish, and trap animals and to prepare the meat and cook the game. There was very little formal instruction the way most teachers would imagine; these were skills I learned just being with my dad, my uncles, and my older brothers. I tagged along. I watched. I helped. Eventually, I learned how to do it on my own. Not only was it experiential education at its best, but what instruction was given was given in offhand, informal storytelling. "Do you remember that one time we went coon hunting?" and embedded in the story were little gems of information shared in a humorous—and dare I say—enlightened manner.

We also talked about different cultural styles of listening and how in the African American Baptist Church the congregation is not a silent witness but a participatory congregation that shouts affirmation. In several American Indian and African storytelling traditions, there is a built-in call and response; the storyteller cannot go on unless the audience calls back. Yet in most American classrooms, students are required to be silent and can be punished if they respond to the ideas in a reflexive yet creative manner.

In contrast, I relish the moments when a student blurts out the next word when I consciously make a pregnant pause. As in a Close exercise they are finishing the thought; the students are right there with me in the flow of the moment. Clearly there is a difference between a distraction and a constructive comment given out of turn.

In our conversation, we bemoaned that television has replaced the tribal storyteller in most families, yet in some pockets of the world, among my Irish Catholic relatives and Jewish friends, there is still a lively storytelling tradition. Although the whole conversation lasted about fifteen minutes, seeds were planted that continue to sprout to this day.

How can storytelling cross cultural barriers and make bridges? How can educators develop cultural sensitivity and use storytelling to reach out to students, especially the hard to reach?

STORYTELLER-IN-RESIDENCE

While teaching in Charlotte, North Carolina, I created a position as the storyteller-in-residence. Much like a reading specialist, I worked with Chapter 1, Title 1, and Reading Recovery teachers. If you follow national statistics, you might know that North Carolina has had some of the lowest test scores in the nation—usually ranking forty-eight out of fifty states—and Charlotte-Mecklenburg Schools ranked lowest in the state. I worked at the ten worst schools in the city. Although I met some of the most inspiring and hardworking educators, as well as many caring and engaged parents, by this one standard—test scores—these schools were the bottom of the barrel.

There were drive-by shootings on the playgrounds. That year Charlotte won the prestigious award of Murder Capital of America if you ranked the number of murders per capita. The kids I worked with were quite literally what "crack babies" grow up to be. In the last two decades of the twentieth century, Charlotte also received wave after wave of immigrants, including Southeast Asian boat people after the war in Vietnam ended, Eastern European immigrants after the wall came down, and Latin American and African refugees fleeing revolutions and genocide. There was one elementary building in which more than twenty different languages were spoken by students who knew very little English.

In the midst of this difficult reality, we had a truly visionary school administrator, Dan Saltrick, who said, "We can wring our hands about these kids coming to school not ready to learn or we can do something about it!" Dan then told me this was my job—to do something about it!

He hired an expert team of reading specialists and me, the storyteller-in-residence. With previews and follow-up visits, I spent more than two weeks at each of the ten schools, presenting oral language development through storytelling. Every child in all ten buildings learned at least three traditional folktales, wrote an original story, and performed for the class. Many of them performed for other classes and for family literacy nights. I presented parenting classes and worked with family resources to provide collections of folktales to honor our rich cultural milieu. I worked extensively with staff development, teaching teachers how to teach storytelling (and also created several of the lesson plans now in this book).

We also filmed several episodes of a television program in which I told stories to a small group of students in the library. Teachers could then play the videos in class, and kids could go home and watch storytelling on local access cable to learn more stories. But our primary goal was to enrich the community with tales—tall and true.

During the two-week residency, I always began with a few large school assemblies so that everyone would get a chance to see and hear storytelling. I also used these performances to introduce some of the content teachers had asked me to cover in science, math, or social studies. I then visited each classroom three times. One visit to teach creative writing and get them started on their stories, historical fiction, creative nonfiction, personal narrative or fairy tale—whatever the teachers requested. In a second classroom visit, I would teach storytelling and a few simple folktales. During the third visit, we put it all together, using storytelling and rehearsal to teach rewriting and prepare for the performance. Each teacher chose a student or two whom I would meet with for one-on-one coaching. The second Thursday, we had a family literacy night, and because their children were performing, many more parents attended. I also included at least one teacher-training program tailored to their school improvement goals. We ended the week with a storytelling festival in which many students, teachers, and other staff members told stories. (For more about hosting a storytelling residency please see page 223.)

There was one Jamaican lunch lady who told a hilarious "island" version of the "Three Billy Goats Gruff" and won great respect from the students and staff. Several staff members commented later that from that day on, she came out of her shell and felt more connected to the school community.

During one family night, a shy kindergarten girl stood up and told a southern-fried version of "The Gingerbread Man" and mixed in a piece of "The Dark, Dark House," for which she received a standing ovation. You could see her little ego soar through the roof! It is much easier to build success on success, and every student can tell stories. Who wouldn't want to be her first-grade teacher?

I will never forget one festival performance when a student in the front row vomited on my shoe. I will admit I was appalled and nearly lost my cookies, too. But the principal wisely reframed the experience. She said, "Think about it: How many kids fake sick to skip school because they don't want to be there? This child was physically ill and came to school anyway because he did not want to miss his chance to tell his story!" She double-checked and determined that attendance went up over the course of the two-week residency.

I have since checked with other principals and found that this is often the case. When I present a school residency, attendance improves. In complete humility I know it is not about the fun and excitement I bring to the school; rather, it is because these students are finding their voices and are truly being heard.

This was one of the most rewarding years of my career to date! I learned so much, including these key concepts, the cornerstones of this book:

- Every student can learn to tell stories!

- Through storytelling, students can learn reading-readiness skills.

- Stories are the foundation for teaching about character, setting, and plot; beginning, middle, and end; and sequential order.

- Through storytelling, the more complex concepts of literature, irony, suspense, foreshadowing, flashback, and metaphor and symbolism can be taught and used by even the youngest students.

- Stories can introduce key concepts in science, math, and social studies, and students can reflect on these concepts through the stories they write and tell.

- Students from diverse cultural backgrounds can feel more connected to their school community through sharing stories from their culture.

- Students who previously hated school—often because they felt disconnected—now had incentive to attend because they wanted a chance to tell their stories!

- Illiterate parents can teach reading readiness and help their children connect with their culture of origin through storytelling.

- Teachers can learn to use storytelling to teach most any subject.

- And most important for administrators, storytelling can improve student test scores in reading and writing.

TEACHING READING AND WRITING IS ABOUT TEACHING THINKING

Working with so many students from so many backgrounds, I gained insight into one universal idea: Teaching reading and writing is about teaching thinking. Helping students to write in different genres is really about teaching students to organize their thoughts in different ways. Teaching writing through storytelling gives students a chance to think out loud, to organize their thoughts and get live feedback from a live audience.

Singing and reciting poetry make metaphor and simile tangible. Telling family stories makes the personal narrative visceral. Sharing fairy tales and folklore lays a solid foundation for the conventions of good fiction. Hearing true stories helps history come to life. Even the most complex math and science concepts become easy to grasp when taught through storytelling.

Furthermore, what is expository writing but a good lecture embedded with anecdotes and metaphor to make a point? In the same vein, when students get a chance to debate and discuss controversial ideas, their persuasive writing is greatly improved. Just a few generations ago, everyone memorized a few poems, and relatively uneducated people like Abraham Lincoln joined debate clubs, Lyceums, and attended an annual Chautauqua to hear scholars discuss ideas.

One of my favorite lesson plans, "Bird Is the Word" (see page 148), is built on the idea that poetry, storytelling, and debate are potent ways to teach thinking. I ask the students to make a list of facts about their favorite bird. With very little editing, these facts can be turned into a poem. The poem is the outline of a story. The story is the frame for an essay. The essay is the foundation for a persuasive piece concerning the relationship of their birds to habitat restoration. I have presented this same series of lesson plans on a wide range of subjects from pizza to geology, zoos to the American Revolution.

Students respond well to this game of playing with words and ideas. They get hands-on experiences with the differences between genres. Although I only have anecdotal evidence and a few letters from teachers and principals to back my claim, I firmly believe that storytelling and playing with genre helps students to write to the prompt in the writing portions of standardized tests improving test scores. More important, there is joy and fun in their writing and they begin to see the connections between things.

STORIES TIE THE WORLD OF IDEAS TOGETHER

I must admit that this connection between content areas is what makes my heart go thump-thump. I am always looking for the webs that tie diverse ideas together. I must also admit that I had a lot of trouble as a student when everything was broken down and put into little boxes—especially in high school and college—when algebra did not make sense because I could not see real-world applications. I was frustrated when my teacher made me close the science book because it was time for math, yet math is an important component of all good science. Ironically, I hated history class when it was just about names and dates, but I now make my living as a historical interpreter and museum consultant because history is about stories!

It was my college history professor, Larry Gara, who made history vivid in his ranting one-man debates with himself and dramatic retellings of America's story. He was also an avid bird watcher who would take me birding during spring migration. Through him I became involved in the Audubon Society. This led to my one-man show as John James Audubon in which I weave history, ornithology, art, and literature into an exciting tour of America's wildest landscapes.

My biology and ecology professor, Fred Anliot, was a published poet and skilled artist who challenged me to think about ethics and philosophy and encouraged me to use storytelling while studying to teach secondary biology. He rarely lectured in class. We were either in the field doing science—because science is a verb—or he would tell us scary and funny stories about the time he was trapped on a remote island for a month longer than expected and lived off of lichens and seaweed, waiting for his rescue plane, not sure if it was ever coming.

Earl Redding not only taught religion and peace studies, one of my minors, but he also exemplified this style of teaching through stories drawn from history, industry, good fiction, and recent movies. I often found myself drawing a line down the middle of the page and taking notes on his content and notes on how he brought the content to life. Within a story, he would weave together scientific experiments from the past and the math needed to accomplish the study, and then he would leave us with an ethical quandary that we could only solve through candid discussion, thinking out loud with our peers and reflecting on our personal experiences. His teaching style inspired me to strive for some of these same connections woven together through storytelling. Good stories also raise questions such as the Quaker-ly query or the "drawing from within" of Socrates or Confucius.

If you accept my earlier premise that we tend to teach the way we were taught, take a moment and sift through your experience as a student. Who were the teachers who inspired you? Who are your positive role models, and what did you learn from them about education?

I am willing to bet that many of these teachers were great storytellers and used storytelling to help you make sense of your world. Stories make connections between history and our personal journey. Stories demonstrate that great scientists use math in creative ways to solve problems and to answer difficult questions. Stories distill meaning from our experience, yet they open doors to new worlds and challenge us to walk through those doors. Stories bind us to the world and help us make sense of the world in which we live. Your students will thrive when their world is woven with stories.

As teachers we can design lesson plans that flow naturally from storytelling to hands-on experience into a chance for students to tell their stories, allowing them to make meaning from their experiences.

Today as I type this introductory essay, I am working on a riverboat on the Illinois River. The boat cruises up stream at seven miles an hour against a strong current; we have had a bit of rain this week, rain that is the remnant of a tropical storm that gathered its waters from the Atlantic Coast of Africa and crashed into the Gulf Coast a few days ago. I watch a beautiful snowy-white egret stalk fish along the river's shore. I watch as she wades in the shallows, silently stalking her prey. Her head darts into the water and she struggles to swallow a large squirming fish. She stands still for several moments, glancing around. The egret simultaneously leaps up and flaps her wings to get lift, rising from the river. I know we are in the midst of the fall migration, and in the next few weeks, millions of birds will wing their way from the Great North Woods to the Tropical Rain Forest, from the Arctic plains to Tierra del Fuego. They all stop to rest along this river. My imagination longs to follow them south.

Global climate issues and deforestation, the algebra and geometry of a storm's travel and river's rise, the aerodynamic flight of birds, migrations and predator-prey relations are all brought to life in that small poetic passage, a small piece of a story. Come on, climb aboard, and take a ride to see where stories just might lead you!

CHAPTER 1

HOW TO TELL AND LEARN THE TALE

INTRODUCTION

Storytelling is as simple as opening your mouth and letting your thoughts and experiences spill out to an engaged listener. Like anything else, the more we do it the better we get. Storytelling is something we all do every time we tell someone about our day.

Have you ever done something really cool and then thought to yourself, "I can't wait to tell my friends?" Did you begin to rehearse in your head how you would tell the story? Then you have told stories to yourself!

Storytelling is built into our basic makeup as a species. I disagree with the common argument that there are some born to tell a tale and others who cannot. I have been teaching storytelling for more than twenty-five years and know from experience that it is something we all can learn to do and get better at with time and practice.

I will also admit that I have learned a great deal from my workshops. As I have worked with many different tellers, I have spent less time teaching storytelling and more time simply striving to create space where folks feel safe and encouraged to tell their stories.

Storytelling is something you learn by telling stories. Create space for your students to tell their own tales. Provide positive feedback and constructive questioning to teach self-analysis.

In the following set of articles, you will find a series of theater games to help beginning tellers move from whole to parts to whole.

Begin by telling a few good stories to model the process and set a high standard for excellence. As time allows, play a few theater games to warm up your students and teach the components of what makes a great performance. Then end with them telling stories to each other so they can put the skills to work.

WHEN TIME IS SHORT: A QUICK ONE-HOUR INTRODUCTION TO THE ART OF STORYTELLING

When presenting a weeklong residency in a school where I only have one hour to teach storytelling, I race through this series of games and activities:

1. I start with a short story like "Once There Was an Old Witch" (see page 3).

2. Everyone echoes each of the four lines, and they learn the story.

3. Then they tell the story to a partner.

4. As a class we discuss how we use our voices, bodies, and imaginations to tell a story.

5. We then choose a partner and play a quick series of games to exercise these skills.

6. VOICE: We sing to warm up our voice. We count to five with feeling and then take turns counting to five in different voices. We make sound effects (see page 5).

7. BODY: We play the magic something with our partners (see page 6).

8. IMAGINATION: We close our eyes and float into an imaginary world (see page 9).

9. Then we put it all together. I tell another short, simple story like "The Big Mouth Frog," and they turn to their partner and take turns retelling the tale.

If you have a full semester or a yearlong unit revolving around storytelling, then take your time and play all of the games and activities in the following series of articles. Many of these activities are also referenced in the pivotal chapter on using "Storytelling as a Rewriting Tool" (see page 71), so beginning a unit on storytelling with these games is a fun way to lay a solid foundation for great stories to come!

"ONCE THERE WAS AN OLD WITCH": I TELL, WE TELL, YOU TELL

Grade Levels: Preschool through adult

Time Estimate: 10–15 minutes

Objectives: To teach everyone one simple story they can tell while introducing basic storytelling skills.

Materials: An active imagination and willing participants.

Introduction: I believe that once you learn one story and the process for telling that story, it becomes very easy to learn and tell many stories. If you can tell this simple story, you are ready for Shakespeare! You use all of the same skills in "Once There Was an Old Witch" that you would use in Shakespeare's "MacBeth."

The Story: Once there was an old witch. (Cackle like a witch.)
Stirring her pot. (Stir with your whole body, arm, shoulders, and entire torso.)
Along came two ghosts. (Change your voice to sound like a ghost.)
"I wonder what she's got?" (Act curious, point.)
Tip-toe, tip-toe, BOO! (Use your hands like feet to tip-toe and then scream BOO!)
I got you! (Jump at the audience. Take a bow.)

Instructional Procedures: The process for teaching this story is quite simple. I tell the story to the audience. We tell it together, and then they tell it to a partner. With younger students, I insert an extra step by having them listen and then repeat while I tell the story in pieces, call and response.

Tell the story with great panache. Cackle like a witch! Talk in an Old-English ghostly voice. Tip-toe with a whisper and then scream BOO! to scare the listeners. With this type of jump tale the important thing is timing. As Mark Twain said, "The pause is the most fickle thing." If you lower your voice and pause with each tip-toe, you draw them in and set up a suspense that you can shatter with a good loud boo.

After you tell the story, invite them to listen as you tell one line and then they repeat it. Go through the story step by step. With a large class or auditorium, I invite all of them to tell the story at the same time along with me. Then they turn to a partner and take turns telling the story. Challenge them to work on their timing and to try to scare their partner even though they know what's coming. If time allows, ask a few students to stand up and tell the story to the class. Always follow one of these performances with a round of applause and a compliment.

Assessment: I often ask students to go home and tell their story to their mom, brother, sister, dad, grandma, uncle, and aunt. I write a note for them to get signed by every person who hears them tell their tale:

I heard _____ tell the story of _____ .

Signed _____ Signed _____

Signed _____ Signed _____

Comments: This basic idea is used to teach many participatory art forms from dance to pantomime, but I first found this strategy used in storytelling by Margaret Read MacDonald, a librarian and storyteller who is the author of dozens of wonderful story collections. There are many short, simple stories like this that you can use in this process, but the "old witch" is my favorite. Once they learn a few short stories, you can use this same process to teach them a little longer story, like a fable or fairy tale.

THE GOLDEN VOICE OF THE STORYTELLER

One of the most important tools of a storyteller is the emotionally charged, clear, and compelling voice. How can you acquire that rich, resonating tone that catches the ears and hearts of your audience? I do not pretend to have any secret formulas or incantations. Simply exercising the muscles and becoming more conscious of your instrument is the key to unlocking the wealth we are all given.

The following are a few games and voice exercises that you can share with your students. Please sing along to model the process and strengthen your golden voice. The key ideas are volume, enunciation, emotion, and character.

First, ask students to focus on the voice as a series of muscles. Relax your throat as you breathe in a deep, open-mouthed breath. To exercise these muscles, to warm up, sing the scales. Listen and repeat: DO-RAY-ME-FA-SO-LA-TI-DO, or better yet sing, MA-MAY-ME-MO-MOO. The "M" sound helps you to loosen the vocal chords, while the vowel sounds help you to open your mouth, open your instrument and let the sound out. Repeat several times to exercise clarity.

To work on volume, I always say, "The larger the audience, the larger your voice needs to be." Project! Ask students to sit up straight, put their hands on their abdomen, and take a deep, full breath. Sing, "How ARE you?" Gently push the word "are" to the full capacity of your volume without screaming or straining your voice. Try it again, this time focusing on letting your vocal chords relax, while gently pushing with your diaphragm. It is difficult to have enough volume without straining. Focus on relaxing your voice.

The next activity is a simple yet effective way of emphasizing the emotional content of your words. With a partner, ask students to take turns counting to ten with feeling. Numbers have no feeling, so this is a chance to ham it up. We all know the way you say a word is often more important that what it means. Saying, "I'm *okay*. Leave me alone!" with tears in your eyes and repressed anger in your voice is a clear example of this concept.

Next play the same game counting to ten with feeling, but add the layer of accent. Count in someone else's voice. This gives students a chance to experiment and have fun pushing the limits of vocal inflection and range. Remind students to be careful in the context of a story; do not confuse the little girl's voice with the voice of the giant. Sometimes it is easier and just as effective to change your tone or pace and still delineate characters. For example, a child may speak a little faster, while an elder may speak slower—both with your natural voice, but clearly different characters marked by the change in pace or speed.

Now it is time to begin to put these exercises to practical use. Ask students to choose one of their favorite stories and read it aloud, to themselves, ALL at once, so the class will get very noisy! As they read, encourage them to practice changing their volume to match the imaginary setting. Imagine you are in a room with thirty people, one hundred people, three hundred people. Continue reading. Next ask them to focus on the emotional aspects of the story. Play around by rereading passages with different feelings. Try a twist of irony by reading joyful text with a hint of melancholy in your tone. Next ask students to focus on the characters in the story. Read some of the dialogue with distinct character voices. Again, play around with subtle changes in tone and pace. Put it all together and read the story start to finish, practicing the various aspects of their vocal range.

With the right kind of practice, anyone can develop the golden voice of the storyteller!

GROWL, HOWL, MOAN, AND GROAN: SOUND EFFECTS AND STORYTELLING

The importance and power of sound effects were lessons I learned early. In one of my first professional appearances, I was performing in a high school gymnasium that was acoustically atrocious. I was two-thirds through a story that was not working. I could hear the chatter beginning in the back corners of the room. The noise grew and swept down from the top corners like a wave through the crowd. I was losing them. I needed to act immediately. At this point in the tall tale I was telling, I was hunting ducks. Call it divine inspiration, call it dumb luck, but the next moment I made a big exploding noise with my mouth, *kaboom*! and did a double backward somersault across the floor.

At the time I knew it was a cheap trick, but it worked. Everyone's eyes were glued to me, and they listened and watched for whatever might happen next. The exploding noise got their attention. I also knew that the stories needed more substance if I was going to continue to hold their attention. I quickly ended that story and switched gears into something a little more mature, thinking it might challenge them to listen more closely.

Although this example is a little rough, it clearly shows how a simple sound can capture the attention of the listener. Beyond that, sound effects can help to create a mood or set the tone for the story. A well-chosen, well-timed noise can also add humor or grief, fear, or suspense, deepening the emotional impact of the tale.

As the father of twin daughters, I relish the times when they were little and sat on my lap reading together. When I read aloud to them they would point to all the animals and moo, cackle, baa, or bark along with me, and then we all laughed together. This memory came up in a workshop I recently conducted for parents. One parent commented that her children, now in the third and fifth grades, still laugh at a parody of an animal sound. We are never too old to laugh at this kind of silliness.

As a quick and simple exercise, rattle off a list of common animals, and then after you name each animal, point to your class and invite them to make the animal sound. Can you quack like a duck? Quack-quack! Can you moo like a cow? M-m-m-o-o-o-o. Can you hiss like a snake? His-s-s. Beyond animal sounds, list other sounds and ask them to make the noise. Can you blow like the wind? Who-o-o-osh. Can you boom like thunder? BOOM! Can you ring like a phone? R-r-r-ring, and so on.

When learning a story, during rehearsals challenge students to keep their ears open for a place to growl, howl, moan, or groan. When Abiyoyo, a terrifying giant, swallows a cow in one bite, a loud burp always gets a laugh. A great horned owl's who-oo-who-who-who adds a level of authenticity to Jane Yolen's *Owl Moon*. These sounds are rarely written into the book, so students can be inventive with the sounds they make and when to use them.

On another plain, these sounds create a cognitive dissonance that catches the listener off guard, shatters his expectancy, his sense of, "Ho-hum, I know where this is going." The listener is more engaged mentally and listens more closely, trying harder to figure out what is going to happen next.

Jump tales, scary stories with a lot of crash-boom-bang, are based on this idea. The trick in this instance is timing. If the listeners expect the bogeyman to jump out now, make them wait a minute until their guard is down. If they know it is going to happen in a few minutes, make it happen now, before they are ready. There is one jump tale that I tell with lots of squeaking doors and soft spooky voices that startles 90 percent of the audience at five different points when I shout, "It got him!" By the third or fourth time everyone is expecting it, but if the timing is right, they will jump anyhow!

Whether a sound effect is a cheap trick or a master's tool is measured by how well it supports the underlying goals of most storytellers: Is it entertaining? Does it challenge the listener to enter more deeply into the story? Does it add to the experience in a way that is artful and thought provoking?

LEARNING THE LANGUAGE OF YOUR BODY AND HANDS: ADDING THAT MAGIC SOMETHING TO YOUR PERFORMANCE

Mime and pantomime, gesture and body language, can add another dimension to the art of storytelling. With the right gesture or motion, you can create images from thin air. Hands can hold and use an invisible prop that becomes real in the imagination of the audience. With a carefully modulated use of rhythmic motions, you can ride an invisible horse across an imaginary meadow.

There are several games and activities that can help your students learn to master this silent language that can say so much.

One game is called the magic something. Begin with an example: First I reach into my back pocket to give the audience a clue. I pull something out of my pocket and by holding my hands close together, I show them that it is flat and skinny. I imagine looking at my reflection in a mirror as I pull this object through my hair. I use my fingers to straighten my part. What is this piece of magic? A comb.

It should be that easy. The important thing is that every gesture is clear. Just as you do not slur your words, you do not want to make sloppy gestures. If the audience does not know what it is that your body is saying, then the gesture is a distraction. Whoever guesses correctly gets to go first; but wait, before I give them the piece of magic, I explain the game.

Ask students to choose a partner. The game is played in four steps: First imagine it, then shape it, then use it, then your partner guesses. First decide what you want to make the piece of magic into; choose something that you can hold in your hand—something ordinary that you use every day at home or at school. Next reach into a pocket and pull out an invisible bit of magic. Peek into a closed hand. With facial expressions make believe there is really something there. Then carefully shape the object. Do not draw it; it is hard to see what you are drawing in thin air. Hold it; show us with the shape of your hands and body—is it round, flat, big and heavy, or long and skinny? Then use it. Do you swing it (a bat)? Do you eat it (a sandwich)? Do you read it (a book)? Finally your partner tries to guess what it is. But if your partner is wrong, it is not his fault. Your job is to tell your partner what the item is without any words so that he does not have to guess. He should know immediately.

Part of what makes each object work is that the gesture is sharp and distinct. If you are drinking a cup of tea, then one hand becomes the saucer while the other holds the cup. If it is British tea, you hold the handle. If it is Japanese tea, you grasp the whole cup.

After mastering individual gestures, put them together to tell a silent story. Wordless picture books are a fun place to start. The first story I told in pantomime was a combination of *The Snowy Day* by Ezra Jack Keats (1962) and *The Snowman* by Raymond Briggs (1978). Children giggle with delight when I throw snowballs at them or lean against a chair and pretend to make snow angels. I have also made up several short pieces that depict scenes from everyday life. One of my favorite pieces to perform is called "Waking Up." I stumble out of bed and into the bathroom. I turn on the water and wash my face. For older children, I pop a zit on my forehead. Then I get out my toothbrush and toothpaste and brush my teeth. They usually laugh when I spit out the foam and brush my tongue. An easy illusion to help illustrate this story is to brush your teeth with an imaginary toothbrush. Simply move your hand back and forth to the right side of your face while moving your tongue back and forth inside your closed mouth. If you can get the timing right, moving your hand and tongue at the same time in the same direction, it really looks like you are brushing your teeth.

The trick to making it believable is to pay attention to details like twisting off the lid to the toothpaste and setting it down and remembering to turn off the water while you brush your teeth. These little gestures link the large ones and add clarity to the story.

After modeling a simple story in pantomime, challenge students to make up their own little story. Ask them to pick a scene from everyday life, such as making a sandwich or mowing the lawn, and to try to tell the story without any words. Give this assignment as homework: Go home and make up a one-minute story that you can tell without any words. Over the next few days when the class has an extra minute, have students take turns telling their mime tales. Remind students that it is okay to laugh, but it is not okay to talk during their story. When they are finished, discuss what the story was about.

Again, paying attention to details is what makes the story work. Remember, if there is a table and you set things on it, make sure you come back to the same spot each time. This is called staging, and it makes the illusion much more believable.

A simple exercise that helps students to stage the story is to drop a handkerchief or a coin on the floor. Walk away from it several steps. Close your eyes, turn around, walk back to the object, bend and pick it up with your eyes closed. If you can put your hand on it most every time, this shows that you have a strong spatial awareness. Try it!

These are only a few of the many exercises you can learn to help use your body while performing. Mime and pantomime, gesture, and body language can add a bit of magic to your program that speaks directly to the imagination of your listener.

HAS YOUR MOTHER EVER TOLD YOU NOT TO MAKE FACES? FACIAL EXPRESSION AS A TOOL IN STORYTELLING

Several years ago I was presenting a storytelling workshop at a small college in Ohio. In the theater department I saw a tiny poster that was a huge inspiration. On the poster were one hundred photographs of the same man's face, 10 by 10 inches, but no two pictures were the same. The next morning while brushing my teeth, I tried making one hundred faces—well, I tried to make as many faces as I could. I worked with a broad range of emotions. Then I challenged myself to attempt subtle variations on a theme from sad, to blue, to downright depressed, from happy, to excited, to overjoyed! This is a really fun game that you may want to try. Make sure you close the bathroom door so your family does not think that you have lost your mind!

As an exercise that illustrates the point, ask the participants to turn to a partner and play a little game called "Face Dances." Before the game, invite everyone to do the yoga stretch called the lion's growl: They should take a deep breath and jut out their lower jaw; open their mouth, eyes, and face as wide as possible; and let out a deep belly growl. Do this three times, remembering to breathe deeply.

The game begins with one partner silently expressing a clear emotion with his or her entire body but with an emphasis on facial expression. The partner then responds silently with a different but related expression. This is passed back and forth a couple of times. As time and interest allow, partners can trade and try other expressions.

This can also be passed around a small circle. One student makes a face at the student nearest, and that student responds silently with a different face. This second student then turns to the person near him and repeats the response, which elicits a different reaction. This is passed around the circle, from person to person with great gales of laughter!

The next step in this process is application. Think about a story that contains strong emotions—most do. How could facial expressions enrich the telling? When you change character in the dialogue of a tale, how can your face tell us who is speaking? When you are singing, how is your face conveying the feeling in the lyric? In all three instances, rehearsal in front of a mirror is a valuable technique. In the mirror, you can see if the facial expression is adequate or exaggerated. You can practice the subtle nuance in a sly smile and the outrageously wide watermelon grin and wink. Try them both. Gently lift your eyebrows and turn up one corner of your mouth in a half smile. Think a devilish thought to add to the effect. For the opposite extreme, wink and smile with your whole body.

Once students have mastered the technique it is important to move beyond mere technique. Encourage them to check in with their hearts to ensure that the feelings and expressions are genuine and honest. A simple method-acting idea is to remember a time when they felt the same emotion as the character they are portraying and to draw on that experience, allowing their feelings to mingle with the emotions of the character.

I often look into the faces of the audience to appraise their responses. The eyes of the listeners will always reveal their feelings. If they are with me, I can delight in that most human of emotions, empathy. If they are not with me, well, I try something else.

To give you an idea of the effectiveness of facial expressions in a story, allow me to share a piece of a story in which a man is walking down a path and falls from a cliff . . . A-H-H-H! He grabs onto a limb. He looks up and sees a tiger growling, licking his jowls. He can't climb up to escape. He looks down (here, I make a drop-jawed gasp); it is more than a thousand feet to the bottom. That moment of pause and the facial expression gives the audience a chance to imagine and empathize. It conveys much more than words can say.

As students begin telling stories, give them time to experiment with facial expressions and body language—put their entire self into the story, into each character. It should not come across as hollow technique but genuine heartfelt emotions. Facial expressions can become a powerful tool in their repertoire that enables them to pluck upon the heartstrings of their listeners.

Open your eyes wide or wrinkle your nose, twist up your mouth, or stick out your tongue! In the context of the story, forget what your mother told you and make faces at your friends!

FLOATING AWAY ON THE RAFT OF IMAGINATION

Many of us know the famous quote from Einstein, "Imagination is more important than knowledge," but I did not know the rest of that quote until recently, "For knowledge is limited to all we now know and understand, while imagination embraces the entire world, all there ever will be to know and understand."

Anyone who has had the opportunity to witness the magic of storytelling will affirm that storytelling embraces the entire world, exercises the imagination, and allows listeners to float away on that magic raft that will carry you into any future knowledge you want to know.

I vividly remember a scholarly study in which electrodes were hooked to children's brains, and the children were then set in front of a TV. There was very little neural activity, especially when compared with those same children's brains that lit up all over while they listened to a story. I know this is true because I saw it on TV!

My interpretation of this research is that television feeds viewers too much noise and lights. It does not allow space for you to create or imagine. While listening to stories, you must imagine what the monster looked like, sounded like and smelled like. In this way, storytelling stimulates all of the senses so more of your brain is firing. I like to tease kids, "I am not a TV—you have to make your own pictures!"

The best exercise for the imagination is to tell stories. After the story, ask your students to draw the monster or dog or their favorite moment in the story. These pictures can then be discussed as tools for both interpreting and retelling the tale. In a similar vein, ask students to make a series of five quick sketches, a story map that helps them remember the outline of main events. Allow a little flexibility, at least three pictures, beginning, middle, and end, but no more than six or seven, because that is too much detail for an outline. Like the story map included on the title page of every story in this book, this series of pictures can help them learn and tell the story to a partner.

Another simple exercise for the imagination, and one used frequently throughout this book, is the deep memory. Invite your students to sit up straight with both feet flat on the floor and to breathe deep. By sitting up straight, aligning their posture, and focusing on their breath, students can access more of their imagination. Tell them that you are going to help them remember a favorite story or folktale as if they were there when it happened. Here is a script you can read aloud or improvise with:

Sit up straight, close your eyes, take a slow deep breath, hold your breath for just one second and then slowly breathe out all of your air. Hold the out breath for one second and then slowly fill your lungs. Take five or six breaths this way, in and hold, out and hold, at your own pace, slow and deep. With every breath, feel your body relax, sit up straight, but let your muscles relax, and just think about breathing. By breathing deep and sitting up straight, you get more oxygen to your brain, you are smarter, and you feel your imagination light up.

Start with something you know. Imagine right now that you are sitting on your bed in your bedroom. Feel the quilt or blanket underneath you. Sit still, but imagine looking around the room at the things on your wall and your floor. Sit up straight, but imagine lying down on your bed; feel how soft it is, how warm and safe you feel.

Now imagine that your bed is a raft, and your bedroom has become a quiet river. Listen to the gurgling of water as the raft floats gently away. Feel yourself beginning to float down this lazy river. There is a gentle rocking as you drift toward a forest, seeing the trees rise up around you. The river enters the trees, and it becomes darker. You are so relaxed, it is almost like you are dreaming. There is a light in the distance, and you float gently toward it. As the raft moves down, down, down the river.

You see the characters from your favorite story up ahead. You know which story it is, one of your favorite folktales or picture books from when you were a kid. Right now, see the people or animals from this story—not a cartoon but the real thing. They don't see you. The raft slows and stops and you watch. Carefully watch what they are doing. Listen, listen to what they are talking about. It is one of your favorite parts of the story! Watch and listen (LONG PAUSE).

As this scene draws to a close, see them slowly fade away; you remember, you are lying on your bed, dreaming a wonderful dream. Feel yourself waking up. The blood flows through your whole body. Imagine sitting up, oh, you are already sitting up. Wiggle your toes and fingers, feel yourself wide awake (clap twice). Turn to a partner and talk about your dream.

This can be followed with each student drawing a story map, or not; maybe the daydream itself is sufficient to exercise the wondrous gifts of the imagination!

SING ALONG! ACT IT OUT! EVERYONE JOINS IN! TELLING AUDIENCE PARTICIPATION STORIES WITH YOUNG CHILDREN

Young children love to squirm! Let's face it, human bodies are not designed to sit still and passively listen for long periods of time. Storytellers are always faced with a choice: invite listeners to wiggle in a manner that adds artistry to the tale, or allow them to fidget in a way that is destructive and distracting. Active listening is an important skill to develop. Audience participation stories can help children learn when to be quiet and when to join in.

Have you noticed that when the listeners join in, they enjoy themselves more? There is a deeper involvement with the material, the concepts, and the inherent wisdom in the story. When invited to become the main character and chant the refrain along with the teller, they internalize the lessons to be learned. It is also a lot of fun to hear three hundred children shouting in their best giant voice, "I challenge you to a duel, choose your weapon and I shall more than match you!"[1]

Most collections of folklore do not include side notes on what the teller should do while telling the tale to engage the listeners. One of the jobs of the storyteller is to be "the artistic interpreter," to add the element of audience participation. Ask students to read the text of a tale and look for repetitive lines the audience can repeat or actions they can pantomime with you. The question is, how can you engage your audience emotionally, kinesthetically, and intellectually?

The audience is a partner in the storytelling process. The teller, the tale, and the listener are a dynamic team. I do not have a series of games to teach the process, but I will admit, I love it when students see me use a choral refrain or make it rain in a story and then, without my bidding, mimic these techniques in the telling of their tales. If you model the process, they will follow the model. It is also helpful to discuss the various strategies with your students, especially if your class is performing for younger grade levels where this kind of participation is key to a successful experience. The following is a list of ten techniques that I have found useful, moving from simple to difficult.

1. Make eye contact! Simply looking into each person's eyes, speaking to individuals, is the best way to emotionally hook the audience. I like to tease young tellers that they are not telling the story to their shoes. They are not talking to the ceiling. They are talking to people so look at them.

2. Ask rhetorical questions. Have you ever felt (seen, done) this before? Do you know someone like this? How many of you have been fishing? Rhetorical questions hook the audience intellectually.

3. Use local metaphors! Compare elements of the story with tangible places, events, and people. Say, for example, "The rock was as big as this room," or "The owl's wings were as long as my arms." It is like saying, don't think about purple elephants. What are you thinking about? A local metaphor hooks the audience's imagination.

4. Use refrains! Many stories have a chorus or a key line that repeats several times through the story. Invite them to repeat key lines with you like a chorus. For example, if you are telling "The Three Little Pigs," you can split the audience in half. Half will say "Little pig, little pig, let me in." The other half will say, "Not by the hair of my

chinny-chin-chin." If a story does not include a choral response, you can always make one up!

5. Build cumulative lines. Some classic folktales contain cumulative lines, where you repeat the first line and add a second, repeat the first two lines and add a third, and so on. Invite the audience to chant these lines with you at first and then let them say them on their own as they learn them. The African story of "The Talking Yam" is a perfect example of this (see page 200). Invite the audience to say everything that is underlined. The first time they repeat after you. The second and third time, they say it with you. And the fourth and fifth time they say it on their own.

6. Give listeners a job! With the story from my first book, "The Seed,"[2] I start by teaching the audience a simple wind song. Say "Shoeee" as you breathe out and "Aaahh" as you breathe in, "Oohh" as you breathe out and "Eeee" as you breathe in. Let's try it all together, but make it sound like the wind, "Shoee, Aahh, Oohh, Eeee." Now you can be the wind and make wind sounds. Whenever I say "the wind blows" and raise my right hand that is your cue.

    In the British tale, "The Old Woman in the Vinegar Bottle,"[3] the audience can say the fairy's part, "In the morning when you arise, spin 'round three times before you open your eyes and say, 'I wish to see what I wish to see.'" Or they could be the old woman who keeps "complaining and complaining and complaining."

7. Invite listeners to join the lineup! There are dozens of stories that contain a string of characters who are working toward the same goal. "The Giant Turnip," a classic Russian story, is one of my favorites in which I keep adding kids until I have five to fifteen helpers including my grandson, wife, granddaughter, horses, cows, goats, dogs, cats, and a mouse all pulling on the turnip. We link arms and grunt three times, "uhng, Uhng, UHNG!" The last time I invite the entire audience to grunt with me so no one feels left out.

8. Play puppeteer! Another way to include the audience as actors is for the storyteller to act as a puppeteer. You can choose as many actors as there are characters in the story, calling on listeners as you need them and then returning them to their seat when their scene is over. Grab their hands as you stand behind them and manipulate them as you would a puppet. When it is time for them to speak, ask them to repeat after you, but make sure you are loud enough for the audience to hear in case the child does not speak up. For example, when I say, "and the hunter went walking," I want you to walk in place. When I say, "and the hunter said, Good Morning," you just say the good morning part.

9. Let them co-create! It takes a lot of nerve and a flexible storyteller to let go of the reins even a little, but if you are brave, you could invite the audience to participate as coauthors. At first you may ask for help in naming the characters or describing the setting, but as you grow in ability and confidence, you could let them shape the plot by asking, "And then what happened?" or "How would you solve this problem?" Then use their suggestions in the completion of the tale.

10. Teach them a song! Everyone loves to sing even if they won't admit it in public. A simple sing-along song can also be a fun transition from one story to the next. The best way to teach a short song or chant is to sing it through to give listeners a feel for it. Then ask them to repeat lines until they get it and then sing it all together. A well-chosen folksong or an original song written just for the story can also deepen the impact of the story by repeating the main idea in new words.

There are many ways to involve the audience and create a space for them to play along, become a part of the story. Rarely is this written into the book, but using these ten examples as a guide, there are always at least a few baits you can use to hook them. With a little imagination and rehearsal, you can find ways to celebrate and build on the relationships between the teller, the tale, and the listener.

Notes

1. From "The Giant Who Was More Than a Match," by Aaron Piper in *Lighting Candles in the Dark*. Friends General Conference, Philadelphia, PA, 1992.

2. "The Seed" from *Learning from the Land: Teaching Ecology Through Stories and Activities*, by Brian "Fox" Ellis, Teacher Ideas Press, Englewood, CO, 1998.

3. "Old Woman and the Vinegar Bottle" from *Favorite Folk Tales from Around the World* by Jane Yolen. Random House, New York, 1986.

SETTING THE STAGE FOR A SUCCESSFUL SHOW! MANAGING PERFORMANCE DYNAMICS

One of the most difficult things about storytelling with students—or beginners of any age—is managing the house, the agenda, the order of tellers, the sound equipment, the intercom interruptions, the student who vomits in the front row, and the plethora of possible problems that can, have, and will come up in any performance and are certain to happen when students take the stage. With experienced tellers who know their material and have some wisdom in regard to jumping these hurdles, it is amazing to watch how they never lose their stride no matter what falls in their path.

When you host student tellers, whether in your classroom or at a large family literacy night, you just need to prepare the storytellers as best you can and manage the difficulties as they arise. Here are a few questions to consider:

How does the sound system work? Who is the point person or problem solver if something goes wrong? Are the students comfortable with a microphone? The first two questions are easy to answer, but I am perpetually amazed at the number of professional speakers who do not know how to use a microphone well. I always spend a little time teaching mic etiquette and letting children introduce themselves to an empty room to get used to the system. Such as, "Hello, my name is _____, and I would like to tell a story about _____."

A simple rule of thumb about microphones is to hold your thumb up to your chin and stretch out your pointer finger; that is the ideal distance from your mouth and the microphone. Do not eat the microphone. It does not taste good even with ketchup. If you are too far away, it will not hear you. If you do not hear yourself coming out of the speakers, you are too far away. Hold your thumb against your chin, and your pointer finger should touch the microphone.

How are the sight lines? How do you want the chairs arranged? What are the distractions, lighting issues, acoustic issues? I like a gunfighter's seat, with nothing behind the teller, like a door or window, that can become a distraction. I always prefer that younger children sit on the floor and older students and adults sit in chairs or bleachers, because if they are comfortable, they will listen better and longer. A half circle or regular theater-style seating is much better than a circle, because with a circle there is always someone behind you. In a rectangular room I prefer a wide audience to a deep one, because it is easy to move side to side and the back row is not so far away. I also prefer to keep the house lights up so I can see the listeners, they can see each other, and we can all watch the story unfold. Darkening the room, especially for ghost stories, invites distractions.

Who's on first? Who is the Master of Ceremonies? Someone should always be in charge of managing the house, keeping things moving along, and problem solving for the tellers so they can focus on the story. A lively MC pumps up the audience, introduces the tellers so that they feel welcome and the audience is eager to hear their story, and then makes sure there is gratitude at the end of each story. When I MC a student program, I often add a sing-a-long song or two to help break up the list of telling, like a sorbet to clear their pallet to help them appreciate the next tale. Sometimes I get the listeners up on their feet to do a wiggle dance about halfway through the list. But the most difficult issue is the order of tellers.

What is the order of tellers? Knowing that student stories are often very short, one to two minutes, it is easy to string together five or six, lead a wiggle dance and line up five or six more. I always try to start and end with the strongest material and make sure that some of the livelier, funnier stories are sprinkled evenly throughout. It is also fun to group a few similar stories together, like three animal stories in a row or two compelling pieces of historical fiction, but make sure they are not too much alike. And of course, it is always nice to alternate between boys and girls and to mix it up culturally. The most important thing is to have a flow, a roller-coaster of storytelling styles, types of stories, energy, and emotions so the audience is kept engaged.

What do you do if IT happens? Sometimes you cannot control the intercom or the fire alarm; you just have to roll with the punches and give them a chance to tell their story!

LEARNING A STORY

The most important part of learning the story is choosing one that you really enjoy and can imagine yourself telling one hundred times. If you don't love it, do you think they will?

Once you have a story that you love, read it over several times:

- Once out loud for feeling, rhythm, and tone.

- Once to get to know the characters. (Imagine you are each of the characters.)

- Once to get to know the place or setting. (Imagine you are in that place.)

- Once to learn the order of events. (Write a brief outline of the five main events.)

Do not memorize! Simply remember the important scenes, feelings, images, and phrases. Remember the bare bones, and flesh it out differently each time you tell it. Be in your story and let *your* words describe what is happening in your mind.

STORY MAPPING

The easiest way to learn a story is to make a sequential picture map of the story. In five pictures or less, draw what happens first, second, third, fourth, and at the end of the story. The illustrations on the title page of every story in this book are story maps designed to help you to learn the stories!

Encourage students to turn their papers sideways and draw five large circles that fill the page. This is how Steven Spielberg and Disney make their movies; they call it a storyboard. For a 90-minute feature film, they need about twenty sketches, but I once saw an HBO special on the making of *Jurassic Park* in which Spielberg showed his rough sketches that were hardly better than a school-age child's doodles, but you could see the outline of the entire movie in about fifteen storyboards!

Here is a story map for a story I developed about Abraham Lincoln's trip to Illinois, part of a program on Lincoln's youth:

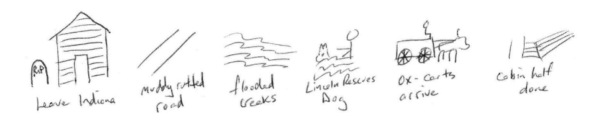

It would be easy to say older students should make an outline with words, not pictures, but sequential pictures are better cues. In preschool through graduate level teacher training, I encourage storytellers to make these simple story maps. You can even allow student storytellers to use these maps as a cheat sheet when they are first learning their stories. With older students, it is sometimes a nice change of pace to ask them to write a synopsis of their story in five brief sentences, but the maps help them to move away from memorizing the words and to focus on the order of events. Story maps also give them the freedom to improvise within the flow of the story so that they can readily adapt the tale to a new setting or new audience.

There are several lesson plans in the next few chapters in which a variation of the story map is the key to outlining their ideas when creating a new story. Make story maps a regular part of your storytelling classroom.

RESEARCHING CULTURAL VARIANTS

One could write a doctorial thesis on the cultural variants of "Little Red Riding Hood" or "Cinderella," and I am sure several scholars have already done so. But even in the elementary-level classroom, it is a valuable exercise for storytellers to spend a little time in the library looking for other versions of the folktale they plan to tell. If you visit 398.2 in the Dewey Decimal section of your bookshelf, you might be delighted at what you will find!

When I first began proposing this to teachers twenty-something years ago, in a unified voice I heard, "We don't have time!" Thankfully, you do not have to travel the world and spend years integrating into diverse cultures to collect these diverse versions of the same story; people like the Brothers Grimm, Joseph Jacobs, Harold Courlander, Virginia Haviland, and Margaret Read MacDonald have done your homework for you!

As an important aside, these are six folks every serious student of folklore should know. Each in their generation raised the bar on the scholarly appreciation of the world's folklore. The Brothers Grimm collected German folktales and gave "Housewife Tales" their first glimpse of fame. Jacobs followed on their heels collecting first English, then Scottish and Irish stories before exploring the British Colonies with a collection of East Indian stories. Courlander traveled the globe from his office in New York, making African, Asian, and American Indian folklore accessible to the world. Haviland (1965) built on this foundation with her delightful collections of "Favorite Folktales Told In … (Name a country!)." And Margaret Read MacDonald has helped countless storytellers, including this author, in their ability to straddle the worlds of print and the oral tradition through her rigorous scholarship on cultural variations. You will find titles of their books in the bibliography of "Ten Books or Authors Every Storyteller Should Know" (see pages 239–241).

Storytellers love their fruitful tangents, but back to the task at hand. A three-step process that will introduce your students to this fascinating pursuit includes:

1. Begin with your own research into three or more cultural variations on a single story. *Cinderella* in France is *Ashenputtel* in Germany and the *Rough-Faced Girl* among American Indians. *Little Red Riding Hood* is an Anglicization of Germany's *Rotcapchen* or *Lon Po Po* in China.

2. Tell one of these stories to your class and then read aloud a second version of the same tale.

3. Lead a classroom discussion of how these two stories were alike and different. The two pivotal questions are: What is the same in each story and how does this relate to ways in which all people are alike? What is different in each story and how does this relate to the cultural differences?

Because I believe this kind of work is so vital to an understanding of storytelling—our deeper selves and our relationships to the world around us—there is a more in-depth version of this lesson plan in the chapter on social studies (see page 83).

From a legal and aesthetic perspective, if you copy a story from a book, doing so is plagiarism and clearly lacks creativity. In the storytelling community, the etiquette is to find three different versions of the same story and then use these to make an original version. If you can find three versions of a tale, then it is public domain and copyright free. The goal is to take an old story and make it new.

Once students have a story map in hand and have looked into different versions of a folktale or written their own original story, it is time to practice telling it.

PRACTICE, PRACTICE, PRACTICE:
THREE KEYS TO SUCCESS

Practice may not make it perfect, but it certainly helps you get better! I would never ask a student to stand up in front of his peers and tell a story without enough practice to make sure he feels confident in the material and the telling. I love to tease students, "There are three things you need to know to be a better storyteller: Number one, you must practice; number two, you must practice; and number three, you must practice!" There are many ways to help your students create time and space to practice their story.

As outlined near the beginning of this chapter, using "Once There Was an Old Witch," and other short, short stories, you can give students two chances to practice with the exercise "I Tell a Story to You, We Tell It All Together, and Then You Tell It to a Partner." At the end of that section there is a note to send home that I use every day during an artist-in-residency program. I gleefully admit that when I present a family literacy night near the end of a weeklong residency, I love it when parents come up to me and say, "My daughter and son have been coming home every night and telling stories you taught. I just had to come and listen for myself!" Little does the unsuspecting parent realize that it has been their children's homework to go home and tell a story every night! Please use this note often (see page 4)!

In the following section, "Coaching Young Storytellers," is a musical-chairs variation that can be used to allow everyone in the class at least three chances to practice their story with three students (see page 18).

A similar method is the round robin. Arrange your class into two concentric circles of chairs, with the inner circle facing out and the outer circle facing in. Put a little space between chairs so students have elbow room. Students take turns listening and telling stories to a partner. At the gong of a bell or bang of a drum, everyone moves to the right so they have a new partner and a new chance to practice their story. When working on rewriting strategies, time can be scheduled between telling to make notes on their rough draft about what worked and did not work and notes regarding their partners comments or questions.

Another great way to build confidence and get several rehearsals in a short period of time is to have everyone practice with a partner. Then have partners choose another set of partners, so each student is now practicing within a small group of four. If time allows, encourage each listener to give one compliment. Then each group of four finds another group of four, so students take turns telling their story to seven others. Encourage those who have heard the story before to say one positive thing about how the story has improved; what did the teller do differently that made the story better? This encourages storytellers to take advantage of the practice to truly improve and not just repeat. This method also builds confidence for speaking before ever larger groups of students.

However you slice it, it takes time to allow every child a chance to practice his or her story. These strategies allow everyone several opportunities to practice in a time-efficient manner. With the homework sheet, "I Tell, We Tell, You Tell"; musical chairs; round robin; and small-to-larger group methods, you now have several tricks up your sleeve so you can vary the method for various lesson plans throughout the year.

COACHING YOUNG STORYTELLERS*

There is a four-step process that grew out of the world of dance and theater workshops. It is an artist-centered approach in which the class acts as listeners and provides feedback, but the artist is given room to make choices and maintains artistic integrity. It was developed and promoted by storyteller Doug Lipman. I have found it to be very effective, encouraging, and empowering in my work as an artist. I have seen students rise to the challenge and blossom under the encouragement and nurturing environment this process provides.

The emphasis should be on letting the storyteller control the session: The student directs comments, chooses whom to call on, and then makes choices as to how these comments shape the rewriting or the retelling. After explaining the process, I ask the teller to call on the people they want and the other students to speak directly to the teller in specific terms—not "I think she did a good job," but "Sally, I really liked the funny part about you and your mother both bending over to get the softball and conking your heads!"

* These notes are based on my experience adapted from a workshop given by Doug Lipman at the National Storytelling Conference in 1998. For more information, please consult his insightful book *The Storytelling Coach*, August House Publishers (1995).

1. First and foremost it is important that the coach practice engaged, active listening. The better job you do listening, the better job they will do telling their story. Give them your complete and enthusiastic attention. Actually, if this is all you did, it is often enough. Tellers know where the weak spots are, they notice their mistakes, but your undivided attention and enthusiastic listening will guide them through a successful telling. I always challenge the class to practice good listening.

2. The first round of comments should be entirely positive, sincere compliments. What did you like about the story? What did you like about the telling? Try to be specific—not just "I liked your hands," but "I liked the way you used your hands to reach up, grab the branch and climb the tree. I could really imagine that." Again if you stop here this is often enough. With beginning tellers and young students, I only allow compliments the first few times we critique.

3. After giving several compliments, the next round of comments should be guiding questions. For example: "I would like to know more about _____." or "How might a giant say that?" or "Could you show me how you might row a boat?" or "Where in the story could you add a sound effect to add to the scary feeling? What sound might you make?" This questioning phase is the most important part of helping a teller to improve a story while they maintain decision-making power over the final version of the tale. With beginning tellers or rough tales, the questions can be pointed and directive. With more experienced tellers, and truly with everyone, it is best to strive for open-ended artistic questions that draw something deeper from the teller.

4. Finally, and rarely, a few suggestions might be offered . . . but the best suggestions are phrased as questions! By phrasing suggestions as questions the storyteller gets to decide how to answer the questions, thereby retaining control over their story and how to tell it. Even direct suggestions can be made in a more passive, non-commanding

voice, such as, "I wonder how it would sound if _____?" Even if there are elements of the story that you as a teacher feel strongly about, these are best handled through feeling statements and questions. For example: "When I heard about the dead frog, I felt sad, almost like the story was over too soon; what could the frog do differently to give the story a happy ending?"

At first I only allow compliments from the students. After student tellers have built some confidence, I still only allow compliments from the students, but I model step three and four. After they have seen this process at work, we discuss the four phases and I let them critique one of my stories with questions and suggestions. Then we might work on one or two students who are strong and self-confident tellers. Once they get the hang of it, most of the critiquing sessions are done in small groups or with partners because this is a time-consuming process.

A simple storytelling game that allows everyone a chance to hear and be heard is a variation on musical chairs. With two rows of chairs facing each other, divide your class in half. Allow the students on one side two minutes to tell their story to their partner. The partner first and foremost practices good listening. When the story is done or time is up, ring the bell or flick the lights, and the partner gives a compliment. Then the partner tells his story, which is followed by a compliment. Everyone moves to the right, with the students on the ends moving to the other row, and now you tell the same story to a new partner, taking turns. This time allow a compliment and a question. Again, everyone bumps to the right. *Only* if the class is ready, the third time, they can give a compliment, ask and answer a question, and maybe make a suggestion, remembering that the best suggestions are phrased as questions. In this quick round robin, everyone gets three turns within about a half hour of storytelling/listening/coaching.

A RUBRIC FOR EVALUATING STORYTELLING IN THE CLASSROOM

Because different storytellers will have different styles—and this is a good thing—it is difficult to hold everyone to the same standard. At the same time, there needs to be a general standard for excellence. You know when a story works, but how do you measure success? Because these are the characteristics of storytelling being taught, the following elements are the ones to be measured.

Within one category, for example, "Audience Rapport," it is not necessary for students to exhibit all of the characteristics noted to get a high score of five, as long as they have a great rapport with the audience. In a similar vein, you do not need to have any accents or sound effects at all to score high on the vocal elements as long as you are articulate, well heard, and the voice is rich, full of emotion, and enthusiastic for the story. You'll know when it works and score accordingly!

The notes within each category are there to give you cues to watch for when evaluating student storytellers. It is also fair to let students see this sheet before they are graded. You might even let them take turns working with a partner, scoring each other and discussing the positive aspects of this rubric as a way of improving their storytelling. The question being: How can these notes and the feedback from my partner help me be a better storyteller and writer?

To help with this process, beyond a simple point score, I usually circle the characteristics that were strong, draw a line through the ones that were weak, and do nothing with the ones that were less important to their style or story. And of course, the comments and compliments are the most important part of this form.

STORYTELLER _____ STORY _____

	weak				excellent
VOICE	1	2	3	4	5
Volume - Inflection - Emotional Timbre - Accents - Sound Effects					
BODY LANGUAGE	1	2	3	4	5
Facial Expression - Clear Gestures - Movement - Staging					
AUDIENCE RAPPORT	1	2	3	4	5
Introduction - Prepare Audience - Eye Contact - Audience Participation - Rhetorical Questions - Metaphors - General Ability to Relate					
THE STORY	1	2	3	4	5
Pacing - Flow - Captivating - Intriguing - Clear Characters - Stick w/ Theme - Tight Story - Sequence of Events-Beg/Mid/End					
THE STORYTELLER	1	2	3	4	5
Stage Presence - Poise - Confidence - Teller knew the tale					

TOTAL SCORE_____

Compliments:

_____
_____
_____

STORYTELLER _____ STORY _____

	weak				excellent
VOICE	1	2	3	4	5
Volume - Inflection - Emotional Timbre - Accents - Sound Effects					
BODY LANGUAGE	1	2	3	4	5
Facial Expression - Clear Gestures - Movement - Staging					
AUDIENCE RAPPORT	1	2	3	4	5
Introduction - Prepare Audience - Eye Contact - Audience Participation - Rhetorical Questions - Metaphors - General Ability to Relate					
THE STORY	1	2	3	4	5
Pacing - Flow - Captivating - Intriguing - Clear Characters - Stick w/ Theme - Tight Story - Sequence of Events-Beg/Mid/End					
THE STORYTELLER	1	2	3	4	5
Stage Presence - Poise - Confidence - Teller knew the tale					

TOTAL SCORE_____

Compliments:

_____
_____
_____

STORYTELLER _____ STORY _____

	weak				excellent
VOICE	1	2	3	4	5
Volume - Inflection - Emotional Timbre - Accents - Sound Effects					
BODY LANGUAGE	1	2	3	4	5
Facial Expression - Clear Gestures - Movement - Staging					
AUDIENCE RAPPORT	1	2	3	4	5
Introduction - Prepare Audience - Eye Contact - Audience Participation - Rhetorical Questions - Metaphors - General Ability to Relate					
THE STORY	1	2	3	4	5
Pacing - Flow - Captivating - Intriguing - Clear Characters - Stick w/ Theme - Tight Story - Sequence of Events-Beg/Mid/End					
THE STORYTELLER	1	2	3	4	5
Stage Presence - Poise - Confidence - Teller knew the tale					

TOTAL SCORE_____

Compliments:

_____
_____
_____

CHAPTER 2

STORYTELLING AND THE READING-WRITING CONNECTION

INTRODUCTION

The premise of this chapter is the foundation of this book, as stated before, but worth repeating: Storytelling and oral language development is the cornerstone for reading readiness and improving writing skills.

If you want your students to be wise in the workings of great literature, tell them lots of stories. If you want your students to develop decoding skills, a richer vocabulary and better comprehension, tell them more stories. If you want your students to create fluent, readable, well-constructed writing samples, allow them to tell stories. If you want them to play with genre, demonstrate flexibility in their writing, and find their voice as writers, allow them to tell more stories.

Whether it is a simple joke like "Once There Was an Old Witch" or an epic Greek myth like "Atalanta," the more stories your students hear and tell, the deeper their appreciation will be for what makes a good story work. When children hear lots of stories, complex ideas like pacing, suspense, and irony become familiar tools that pop up unexpectedly in their writing. As children get a chance to play with storytelling, simple ideas like character development and a well-defined setting, beginning, middle, and end, will all grow in complexity.

STORY FORM AND STORY GRAMMAR COME TO LIFE THROUGH STORYTELLING

Most of my fondest memories from my education are intertwined with storytelling. I remember Mrs. Ford, in kindergarten, teaching us simple finger plays and songs, the whole class singing along. This was a wondrous introduction to the joys of language, phonemic awareness, rhyme, and rhythm. I will never forget the first time I stood up and told the story *Where the Wild*

Things Are by Maurice Sendak (1963) in Mrs. Campbell's second-grade class. I gained firsthand knowledge about paying attention to your audience, the roller-coaster of pacing, and the satisfying arc of a story that ends back near the beginning. In the sixth grade, Mrs. Sahloff read aloud to us from *James and the Giant Peach* by Roald Dahl (1961). We had lively conversations about the odd characters, the unexpected twists, and the deeper metaphorical implications of each turn of events, all the while unknowingly learning literary analysis. In my high school honors English class, Mr. Hoffman shared with us a story about a relay race written by one of his college students; the descriptive detail and the anguish of the runner still haunt me every time I run a few laps around the neighborhood, instilling in me the power of words to change lives.

More than fond memories, these experiences with storytelling were also some of the most important instruction that I have ever received—obviously, because I remember these moments more than thirty years later.

The lessons became a part of me, informing my work as a writer and my strategies as an educator. It was not the teacher who hammered us about spelling lists that taught me to spell; it was the drive to publish and share my work with my class, to avoid embarrassment and look good in front of my peers. This opportunity to share motivated me to pay attention to the details. It wasn't a rote grammar exercise that taught me diverse patterns for sentence construction; it was the exposure to great stories that gave me a natural sense of what sounds right and nurtured a willingness to experiment with form.

Just as an artist goes to the museum to learn to paint by copying the masters, your students will develop their reading and writing skills through an immersion in classic literature. In this chapter, they will hear stories from Chinese, African, ancient Greek, and the American Indian traditions. They will rewrite folktales, fables, myths, personal narratives, and tall tales masquerading as ghost stories. They will gain an inherent sense of story grammar and story structure, while falling in love with the literature of the world.

GRAPHIC ORGANIZERS AS A PREWRITING STRATEGY FOR IMPROVED WRITING SKILLS

The various structures used to create different genres of folktales also provide models for original writing. As you walk your students through the series of lesson plans, you will note several prewriting strategies that involve graphic organizers. The most vital prewriting strategy is the art of storytelling. As I often tell students and tease teachers: If you tell it first, writing becomes a whole lot easier!

If imagination is a key to unlocking creativity, and imaging is the foundation of imagining, then it makes sense to help students think visually. If teaching writing is about teaching thinking and giving students the tools for organizing their thinking, then graphic organizers are a great way to teach different patterns for thinking. Graphic organizers can help students organize their thinking and improve their ability to write and think more clearly.

Thinking about thinking—metacognition—is a powerful tool for improving mental acuity. Allow me to highlight some of the thinking strategies in the following lesson plans. Throughout this book, you will notice recurring patterns and the recycling of several graphic organizers for teaching prewriting.

In the first chapter, the section "How to Learn a Story" offers an example of a story map, one of the simpler graphic organizers. A "Story Map" is a series of images, four to seven circles that outline the story visually. Every story in this book comes with a story map. This is a quick and easy way for a student to take visual notes after telling a story to a partner. These notes can then be used to write the story by turning each image into two or three sentences, a paragraph, or a full chapter in a longer piece.

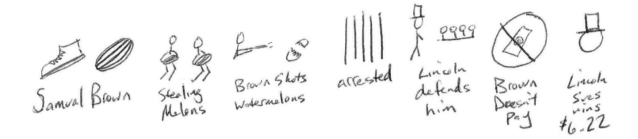

Students can use story maps all of the time when outlining ideas in a quick shorthand. This makes it easier to come back to a story later when they have more time to write it down.

The first story in this chapter, "The Stonecutter," exemplifies two different graphic organizers. The handout on sequential pictures is very much like a comic strip, using eight boxes to map out a detailed sketch, including (1) Characters, (2) Setting, (3) Beginning, 4) Problem, 5) Middle, 6) Try and Fail, 7) Solution, and 8) End. This is a variation on the story map that asks for more elaboration and gives students a more structured outline of all of the story elements.

Another variation on the story map inherent in "The Stonecutter" is the circular story. Ask your students to use this story as an example for writing their own circular story. They can make a series of seven circles that form a larger circle. Each leads to the next event and eventually back to where they started. My first children's picture book, *The Web at Dragonfly Pond* (Dawn Publications 2006), was written using this strategy, inspired by "The Stonecutter" in both form and content.

The Native American pictographs used to tell the story of "The Buffalo Brothers" can be used to write any kind of a story. More abstract, more of a mural, and less structured than the sequential pictures, students can use this strategy to brainstorm ideas, allowing their imagination and the pictures to lead them through their creative process.

In rewriting "The Nail" or a Greek myth, the chart for the five Ws and the H, though less artistic, is yet another kind of visual aid that helps students to think through the elements of their story, both the traditional version and their new creation.

"The Recipe for a Story" is another chart for helping students to organize what they know about traditional story forms as well as a tool to help them create original stories. These charts help students to classify and organize their thoughts before they start writing. Like a menu, they have all of the ingredients for a happy meal, but this process allows them to choose which side dishes and flavors they want to use!

Later in the book, in the chapter on science and storytelling, you will see an adaptation of the circular story to teach the Water Cycle. This idea of using a circular story to follow a drop of water through the stages of evaporation, condensation, precipitation, and collection can be used with a simple circular story map like "The Stonecutter," or as a mural like the pictographs in "Buffalo Brothers." The circular story map can also be used to write stories for all of the cycles of nature, from the food web and mineral cycles to the circulatory system and electrical circuits.

The "Talking Yam" uses a dynamic flow chart similar to the ones we used way back in the early 1980s to write computer programs in Basic. It is a hybrid of the story map, circular story, and computer graphics, and it is the crowning achievement of this author! It is included as an end in itself, but also as an example of a keystone concept: Graphic organizers as a prewriting process is a fluid strategy that should not be taught as rote exercises to be memorized and used exactly as prescribed. They are loose models to be used as inspiration. The story, the content, and the creativity of the writer should lead the author to adapt and invent new forms.

As you walk your class through the various lesson plans, please highlight the underlying format of the story. Give your students a wide variety of models to choose from when creating their own stories. Discuss flashbacks, tangents that loop back to the core idea, foreshadowing, parallel scene construction, stories that begin at the climax—digress for background—and then push through to the conclusion. Teach them to see the strategy behind the story structure, to *think* about their thinking.

The first couple of lessons in this chapter are most appropriate for preschool and early elementary, while the later lessons are better suited for upper elementary, junior high school, and high school students, but all of these lessons can be taught to most grade levels. You will notice layers that overlap in a few of the lessons; there is value in repetition, but you will also notice additional layers of subtlety and complexity as your students make progress through the series. Also know that the first few lessons can be easily adapted for teaching the upper grades how to write fairy tales and fables; then these older students can adapt the lesson plan and help a younger student write a story through a big brother/big sister story-buddy program.

"THE STONECUTTER": SEQUENTIAL PICTURE STORY MAPS

The Stonecutter

A Traditional Chinese Tale Retold by Brian "Fox" Ellis

Kachunk! Kachunk! Kachunk!

Once there was a stonecutter who worked hard all day, with a chisel and a hammer, Kachunk! Kachunk! He cut square stones to build a school or temple, Kachunk! Kachunk! He cut flat round flat stones for a garden walk, Kachunk! Kachunk! He sweated and strained, lifting huge heavy stones, heaving them into a wheelbarrow and taking them to the building site.

One day while he was working a wealthy merchant walked by. The stonecutter said, "I wish I were a merchant. My life would be so much easier."

The Spirit of the Mountain heard him and *gong* . . . He became a wealthy merchant.

He lived in a grand home with a fine chef to fix him fantastic meals and a servant to clean up after him. Now his job was to count his money. His favorite part of his job was spending his money, investing it, so he could make more money.

One day while the wealthy merchant was walking through town, the Emperor marched past. The merchant said, "I wish I were an Emperor. Then I would be the most powerful person in the land."

The Spirit of the Mountain heard him and *gong* . . . He became an Emperor.

He no longer walked around town; he had four strong men to carry him everywhere he went. He had armies at his control. He could have your head if he wanted it! "Certainly, now, I am the most powerful person in the land!" he said.

One day while the Emperor was parading through town the sun beat down on him. "Everyone must sweat under the sun," he thought. "The sun is more powerful than I. I wish I were the sun. Then I would be the most powerful thing in the world."

The Spirit of the Mountain heard him and *gong* . . . He became the sun.

He had the power to make flowers bloom. He could scorch the land, cause a drought—the people would starve if he willed it! "Certainly, now, I am the most powerful thing in the world!" he thought.

One day while the sun was beating down a big black cloud moved in and blocked the sun, shading the earth. He tried to boil it away, but the cloud was too big. "Something is more powerful than the sun? I wish I were the cloud." He said, "Then I would be the most powerful thing in the world."

The Spirit of the Mountain heard him and *gong* . . . He became the cloud.

He could make gentle rains to help the rice grow. He could cause a flood, wash away the village! "Certainly, now, I am the most powerful thing in the world!" he thought.

But, whoa, he had no control over which way he went. The wind could blow him here and there. "Something is more powerful than the cloud? I wish I were the wind." He said, "Then I would be the most powerful thing in the world."

The Spirit of the Mountain heard him and *gong* . . . He became the wind.

He could be the gentle breeze that tousles your hair. He could become a tornado or hurricane with winds so strong he could tear trees from the ground and toss buildings into the air! "Certainly, now, I am the most powerful thing in the world!" he thought.

But, swoosh, one day he blew into the mountain. Swoosh! No matter how hard he blew, SWOOSH, he could not move the mountain! "Something is more powerful than the wind? I wish I were the mountain." He said, "Then I would be the most powerful thing in the world."

The Spirit of the Mountain heard him and *swoosh* . . . He became the tallest mountain in all of China. "Certainly, now, I am the most powerful thing in the world!" he thought.

Strong winds would blow, but can the wind move a mountain? No! The sun would beat down on him, but can the sun move mountains? No! The rain might wash a few pebbles to the sea, but a cloud cannot move a mountain. Can emperors or merchants? No! No one can move a mountain except . . .

Kachunk! Kachunk! The Stonecutter, he can move a mountain, Kachunk! Kachunk! One stone at a time.

Sequential Picture Story Maps

Grade Levels: Pre-K–12

Time Estimate: One hour

Objectives:

- Students will learn a traditional Chinese folktale, as well as a frame for creating their own circular stories.

- Students will make a story map, a potent tool for learning and writing their own stories.

National Standards:

- National Council of Teachers of English (NCTE) 1—Students read a wide range of print and non-print texts to build an understanding of texts, of themselves, and of the world; to acquire new information; and for personal fulfillment. Among these texts are fiction and nonfiction, classic and contemporary works.

- NCTE 2—Students read a wide range of literature from many periods in many genres to build an understanding of the many dimensions (e.g., philosophical, ethical, aesthetic) of human experience.

- NCTE 3—Students apply a wide range of strategies to comprehend, interpret, evaluate, and appreciate texts.

- NCTE 6—Students apply knowledge of language structure, language conventions, media techniques, figurative language, and genre to create, critique, and discuss print and non-print texts.

- NCTE 12—Students use spoken, written, and visual language to accomplish their own purposes (e.g., for learning, enjoyment, persuasion, and the exchange of information).

- National Council for the Social Studies (NCSS) 1—Culture

- NCSS 3—People, Places, and Environments

Materials:

- Paper and pencil (preferably, large 11 x 14 unlined paper)

- Crayons, markers, or colored pencils

- A copy of the worksheet "Sequential Picture Story Map"

- Chart paper and magic marker

Background Information: This is a traditional circular story. Because of the clearly laid out sequential order of events, with each episode introduced with a recurring line, it is the perfect story for introducing sequential picture story maps. Making sequential picture maps is one of the best ways to introduce the idea that stories have a beginning, middle, and end with a problem and a solution. The handout in this section was created more for teachers to help them map out the lesson. With students I just hand out a blank sheet of unlined paper, preferably 11 x 17, large newsprint.

You can use this same lesson with older students because many of us are more creative when the imagination is engaged in images and not so worried about the words, just yet.

When I perform this story, I sometimes use a Tibetan bell to gong the transformation. If you do not have a bell, you can snap your fingers or clap your hands. I also invite the audience to guess what the character will become next with a pause after the phrase, "and then he became . . . ." Pause here and let them fill in the gap, like a Cloze exercise. And I always begin the story with a query: Who or what is the most important thing in this story?

Instructional Procedures

Introduction: Begin this lesson with a quick review of what makes a story. Through Socratic questioning, discuss the ingredients for a story. What does every story need? With early elementary students, we talk about the three questions: *Who* is in the Story? *Where* does the story take place? And *what happens* in the story? And then what happens, and then what happens? With older students, we talk about character, setting, and plot. With all ages, we discuss beginning, middle, and end, problem and solutions.

Then tell the story! If it makes it easier for you to remember it, you can copy the sequential picture map embedded in the story.

Activity: After the story is over, discuss the answers to these questions: *Who* was in this story? *Where* does this story take place? And *what happened* in the story? And then what happened, and then what happened? What problem did he have? How did he solve it in the end? Now turn to a partner and discuss the big question in this story: Who or what is the most important thing in this story? And why did you give this answer? Discuss your answer with a partner. Then discuss this big question as a class.

Now it is time to write a new story. I tell the class, "You will help me write a story, and then I will help you write your own story." Take a large piece of paper and fold it in half, fold it again, and fold it in half a third time. Ask the class to make a prediction: When I open this piece of paper, how many rectangles will I have?

Ask students to think about this next series of questions before they hold up their hands. Always call on several students, get several ideas, and then put a few together to get the best idea. Try to model the creative process; we can come up with a lot of ideas and usually the best idea is a few ideas put together. Ask students to "Help me out here; to make a story, we need to answer those key questions. First, *who* is in the story? Do we want people or animals? How old are they? What do they look like? Please do not give me a one-word answer, like "dog"; tell me what color it is, how big, whether it is missing its tail, walks with limp, or likes to lick your face. Describe the characters so I can draw them."

After calling on several students, draw two or more characters in the first box and tell the beginning of the story as you draw, "Once upon a time, there was a big tiger with orange and black stripes. She had a long tail and sharp teeth. There was a little hairy monkey with whiskers and a long tail up in a tree, but we are getting ahead of ourselves. *Where* do they live?"

Next, discuss the setting. *Where* does this story take place? Again, ask for complete sentences, descriptions with enough detail so that you can draw it. Call on several students you have not heard from and put together a few ideas, telling the story as you draw. "The monkey lived high in a coconut tree on the shore of the sea near a jungle. There were lots of vines."

Then discuss the plot, *what happens*? Ask students to turn to a partner and discuss this one question: "If you were this monkey or this tiger, and you lived in this place, what would you do?" Or, "What problems would you have and how would you solve them?" The idea here is that each of them could make an entirely different story with these two characters! Then discuss this as a class. What happens first? What problem might arise? Maybe they try to solve it and it does not work; then what happens? Then what happens? And how do they solve the problem? How does the story end?

Here is the zinger! Here is a powerful yet simple way to improve the complexity of student writing using storytelling. Ask the students, "How many of you have read a book or watched a movie and they tried to solve the problem, but it did not work, it made things worse? Were you excited and scared? Then the characters try something else and the next time it works. You can do this: Have your characters try, fail, but don't give up; try again and then solve the problem!"

After the rough draft of the group story is done, model the rewriting process. Tell the story to the class with exaggerated drama and make a few changes to the pictures as you go. Ask them for suggestions after you are done telling it. How can we make this a better story? Draw the improvements in a different color.

Tell a story, then write one together, and now it is time for them to write their own.

Next, pass out a large sheet of paper to every student. Walk them through the folding process, asking students to turn and help a neighbor when they are done. Fold it in half, fold it in half again, and fold it in half a third time. Ask the class to make the same prediction: When you open your piece of paper how many rectangles will you have?

Before drawing anything take a moment and think: *Who* is in your story? *Where* does your story take place? *What* happens in the beginning, middle, and end? Because oral language precedes writing, help students find a partner, turn to that partner and describe their characters. They are not to copy from each other, but maybe by listening to their partner, they can get an idea that makes their character better. Now give them a few minutes to draw the characters in the first box.

Invite them to turn back to their partner and discuss their settings. *Where* does your story take place? Ask them to draw the place, the background for the story.

Throughout this process, ask rhetorical questions to help students clarify their imagery. A question worth repeating often is, "Is this just a bunch of pictures, or do these pictures tell a story?" Encourage them to tell the story to themselves as they draw it the same way you did while drawing the group story. The room does get noisy!

Next, ask students to use their imagination; if they are this character in this setting, what problems might they face, and how might they solve them? Maybe they try the first time and it does not work, then what happens? Emphasize happy endings. Everyone likes stories with danger and excitement, but in the end it is a better story when the main character solves the problem. Wander around the room, peering over their shoulders as they work. Try not to make suggestions; instead ask a lot of questions. Pause with students who are racing ahead and ask them to tell you their story so far. With students who are moving slow or having some difficulty, review the basic questions of who, where, and what happens with a little more detail. For example, "Does that dog live in the city or country? How would you describe this place?"

When the class is finished with their rough draft, ask them to turn to a new partner and take turns telling their stories. Remind them that as they go they can think of new things to add. The key question at this point is, "How can I make this a better story?" Ask them to repeat this question with you—chant-like, several times!

At this point you have three choices:

1. You can pass out a clean sheet of unlined paper, help them fold it, and allow them time to make a final edit of their sequential picture story. These can be easily cut into eight rectangles and made into a book. Give each student a piece of colored paper twice as large as one page. Help them fold it in half and wrap it around the pages. Staple it close to the fold and you have a wordless picture book.

2. You can help them to fold a clean sheet of paper into a mini-book and ask them to copy their final draft into this new format. Please visit www.foxtalesint.com to download a free mini-book (in PDF format) that includes illustrations and text for "The Stonecutter." You can give every student a copy of "The Stonecutter" and a hands-on example of this type of book making.

3. You can ask them to use these sequential pictures as a first draft and then write the story out in words. Preliterate students can be partnered with older reading buddies or parents who take dictation and write the students' stories with them. These paragraphs can be paired with the pictures to create a children's picture book. This classroom collection of books can be grouped into a mini lending library to be shared with peers.

Assessment: The stories can be graded with an emphasis on how well they answered the questions who, where, and what happened, and how clearly they defined character, setting, and plot. If you ask students to write the story in words, these papers can be graded for both content and stylistic issues, as well as spelling and grammar.

The students can also perform their stories for the class, and the rubric on page 20 can be used to assess their performances.

More than a grade, it is important that students are writing for an audience. Make a big deal with their final draft and allow them to "publish" their work for a growing classroom library. Create time in the schedule for student storytellers to visit other classes to perform. Send your class out in small groups of three or four to tour the school and perform for their peers or younger siblings.

Follow-up Activities: This same set of lesson plans can be used again and again in many content areas. Here we are focusing on creating new "folktales," but the same process can be used to write historical fiction about a character from a certain period in history. You can help your students write "true adventure" stories about their favorite wild animal in science class. The possibilities are endless.

These illustrations with text can also be loaded onto one of several easy software programs and turned into short animated films with voiceover and a musical soundtrack. I have used Movie Maker from the Windows XP Suite. There are other products that might cost more, but they also do a better job with more editing options.

Comments: This is a lesson I have used literally hundreds of times in dozens of settings from preliterate kindergarteners to graduate-level teacher training. Everyone ends with a fine tell-able tale. With a different emphasis on character development or a specific historical period, this same set of lessons can be used to introduce or deepen students' understanding of the most basic or complex literary concepts. This is a lesson you can come back to again and again.

Sequential Picture Story Map

CHARACTERS—*Who* are the actors in the story? Human or animal? Male or female?

SETTING—*Where* and *When* does the story take place? City or country? Buildings? Nature?

PLOT—*What happens*? Usually there are *Problems* and *Solutions*. What problems would you have if you were this character in this place? How would you solve them?

CHARACTERS	SETTING	WHAT HAPPENS?	PROBLEM
ATTEMPT	FAILURE	SOLUTION	END

Follow these directions to make a rough draft of your story. Remember that this is a rough draft, so it is okay to make stick people; it is okay to change your mind; it is okay to be sloppy!

1. In the first box draw the main character(s) in your story. Like most good writers, you may come up with several ideas. Choose one or two. You can add other characters later.

2. In the second box draw the setting. (I usually blur the line between the first and second box and draw the setting behind the characters.) Where are these characters? This may change as they travel. What time of day or season is it? Draw this in as well.

3. In the third (fourth, fifth, sixth) box, draw some action. What are these characters doing? And then what happens? And then what happens? And then what happens? Do this until you fill all eight boxes. (If you finish your story with seven boxes or need nine or ten boxes, that is okay.)

4. Maybe in the third or fourth box you introduce a problem or conflict.

5. Maybe in the fourth or fifth box, they try to solve the problem, and their plan doesn't work, or worse yet, it creates a bigger problem. What happens next?

6. By the seventh box, you need to come up with a solution to the problem.

7. In the eighth box, you can draw an ending that is satisfying, Ah, it's over.

Use this rough draft to tell this picture story to a friend. This will make it easier to write your story.

"BUFFALO BROTHERS": PICTOGRAPHIC BUFFALO ROBE STORYTELLING

The Story: *Buffalo Brothers—A Traditional Lakota Story* by Luther Standing Bear

At one time great fields of the golden sunflower grew on the plains of the Sioux country. Both the Sioux and the buffalo loved this beautiful flower. Its leaves were so bright and green and the yellow petals more lovely and delicate than gold.

Many little yellow birds, so many they could not be counted, hovered over the fields of sunflowers. They loved the sunflower, too, and their feathers were almost as yellow as the petals arranged so neatly around the centers of brown. The birds picked at these brown seeds and talked a lot while they were about it. No wonder, then, that we boys liked to lie around on pleasant days in these fields and take in all the sights and sounds. Everything interested us.

The buffalo liked to wallow their big heads in the sunflowers, and many times we saw them with long stems wound about the left

horn, for they never wore them on the right horn. Perhaps they did this to decorate themselves, or maybe they liked the smell of the flowers. We only knew that they liked the sunflower.

Of course, we boys did not try to get very close to the buffalo, but we sat on our ponies at a distance and watched them. In the summer, if the flies were bad, the buffalo raised the dust with their horns and the dust-clouds would hide them from us for a while.

Sometimes we saw them play, and sometimes we saw them swim in a lake with only their big black heads above the water. From a distance it looked like a single moving black body on the surface of the water.

One day a great hunt took place. The men killed many buffalo and brought home many hides.

The next day some of us boys rode out on the prairie. No buffalo were in sight. Everything was quiet except the birds in the sunflower fields. I rode alone up a little hill, and looking over, saw two buffalo. I was surprised, for I thought that they had all been killed or had been frightened away. I sat on my pony and watched. One buffalo was on the ground, his feet under him; the other was nosing and pushing the fallen one about with his head and horns. I was curious, and watched for several moments before I realized that the buffalo on the ground was either ill or wounded. The day before, no doubt, he had been wounded, but had been able to escape the hunters. At this spot he had lain down weak from the loss of blood. With the grunted urges of the helpful buffalo, the wounded one would try

to rise. Each time he tried, he got upon his forefeet, but each time sank back again. However, this seemed to be satisfactory, for the friendly buffalo moved on.

The next day my curiosity brought me back to the place, but I came alone. The wounded buffalo still sat on the ground. After I had waited for an hour or so, I saw the other buffalo coming. When he got to the wounded one, there was a greeting with horns and heads. The well buffalo encouraged the sick one with rubbing and poking, and pushing him with his head. The poor fellow rose to his feet and stood for a moment, but sank back to the ground again. The second time he got to his feet he walked for a few steps and again lay down. But he was in a clean place and there was some green grass close by. In a little while the visiting buffalo went back to his herd somewhere in the distance and out of sight.

I could not now help going back to see what was to happen, so the next day I was looking on again. The unfailing friend came as before, and the stricken buffalo must have revived considerably, for after some coaxing he arose on weakened legs, but followed his friend away at a slow but steady pace.

I saw them disappear, and I went home feeling that I had been made better by this lesson in kindness.

From *Content Area Reading, Writing, and Storytelling: A Dynamic Tool for Improving Reading and Writing Across the Curriculum through Oral Language Development* by Brian "Fox" Ellis. Westport, CT: Teacher Ideas Press. Copyright © 2008.

Grade Levels: Pre-K–5

Time Estimate: 60 minutes

Objectives:

- Students will learn about Lakota culture.

- Students will write a pictographic story.

- Students will learn decoding skills that translate directly to better reading and writing.

- Students will be engaged in metacognition—thinking about their thinking—strengthening their ability to translate ideas and images.

- This exercise is especially effective in helping preliterate children learn skills that will prepare them for reading readiness and writing.

National Standards:

- NCTE 1—Students read a wide range of print and non-print texts to build an understanding of texts, of themselves, and of the world; to acquire new information; and for personal fulfillment.

- NCTE 2—Students read a wide range of literature from many periods in many genres to build an understanding of the many dimensions (e.g., philosophical, ethical, aesthetic) of human experience.

- NCTE 9—Students develop an understanding of and respect for diversity in language use, patterns, and dialects across cultures, ethnic groups, geographic regions, and social roles.

- NCTE 12—Students use spoken, written, and visual language to accomplish their own purposes (e.g., for learning, enjoyment, persuasion, and the exchange of information).

- NCSS 1—Culture

- NCSS 3—People, Places, and Environments

Materials:

- Paper and pencil

- Chart paper and magic marker

- Large brown paper grocery bags or brown craft paper

- The buffalo robe story

- Copies of the handout of pictographs

Background Information: Plains Indians relied on Tatanka, the American bison, for their sustenance. The bison, commonly called buffalo, provided everything. The meat was their food; the bones made their tools; and the skin made their clothes, covered their lodges and made drums. (Contact your local museum to see if it has have a buffalo robe story.)

Luther Standing Bear was a boy when General Custer attacked his village and made his last stand. He was a young man during the massacre at Wounded Knee. As an older man he rode a buffalo for the Queen of England in Buffalo Bill's Wild West Show. As an old man he wrote down some of the stories of his youth—true stories, not folktales. These stories were published in 1934, and his book *Stories of the Sioux* has recently been republished by Bison Books, University of Nebraska Press. These stories are a wonderful window into life on the prairie before reservations and the desecration of the buffalo.

Instructional Procedures

Introduction: Without saying anything, write C-A-T on the board. Ask students, "What is this?" When they say cat, ask them if you should feed it or take it for a walk? Then draw a cat face, a simple circle with dots for eyes, triangular ears, and add whiskers. Ask students, "What is this?" When they say cat, ask them if you should feed it or take it for a walk.

Is this a cat or the word for cat? Is this a cat or the picture of a cat? In different languages we have different symbols for the same things. In Spanish it is *gato.* But we all know that this picture means cat, or *gato,* whatever language we speak.

Hold up the buffalo robe story of "Buffalo Brothers." Introduce the idea that stories can be written in pictures. We have all heard the idea that a picture is worth a thousand words. These pictures together tell the following story. Tell the story!

Activity: After telling the story, discuss some of the specific symbols used. Explain how pictures represent more than objects, but also verbs.

Give the students two options: They can invent an original story in the tradition of a folktale, or they can borrow a traditional Native American story from the library and retell it in pictographs. Explain how pictographs make a spiral—not left to write like standard English, but circling in toward the center in a spiral shape. Or in some pictographic stories, like "Buffalo Brothers," there is a mural that depicts scenes from the story as a symbolic memory chart.

Next, invite students to help you write a story using a large sheet of chart paper and a magic marker. I ask students to think about this next series of questions before they hold up their hands, but I always call on several students, get several ideas, and then put a few together to get the best idea. I try to model the creative process, that we can come up with a lot of ideas and usually the best idea is a few ideas put together. Ask, "Help me out here; to make a story, we need to answer these key questions. First, *who* is in the story? Do we want people or animals? How old are they? What do they look like? Please do not give me a one-word answer, like "horse." Tell me what color it is; how big it is; is it a pony or a stallion; does it have a stripe down its face? Describe the characters so I can draw them." Like the last lesson, ask them about *where* and *what happens,* taking notes and creating a story as a class. Tell the story as you draw it.

When the rough draft is complete, retell the story adding details to model the rewriting process. Then pass out a large sheet of unlined paper and ask students to write their own stories.

Remind students that stories are about characters; setting and plot; beginning, middle, and end; and problems and solutions. With younger students, walk them through the same questions as in the last lesson plan, namely: *Who* is in your story? *Where* does it take place? *What Happens*? If you were this person or animal in this place, what problem might you have and how would you solve it?

Throughout the process, remind them that this is more than a series of pictures. These pictures tell a story.

Encourage students to invent their own pictographs and create a key. Although the attached sheet of pictographs sometimes distracts students and they tend to copy their favorite pictographs without a sense of plot, explain that the pictures on the sheet are just examples of the limitless number of pictographs they can invent. Older students can be asked to make a key on a separate sheet of paper. They can draw each symbol they use and write a word or short phrase to define the meaning of the pictograph.

After they make a rough draft on a plain piece of paper, invite students to find a partner and tell their story, with one question in the back of their mind: How can I make this a better story? Then give students a piece of brown craft paper or a paper bag to cut out an animal-skin shape for their stories. If you cut off the four corners and make two half circles on each end, the paper will look more like a piece of leather. Leather stores also sell pieces of leather if students want to make something a little more authentic.

With practice students could then perform their stories for their class, for younger students, or for a family night performance.

Assessment: The pictographs can be collected for a grade. The emphasis should be on the flow of the story—good form with a plot that pulls you along and a satisfying ending. A grade could also be given for the key, if a key is requested upfront and the expectations are made clear. Their performances can also be assessed using the rubric at the end of Chapter 1.

Follow-up Activities: This is one writing exercise in which the pictures are enough. If you would then like them to write out the story using the pictographs as a rough draft, this is an easy option.

Comments: One potential controversy with this lesson plan that can be easily avoided is this: Students who are not Native American cannot write a Native American story. More than semantics, it is important that students are not encouraged to dress up like Indians, whoop it up, and do a rain dance; racial stereotypes should be avoided at all costs.

Using this story-writing process as a model, students can write whatever story they want using the universal language of pictographs. I have had young students help me write stories about a trip to the zoo or a story about two horses on a farm. With older students who are in the middle of a unit on Native Americans, encourage them to write a story about an average day in the life of the culture they have chosen. Emphasize that they can get extra points for cultural accuracy *and* lose points if they mix up cultural details. For example: Do all Indians live in a tipi? Would they be more likely to hunt deer rather than buffalo? For more in-depth information on *Teaching about Native Americans*, I highly recommend the book by that title published by the National Council for the Social Studies (Washington, DC, 1997).

For more information about pictographs visit these Web sites:

www.inquiry.net/outdoor/native/skills/picture_writing.htm

www.inquiry.net/outdoor/native/sign/stories.htm

www.inquiry.net/outdoor/native/sign/pictographs.htm

Native American Pictographs

Drawn by Brian "Fox" Ellis

"THE NAIL" AND "HE GOT OUT!": TAKE AN OLD STORY AND MAKE IT NEW

The Nail

   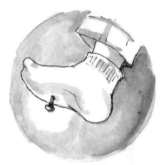

When I was a boy growing up in the North End of Toledo, Ohio, I had a neighbor named Jake. He was a colorful character who got along well with other people as long as he did not have to work with them. So Jake was self-employed.

Jake was a stocky guy, built like a tank, and he could fix anything. Give him a roll of duct tape and a hammer, and he could build you anything you could imagine—or so it seemed. He was always around when I needed help fixing my bike.

 Jake used to buy old cars and fix them up and sell them. Sometimes he would get a rust-bucket for a few hundred dollars, fix the dents, add a coat of paint, soup up the engine and sell it for a few thousand dollars. He also bought old houses and fixed them up. Today they call it "flipping a house." Jake told me about a house that he once bought that he thought was haunted.

He said: "It was an old farm house on the edge of town. It looked like it had been abandoned for years. The windows were broken out. There were holes in the floor and holes in the roof. I got it for a song."

"After I signed the papers the realtor told me it was haunted. I laughed. I did not believe in ghosts. When I went to the hardware store to buy some lumber and drywall, paint and roofing, I told the hardware guy about the house. He turned pale white and stammered, 'You did-did not b-buy that house did-did you? It, its haunted. Something t-t-terrible happened there m-many years ago.'"

"When I asked him what it was he wouldn't tell me. He just said, 'D-don't sp-spend the n-night alone.'"

"Well, I did not have a choice. At that time I would live in the house while I fixed it  up. That way I did not have to pay rent. The first day I fixed up one room as my bedroom. There was no electricity or gas so I used a camp stove to cook my supper and a flashlight to read by."

Jake then turned to us kids and said, "I still read every night before I go to bed. Do you kids read every night?" I nodded. He said, "Readers are leaders and don't forget it." I didn't.

Jake went on with his story: "I forget what I was reading that night, Edgar Allen Poe or Steven King or something. I love a good ghost story. Just as I was getting to the scary part of the book, I heard it (make a scratching sound), a strange scratching kind of noise. It is hard to describe, but it was coming from upstairs. I was not scared, well maybe a little, but I was more curious than scared."

"I grabbed my flashlight and headed upstairs. Squeak, squeak, squeak. Those stairs sure were noisy. When I got to the second floor I heard it louder, closer. Whatever it was, it sounded like it was in the ceiling. I did not know the place had an attic. I looked around and found some of those folding ladder-type stairs that you pull down from the ceiling. I reached up to grab the string, pulled down and AAHH!"

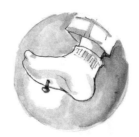

"A bunch of dust, dirt, and leaves fell into my face! I was scared, too. The sound, whatever it was, was definitely louder, closer, and it was up those stairs."

"I shined my flashlight up there but I couldn't see anything. I d-did n-not b-believe in g-g-ghosts."

"I headed up those stairs. Squeak . . . squeak . . . squeak . . . AAHH!"

I stepped on a nail!

He Got Out!

I have a friend who lives on Prospect Avenue near one of Peoria, Illinois' largest, oldest, and most beautiful cemeteries, the Historic Springdale Cemetery. My friend works second shift at a factory on the other side of the cemetery, so every day at about three o'clock he walks across the graveyard to get to work. But when he gets off work at midnight, he thinks about walking the long way around.

What would you do?

Walking around the cemetery means walking almost two miles. Walking through the cemetery is less than half a mile. He has made the walk five days a week for thirteen years. He cuts through the graveyard.

One night, just after midnight, he was walking home through a gentle rain, more like a heavy mist. He could hardly see where he was going, but he knew his way and could walk the paths with his eyes closed. As he walked along—AAHH!* He fell into an open grave!

This grave had not been there when he went to work in the bright light of the afternoon! He tried jumping out but kept falling back down. He tried climbing, but because of the rain the walls were slippery mud. How do I say this nicely? My friend is, um, vertically challenged—not very tall. No matter how hard he tried, he could not get out. Well, he figured there would be a funeral in the morning and someone would come along and let him out. They would get a scare, but at least he would get out, *if* he could last the night.

Because it was damp and cool, he curled up in a small ball in the corner to conserve his heat. He tried to sleep.

About two o'clock in the morning, at closing time, he heard someone else coming through the cemetery. They were quite loud and seemed to be singing some Irish drinking song. The song was getting closer, louder—AAHH!* This other guy fell into the grave. This other guy was

From *Content Area Reading, Writing, and Storytelling: A Dynamic Tool for Improving Reading and Writing Across the Curriculum through Oral Language Development* by Brian "Fox" Ellis. Westport, CT: Teacher Ideas Press. Copyright © 2008.

freaking out. He was screaming, jumping, and trying to claw his way out! The muddy walls caused him to slip and fall repeatedly. In his panic he did not notice my friend curled up in a ball in the opposite corner.

My friend decided to play a little joke. In his scariest, loudest voice [cup your hands around your mouth and vibrate one hand for a scary effect!] he said, "Tr-r-r-ry and tr-r-r-ry, but you will never get out! Ah-ha-ha-ha!"

Oh, but that other guy, he got out!

Prior to the AAHH! in both stories, talk quieter and slower and then make a loud scream! If your timing is right when you scream, the audience will jump! You can usually get two good jumps from both of these simple jokes!

Take an Old Story and Make It New

Grade Levels: 3–12

Time Estimate: 60 minutes

Objectives:

- Students will learn two simple folktales they can rewrite and retell.

- Students will walk through a simple rewriting strategy, by personalizing or localizing a folktale.

- Students will demonstrate an ability to rework an old tale and make it new.

- Students will refine their ability to tell a folktale.

National Standards:

- NCTE 2—Students read a wide range of literature from many periods in many genres to build an understanding of the many dimensions (e.g., philosophical, ethical, aesthetic) of human experience.

- NCTE 5—Students employ a wide range of strategies as they write and use different writing process elements appropriately to communicate with different audiences for a variety of purposes.

- NCTE 11—Students participate as knowledgeable, reflective, creative, and critical members of a variety of literacy communities.

- NCTE 12—Students use spoken, written, and visual language to accomplish their own purposes (e.g., for learning, enjoyment, persuasion, and the exchange of information).

Materials:

- Paper and pencil

Background Information:

"We have heard it all before, but we rejoice in the retelling." —Beowulf

"A bad writer borrows, a good writer steals outright!" —Mark Twain

Great writers from Homer to Shakespeare, Leo Tolstoy to Toni Morrison, have borrowed ideas from the past and made them new. What makes them a great writer is that they can add their wit, their life experience, and their imagination to make it truly a new story. This works especially well with scary stories, folktales, tall tales, and old myths. In the following lesson plan students will walk through this ancient process of updating a traditional tale by making it personal or localizing the story.

Do not tell them the title of the stories because it gives away the punch line. Both of these stories are conversational pieces perfectly suited for small-group telling or a classroom setting, rather than a stage.

Instructional Procedures

Introduction: Ask your class if they have seen a movie based on a book they have read. Which was better and why? How was it changed to fit the format of a movie and why? If your class is a fan of science fiction or fantasy books, TV shows or movies like *Ghost Whisperer, Supernatural,* or the Harry Potter films, discuss how these popular programs are full of references to old mythology and to biblical and traditional stories.

Explain that some scholars say there are seven basic stories that just keep repeating and that everything from modern soap operas and television dramas are simply recycling old ideas. All of Shakespeare's plays can be traced back to events in history or old folktales. Mark Twain even admits in several places that he did not make it up. For example, in his most popular story, "The Notorious Jumping Frog of Calaveras County," he has a droll introduction claiming to have heard the story in a mining camp out West.

What makes people like Twain and Shakespeare such great writers? They add their wit and charm. They add their words and repeat nothing. They rework the story so completely that sometimes it is hard to recognize their source.

A classic example of this is Leonard Bernstein's *West Side Story,* a rewriting of Shakespeare's play *Romeo and Juliet.* It is reset in modern times with gang warfare, racial issues, and some great music. The love story and the family disapproval of that love stays the same, but now the rivalry is between two New York street gangs, instead of two families from Verona. Bernstein also aptly adds a lot of modern lingo. His use of slang and colloquial phrases adds heart and verve to the story.

Discuss the differences between plagiarism and originality. The difference is this: Plagiarism is simply copying from another author. It is illegal and students can go to jail, pay a $10,000 fine, or both. Originality means that writers use their words, their wit, and add original twists and details. If even one sentence reads the same, they are breaking the law! It is not acceptable to copy! Students cannot copy from a cartoon, a modern movie, or a book they have read. Encourage them to start with an old folktale, a classic myth, or some other source material that is in the public domain. Change the details the way Bernstein did. Change the five Ws and H, but most important—use new words.

Anyone can do this. Use a modern dialect, colloquial phrases, or the language of the time period they have chosen. Put yourself in the story and retell it as if it happened yesterday, not a long time ago; as if it happened right around the block, not far, far away.

Before telling the stories, warn students that you are going to ask them to rewrite one of these stories, so they need to listen carefully to the details.

Tell the stories!

Activity: Explain that students can borrow ideas from the past and make something new in five easy steps.

1. First, they must find a story they like.

2. Then, make a list of the five Ws and H: Who, What, When, Where, Why, and How.

3. Change the details to fit their life experience, be creative. Change the who, to you; the when to now; and the where to here. The what, why and how may not change much.

4. Tell the story to a friend.

5. Then they write their own version of the story.

The most important step is the first one. Students should choose a story that they are excited about. Tell them, "If you don't like it, do you think your audience will? If you are enthusiastic, then that passion comes through." Enthusiasm is contagious. Included in this lesson are two traditional jump tales. Students should listen to them both and decide which one they like best.

Put this chart on the board and ask students to copy it so they can better outline their story:

	The OLD version of the story	**My NEW ideas:**
Who		
What		
Where		
When		
Why		
How		

Second, they need to make a list of the five Ws and H: Who, What, When, Where, Why, and How. Make a copy of the chart. Discuss the old version of the story as a class. Based on this traditional telling of the story: Who is in it? Where does it take place? When did it happen? What happened? Why did this come to pass? How did it happen? Most of these questions can be answered with just two or three words, a short phrase or a brief sentence.

Next, working independently, ask students to change the details to fit their experience. Fill in the "new section" of the chart. Ask them, "Who do you know that is like these characters? Where is a place you have visited that reminds you of this place? Is there an old cemetery or abandoned house in your neighborhood? Why would you or your friend be out late at night or doing this kind of thing? When could it have happened to you or your new character? Use what you know. Or use your imagination to make up a new place, a new character, a new time in history."

Explain that some things will stay the same like the major plot feature—what happened—because this is what draws them to this story, this is what makes the story work. Give students a few minutes to finish filling in the chart.

The fourth step is to tell the story to a partner. Invite them to turn to a partner and just make it up as they go. If they tell the story before they write it, then writing becomes easier, more fluid, and more thought through. As they practice, always encourage them to watch their partners watch the story. In this way, their partner will help them become a better storyteller and a better writer. If their partner looks excited, curious, or scared, it must be good; write it down! If they look confused or uninterested, change that part of the story to make it more clear or exciting.

After they have told their story they are ready for step five: write a new version of this old tale. Encourage them to be creative: Add new details, describe the characters and setting, build suspense, or add a twist of irony. Make it funnier or scarier. When they get their story done, they can type it up, do some editing (check spelling, punctuation and grammar), and then put the stories together as a class book.

Assessment: These stories can be collected for a grade. The emphasis should be on how well they walked that line between the creativity and invention in changing the story while maintaining the integrity of the original version.

Follow-up Activities: As an exercise in comparative folklore, it can be fun to see how many versions of "Cinderella" you can find and compare and contrast the cultural details (see page 87). Students can also give a simple peer review of their partners' final draft by making notes in the margin on where they liked their partners' changes. Emphasize that this is not a grade but a positive critique—only compliments. As a class, if these stories were collected into a single book or published online, students could read each other's versions of these two stories and learn a great deal from each other's writing styles.

Comments: This is another lesson plan where you will want to dog-ear the page and come back to it again and again. It works especially well with fables, tall tales, and scary stories, and later in this chapter we will use an adapted version of this lesson plan to rewrite a Greek myth (see page 53). You can also integrate this lesson with social studies by asking students to rewrite a folktale set in a new historical period with extra points given for historically accurate details.

FUN WITH FABLES: A LESSON IN COMPARATIVE FOLKLORE AND CREATIVE WRITING

The Dog and His Bone

It was market day in the village. The village was filled with people, buying and selling goods and haggling over prices. Oh, the smells of the marketplace! Do you know the smell of meat barbequing on the grill? Fresh baked bread hot out of the oven? A perfectly ripe peach sliced into delicate sections?

I talk about smells, because this is a story about a dog. Now, you and I are humans, last time I checked, and most of what we know comes in through our eyes; we watch, we read, we see. But most of what a dog knows comes in through his nose, and all of these smells were making this dog hungry!

Just then he walked past the butcher shop. He smelled fresh smoked ham and sausages, pork chops, and chickens. M-m-m, he was hungry. The dog went inside the butcher shop.

The butcher saw him coming. He shouted, "Hey you dog, get out of here!"

"Aarrf, arrf, aarf." The dog ran out, but he didn't go too far. Outside of the butcher shop he stopped. He waited. He watched.

It *was* market day in the village. The village was *filled* with people, buying and selling goods, and haggling over prices. The butcher shop was busier than any other.

The butcher went into the back room to get some sausages for a customer. The dog was watching. "Aarr, this is my chance!" he thought. That dog snuck back into the butcher shop. He slipped between the legs of the customers. He went right over to the counter and snatched a great big bone.

Just then the butcher came out of the back room. The butcher saw that dog. He yelled, "Hey you dog, come back here with that bone."

From *Content Area Reading, Writing, and Storytelling: A Dynamic Tool for Improving Reading and Writing Across the Curriculum through Oral Language Development* by Brian "Fox" Ellis. Westport, CT: Teacher Ideas Press. Copyright © 2008.

Would you keep on running? The dog did. And I must admit, that butcher was not in very good shape. The dog left him in his dust.

 "Grrr, maybe I'll go out to the woods where I can eat the bone in peace and quiet," the dog grumbled to himself. To get to the forest he had to cross a river. He found a bridge. As he walked over the bridge, he stopped to rest. He was tired from all of that running. He looked into the water, and there he saw what looked like another dog. That dog seemed to have a bone that was bigger than his bone. He was greedy. He thought, "I'll growl at him. I'll scare him. Then he will give me his bone and I'll have two bones." So he started to growl. "Grr-r-rr!"

That other dog seemed to be baring his teeth and growling back.

The dog thought, "I ain't going to take it. I'll bark, I'll howl! That'll scare him. Ouuu Ouuu Ouuu!" But as soon as he opened his mouth to bark and howl, the bone fell out. Splash! His reflection disappeared, and so did his bone, which went floating down the river. That dog learned too late: Greed will get you nowhere. It is better to be happy with what you have!

Fun with Fables: A Lesson in Comparative Folklore and Creative Writing

Grade Levels: 2–12

Time Estimate: 3–4 class periods

Objectives:

- Students will learn to research traditional folktales.

- They will gain a deeper understanding of the cultures who told these tales and their relationship to the environment.

- They will learn rewriting skills and improve their writing skills.

- They will deepen their understanding of what it means to be human while exploring the values of other cultures.

- Students will also improve their ability to think metaphorically.

National Standards:

- NCTE 2—Students read a wide range of literature from many periods in many genres to build an understanding of the many dimensions (e.g., philosophical, ethical, aesthetic) of human experience.

- NCTE 4—Students adjust their use of spoken, written, and visual language to communicate effectively with a variety of audiences and for different purposes.

- NCTE 5—Students employ a wide range of strategies as they write and use different writing process elements appropriately to communicate with different audiences for a variety of purposes.

- NCTE 8—Students use a variety of technological and information resources to gather and synthesize information and to create and communicate knowledge.

- NCSS 1—Culture

- NCSS 9—Global Connections

Materials:

- Paper and pencil

- Handout "Myth into Reality"

- Access to the library or Internet and several collections of traditional fables

Background Information: Fables are really about humans in animal skins; fables can help us all to be better humans by helping us learn from the mistakes of others. Fables are as old as the art of storytelling itself. One of the oldest books in the world, the *Panchantantra* from India, is a collection of animal stories. Aesop lived more than three thousand years ago. More than 250 fables are attributed to him. From the French author Jean de La Fontaine to the Russian writer Leo Tolstoy, fables have been passed on from one generation to another. From the modern

American author James Thurber to the ancient American Indian fables retold by John Ross, these stories are about universal truths. Adding a moral to the story was actually a Roman grammar school exercise that came a thousand years after Aesop. Aesop, and many of the creators of fables, wanted the listener to think for themselves, to create their own interpretation. As you share these fables with your students they get to decide: What is the moral of the story? What can I learn from the comic mishaps and surprising success of these characters?

Instructional Procedures

Introduction: Every culture has a rich tradition of folktales, fables, and myths that celebrate their understanding of the way the world works and their relationships within their world. Through these stories, they taught their children values and appropriate behavior. On one level these stories explained their understanding of science, animal behavior, and the environment, but on another level these stories were about all-too-human creatures clothed in animal skins.

Activity: Begin the unit by telling a few simple fables from various cultures. (For additional fables see also "The End of the World" on page 180, "Hummingbird and Crane" on page 83, and "The Dung Beetle and the Eagle," on page 213.)

Before you tell these fables, briefly discuss how these stories are about animals and their environment and the fact that they are also about people in animal skins. Do you know anyone sly like a fox, cuddly like a bear, or sloppy like a hog? Do not point at another because three fingers are pointing back at you! We are all animals *and* animals are good metaphors for talking about human behavior. Challenge students to listen to the following stories with both ears. As they listen ask them to look for human characteristics modeled by the animals *and* to listen for any new information about the animal in its environment.

Tell several short fables from several cultures.

Discuss the stories. Focus on the information you can glean about both the animal and the human characteristics. For example, in Aesop's fable about the dog and his bone, we learn that dogs are carnivores, they like to eat alone, and they are resourceful hunters, —all good science facts. We also learn that this dog is sneaky and greedy, and greedy people often lose what they have when they try to get more than their share through unethical means.

You may want to draw a chart on the board with three columns. In the first column, list the various animals depicted in the stories. In the second column, list the scientific facts about each animal that you learned from the story. In the third column, list the human characteristics that each animal depicts or symbolizes.

Now you have several choices.

As a follow-up writing lesson, you can ask students to rewrite a fable from their culture. This encourages students to research their own culture, analyze traditional literature, and practice rewriting skills. Use the chart of five Ws and the H from the previous lesson.

As a second assignment, you can also compare three different versions of the same fable and then help students write their own version of it. Photocopy three versions of a simple fable like the Fox and the Grapes or the Pitcher and the Crow. Put them on the overhead projector or pass out copies to each student. Read them aloud and discuss what you like and don't like about each one. Which one has the best beginning? Which one has the best description of the character? Which one has the clearest step-by-step plot development? Why? Which one handles the moral of the story most subtlty without beating you over the head?

As a class, begin to write a new version of the same fable, borrowing ideas from all three versions but using your own words. After the class has started this process and students have a good handle on it, ask them to write the rest of this fable on their own. Ask a few students to share their versions for an informal compare-and-contrast.

As a third assignment, ask the students to work independently as folklorists. Send them to the library to find two or three versions of the same fable. With some fable collections, such as *Aesop's Fables* or the *Jataka Tales of India,* it is easy to find several translations of each story. With other writers, like Tolstoy or da Vinci, you may be lucky to find two translations of a specific story. With a little bit of digging you might find the same fable reworked by Tolstoy, Aesop, and La Fontaine! Remember, 398.2 is the Dewey Decimal number for traditional folklore and the place in the library where you will find fables from around the world. There are also a growing number of Web sites that include complete collections of classic fables from many cultures. You may ask students to find one online version and two print versions of the same fable.

After students have found two or three versions of their fables, ask them to read them over carefully looking for their favorite parts of each version. They can make a brief chart that compares and contrasts these different versions and turn this in for a grade. Using the story you rewrote as a group for a model, ask students to write their own version of this tale. Emphasize the point that you can borrow an idea, but you must use your own words. This is a tricky point to get right, and an understanding of copyright law is helpful. If students can stick to the essence of the story but use some original twists and original phrases, they should be rewarded and held up as models for other students to emulate.

For students who may need a little more coaching, you may ask them to first write a short sentence that expresses the main idea of the story. Next they can make a story map, or flow chart that uses pictures to outline the five main events in the story. Then, using the pictures, not the text, of other versions they can write their own versions. Each picture of their flow chart can be turned into a short paragraph to complete the tale.

Once students have a first draft of the story, ask them to practice telling the story to themselves. Using storytelling as a rewriting tool, found later in this chapter, have them first read the story out loud and listen for ways to make it better. Ask them to stand up and act it out using body language to clarify the verbs and flow of their writing. Ask them to tell it to a partner and watch the partner's response to help them clarify their ideas and smooth out the rough places in the text.

Collect these stories into a classroom book; instead of Aesop's or Tolstoy's fables, your class now has a book called "Mrs. Smith's Fables!"

Assessment: There are several opportunities for the teacher to assess and improve student writing through this series of lessons.

First, collect the various versions of the stories you started as a class and the students finished individually. Grade these papers both on how well they paid attention to the class beginning and their individual creativity with the end of the story.

Second, ask students to turn in a printout or copy of the three versions of the same fable they found online or at the library, along with their critique of these stories. They can answer on paper the same questions the class discussed in regard to best character description, clear setting, and step-by-step plot.

Students' versions of this second fable can be given two grades, one on grammar and mechanics and one on style and originality.

Follow-up Activities: With a solid background in fables, students can then be given a chance to create a brand new fable. Using the information students learn in the lesson "Bird is the Word" (see page 151), students can write a fable for science class in which the emphasis is on the science information contained in a fictional fable. Fables that involve people can be rewritten in social studies classes with emphasis put on the historical period, a piece of historical fiction that uses the fable as the plot line, or rewritten with cultural details and motifs that illuminate a culture being taught in social studies. (For an excellent example of this kind of scholarship, folklorist John Bierhorst has collected Aesop fables brought to America by Spanish missionaries and then translated into the American Indian cultures. See *Doctor Coyote: A Native American Aesop's Fable,* 1996.)

Comments: Children of all ages love fables. Fables are short and easy to learn. Learning a few fables builds confidence for other storytelling adventures. I firmly believe that it is difficult for any child to be an active part of any culture, to have a voice within our democracy, or to be truly wise without a working knowledge of fables. I think Einstein had fables in mind when he said, "If you want to raise wise and compassionate children, tell them stories. If you want them to be wiser and more compassionate, then tell more stories." If your class, as a whole, learns one new fable a month, just think how wise and compassionate they will become!

"ETERNAL LOVE": MYTH AND MIMICRY—REWRITING CLASSIC TALES

Eternal Love Is Born of Eternal Kindness

Down in the far southern end of Illinois near a little town known as Boskydell there is an old white clapboard Methodist church. The small white church with its bell tower rising above the front entrance looks as old as the hills that rise up around it. Out behind that church there are two huge trees growing from the same trunk. One is a mighty white oak. The other is a big beautiful basswood, or linden tree.

Now you might be wondering how it came to be that two such large trees are growing from one trunk. I will tell you the story.

Many long winters ago Saint Peter used to wander the earth looking for a little human kindness, looking to see who may be able to pass through those pearly gates when their day finally comes. He came to Boskydell dressed as a beggar, looking for a bite to eat and a place to rest his weary bones.

He knocked on many doors that day and all of them were closed in his face. He knocked on the doors of both rich and poor and no one would welcome him in. The day quickly passed. This holy man was just about out of hope. Toward sunset he came to the edge of town where he saw a small shack.

Maybe you have seen a shack such as this, it leans to one side and is propped up by timbers. There are holes in the roof and chinks missing in the walls. The yard is tidy and well kept but lacking any of the amenities one would find around a more affluent home.

He was about to pass, when Saint Peter said to himself, "I have knocked on all the other doors I should at least try this one."

When he rapped upon the door, it was opened immediately by a kindly old woman. When she saw a wayfaring stranger, she did not hesitate to welcome him into her humble home. Her husband placed a bench before the fire so Peter could warm his bones. She put a sheepskin upon the bench before Peter sat down. This she did so he could sit more comfortably on the hard wooden bench. While she stirred the coals and kindled a fire, her husband gathered wood from the woodpile. It was not long before a blazing fire burned brightly.

The old woman put a pot of water on the fire and added a few herbs. Her husband reached up into the smoky rafters and pulled down a ham to add some meat to the broth. The two of them sliced carrots and peeled a few potatoes. Within moments a rich stew was simmering.

The wife set the table with their finest dishes, though I tell you they were old hand-hewn wooden bowls. The table was so rickety it required a piece of broken potsherd to keep it from wobbling. The husband slipped into the root cellar and quickly returned with a bottle of his best homemade wine, though it was closer to vinegar than fine wine.

The fare was simple, but within a short while the table was spread with a wonderful banquet. The hosts were completely unaware of their guest's true identity. But never had a meal been served with such love and kindness. The joyful conversation flowed as freely as the wine.

From Content Area Reading, Writing, and Storytelling: A Dynamic Tool for Improving Reading and Writing Across the Curriculum through Oral Language Development by Brian "Fox" Ellis. Westport, CT: Teacher Ideas Press. Copyright © 2008.

No matter how much wine they poured from the bottle, it was never empty; no matter how much stew they ladled from the pot, it was always full. When the hosts realized the miracle before them, it dawned on them that this was no mortal guest. They exchanged knowing glances and bent to one knee in awe. Saint Peter stood up revealing his true self. His rags fell away as glowing white robes flowed around him.

The old man and old woman apologized for their humble meal saying, "If we would have known we would have killed the old gray goose." Presently, they began to chase the goose around. I will tell you they loved this goose as a pet, never intending to make her a meal. And if you have ever been around an ornery old goose you know what a good substitute it can be for a watchdog. This goose would honk when trouble was near and would chase away all but the most persistent pests.

It was actually quite comical to see the fleet-footed goose being chased by the old couple! Around the house and through the yard they went, in the front door and out the back. When the goose sought shelter between the legs of their guest, Saint Peter raised one hand and bid them to stop the chase. "Save the goose's life. The meal you served was more than sufficient, better than any I had ever eaten in Gethsemane. Follow me," he said,

Saint Peter led his hosts up a small hill where they could see the entire village. As Saint Peter said, "I knocked on many doors and only you welcomed me in," he waved his hand and the village sank into a murky swamp. A lake rose up until all the houses disappeared. You may know this lake as Little Grassy Lake. With another wave of his hand the small shack of the old couple became a beautiful white clapboard church with a respectable rectory beside it. Peter said, "Will you care for the House of the Lord?"

The two nodded, wordless from their joy, though their eyes teared with the small splinter of grief they felt from the loss of their neighbors.

Then Saint Peter said, "In exchange for your kindness I am prepared to grant you whatever you want. You may make one wish as long as you both agree."

They knew that with those words they could have anything, anything they wanted. But they already had all they ever wanted and more! The elderly couple exchanged glances. Without words each knew the wish within the heart of the other. With one voice they said, "When our time comes, when you call us home, one of us could not bear to live without the other. Please, all we ask is that when you come to take us home we shall go together."

A wish such as this? Of course it was granted.

Though I tell you they were quite old when this story began, they lived many more long years in wedded bliss. A life filled with kindness and with love.

But eventually their time did come.

One afternoon, the old man was working in the garden, hoeing a row of corn, when he felt an ache. Somehow he knew it was his time to meet his maker. He looked up toward the house to see his wife coming in his direction. She too knew it was time. As they embraced one last time, as their lips touched for one last kiss, their skin began to grow bark. Their arms became limbs and their fingers became twigs. Leaves sprouted from both of them. He became a mighty white oak and she a big beautiful basswood, their branches entwined for eternity.

These trees are still there. You can see for yourself. If you find yourself in Boskydell, Illinois, the locals will tell you this tale. They will also tell you that many young lovers come to visit this shrine. On their wedding day they will bring an offering, a bouquet of flowers to lay near these trees. A silent prayer will fill their hearts:

May we too know eternal love born of eternal kindness.

Eternal Love—Myth and Mimicry: Rewriting Classic Tales

Grade Levels: 4–12

Time Estimate: Three class periods, 150–180 minutes

Objectives:

- Students will be immersed in Greco-Roman mythology.

- Students will gain a better understanding of story form.

- Students will demonstrate an understanding of character, setting, and plot.

- Modeled on ancient myths, students will write a contemporary short story.

- Students will use storytelling skills to learn new rewriting strategies.

National Standards:

- NCTE 1—Students read a wide range of print and non-print texts to build an understanding of texts, of themselves, and of the world; to acquire new information; and for personal fulfillment. Among these texts are fiction and nonfiction, classic and contemporary works.

- NCTE 2—Students read a wide range of literature from many periods in many genres to build an understanding of the many dimensions (e.g., philosophical, ethical, aesthetic) of human experience.

- NCTE 4—Students adjust their use of spoken, written, and visual language to communicate effectively with a variety of audiences and for different purposes.

- NCTE 9—Students develop an understanding of and respect for diversity in language use, patterns, and dialects across cultures, ethnic groups, geographic regions, and social roles.

- NCTE 12—Students use spoken, written, and visual language to accomplish their own purposes (e.g., for learning, enjoyment, persuasion, and the exchange of information).

- NCSS 1 Culture

- NCSS 2—Time, Continuity, and Change

Materials:

- Paper and pencil

- The Handout "Myth into Reality"

- Access to the library and Internet for Greco-Roman mythology

Background Information: I am a big fan of multicultural education, as evidenced by the variety of folktales I tell and the diverse cultural origins of the stories in this book, but I firmly believe that without a solid foundation in the classic Western mythology, it is difficult to be a fully functioning member of the modern world. Greco-Roman mythology informs much of our media and political debate, the Roman Senate is one of the cornerstones of our democracy, even the word "psychology" is taken from the myth of "Psyche and Eros." More than a state or national standard for most school districts, Greco-Roman mythology gives us heroes, hope, and coping strategies. Myths show us the darker aspects of ourselves in a way that helps us handle the tragedies and victories of human existence. Countless soap operas, comic books, movies, and novels draw from the rich well of mythology for character archetypes and plot lines. In this lesson, students will first drink deep from this well and then begin to brew their own modern realistic fiction modeled on mythology.

But then again, I would also argue that with our growing multicultural society, it becomes ever more vital that we learn the classic mythology of India, Africa, Asia, and the Americas. Maybe these other models will help us get past some of the historical mistakes that seem to recur in every generation. As a species, we are always made richer by diversity. That is an argument for another lesson plan; allow me to reassert that a foundation in classic mythology is a keystone of cultural wisdom.

This lesson works best if integrated into a standard unit on Greco-Roman civilization or mythology. Each of the three sections stands alone but work better if followed in order.

Instructional Procedures

Introduction: Begin with a Socratic discussion to see what students know of mythology—an informal prior knowledge quiz. Lead the discussion toward the ideas outlined in the background material, namely, our culture is thoroughly steeped in Greco-Roman mythology, and a better understanding of myths will help the students to be a fully functioning member of our democracy and help them to be better writers. Before telling stories, invite them to think about what makes these stories timeless, "What can we learn about being better humans based on the tragedies, victories and comedies of these classic myths?"

Activity: Tell two or three of your favorite classic myths. Reading aloud will suffice, but if you are asking your students to learn and tell a story, it would be great if you could model the process, even if you read two and perform one—these stories were meant to be told.

Ask students to turn to a partner and discuss the stories focusing on two questions: What was their favorite story and why? What can we learn from each story about being better humans? After a few minutes, open this conversation to the class.

With a brief introduction about how these stories are truly timeless and often rewritten for modern audiences, tell "Eternal Kindness."

Save fifteen to twenty minutes of this first period for them to begin looking for a myth they would like to tell. Visit your school library or surf the Web for myths. If at all possible, help them to find two or three versions of the same myth.

In this first period, it is important that they are immersed in mythology and hear several kinds of myths so everyone finds something they like. For homework, they do not have to write anything; they need to come to class the next day with the myth they wish to learn and tell.

In the second session walk the class step by step through the process of learning a story (see pages 14–20 in Chapter 1.) All of this assumes that the class has played the theater games also found in Chapter 1. First, invite the entire class to read aloud their stories playing with voices, sound effects, feelings, tone, and pitch. The class will get very noisy! Then invite them to stand up and act it out, focusing on the verbs, body language, facial expression, and gesture. Each time they should look at the paper less and less often—forget the words on the paper, and use their own expressions. Next, ask them to make a story map, five simple pictures that create a visual outline of the order of events. Finally, allow them to turn to a partner and take turns telling their classic myth, reminding them to be good listeners for their partner if they want their partner to be a good listener for them. Throughout this process, float around the room, listen in on their rehearsals, and offer suggestions through leading questions.

Save time at the end of the period for two or three students to tell their story to the class. Over the next few days, allow two or three of them a day to tell their story to the class until everyone has had a turn. Students can evaluate their peers using the rubric at the end of Chapter 1. This process will introduce students to a wider variety of myths as well as give them a chance to improve their storytelling skills.

The third session of this lesson involves the rewriting of a traditional myth to create realistic fiction, a modern myth. Introduce the session with a review of "Eternal Love" and discussion of how this story was updated. I set it in a modern town, used real events, like the flooding of Little Grassy Lake, and even shifted some of the Greek pantheism with a soft reference to Christianity and our modern cultural beliefs. This last point is also an old tradition. As Rome became Christianized, Romans began to rework some of the Greco-Roman myths into Christian motifs. Actually, implied in the term Greco-Roman, we know the Romans also adapted Greek myths to fit their cultural motifs.

Referencing the handout, "Myth into Reality," ask students to get out a clean sheet of paper and write a brief outline of their classic myth in five short sentences. If you have used the chart for the five Ws and H, refer to the concept but explain how this is a more complex adaptation of the idea. Also give them a few minutes to write a brief character description of the gods and mortals from the traditional myth and begin to transform them into modern folks. For their modern myth, encourage them to think cinematically, like they are writing an outline for a modern movie about something that happened just last week. What characteristics of the Greek hero are important, and who would they cast as a leading man or woman? Would they set the story in a major city, suburb, their local mall, or a rural area? How can they adapt the major plot elements, keeping them somewhat the same but adding a modern twist? How can they rework the story so it seems believable?

After they have answered all of the questions on the handout and made a chart for the five Ws and the H, invite them to close their eyes and have a daydream, like watching a movie inside their forehead. The more richly they can imagine the story, the easier it will be to tell and write. Ask them to turn to a partner and take turns telling the new version of their story. When they are both done telling, they need to get out a clean sheet of paper and write a new story, based on the old Greek myth.

If time allows or as an additional lesson, when they are finished with their rough draft, ask them to turn to a new partner and retell the story as way of rewriting, rethinking, and reworking their first draft.

Assessment: To help students with literary analysis, you can ask them to write a brief review of the stories you told in the first session. What was their favorite story and why? What did they learn from each of the stories told?

Their performance of a traditional story can be graded based on the rubric at the end of Chapter 1. You could also ask each student to fill in the rubric on each teller, throw out the highest and lowest score, and then average the points, weighted against your assessment, although this is a little more challenging to score.

Each student's piece of realistic fiction can be graded on the basis of creativity and mechanics.

Follow-up Activities: This same set of lesson plans can be used with most any type of folklore: Asian or African mythology, ghost stories, tall tales, or Grimm's fairy tales. To further integrate classic mythology and social studies, you could ask students to rewrite a Greek myth as if it happened during a specific historical period, say, the Civil War or World War II. These could earn three grades, one for creativity and style, one for grammar and mechanics and one for historical accuracy.

Comments: Knowing that most middle or high school students are required to study Greek myths and that these stories deal with so many adolescent issues like loyalty, jealousy, coming of age, romance and scorn, these stories have always gone over well with students. Once during a weeklong residency, I helped a class of seventh graders rewrite myths, and one student used a true event from a recent football game, reframing it with mythological references. Because he made little effort to disguise the names of his friends, he got a lot of laughs. We could also see each of his friends rise a little in their seats as they were made out to be heroes in the victorious defeat of the Titans.

MYTH *into* **REALITY**

Go to the library and find one of your favorite classical myths. This is an important point: It must be a story you love. If you are excited by the tale, then your enthusiasm will be contagious. 398.2 is the place in the library to find myths from around the world. Find a couple of versions of the same myth to compare and contrast the differences. Which parts of each version do you like better?

Read the story out loud several times. Experiment with different VOICES, pacing, tone, sound effects, and dramatic inflection. Stand up and act it out. Experiment with BODY language. Use gesture and facial expression. Close your eyes and see the story in your IMAGINATION. Use your voice, body and imagination together to TELL the story!

You can also rewrite an ancient myth as if it happened in modern times.

First make an outline of the basic plot. In five or six sentences, write a brief summary of the story emphasizing the main events. This is the skeleton of the story that you will flesh out with your own details. Although the details will change, the basic plot should remain the same.

You can change the characters' names and descriptions so that they are more modern. Make a list of the main characters. Next to each name, write a modern name and brief description of what they look like. Hercules becomes Harvey, Zeus becomes Zachary, and Venus becomes Valerie. Although you may change the names and clothing, hairstyle, and jewelry, their basic character should stay the same. Hercules is still brave and foolish. Venus is still beautiful, powerful, and vain.

Change the setting to a place you have been or know very well. The better you know your setting, the more realistic your details will be. It could be a big city like New York or Chicago, or it could be your uncle's farm. To help you outline the story, draw a map of the setting(s) or floor plan of the house(s). Remember that setting includes time: time of day, time of year, and time in history. Do you want to set the story in 2009, the 1960s, or the 1850s? Winter or summer? A bright sunny morning or a dark stormy night? Whatever time you choose will help to determine the types of clothes, houses, transportation, communication, and other "technology" of the times. Consistent details will help make the story more credible.

Next, make a list of the five Ws and H. Who, What, Where, When, Why, and How. Play around with these. Some you will change a lot, some you will change very little. First make a list of the facts from the original story. Then write a sentence or two about your changes. For example: Instead of Phaeton riding Helios' chariot of the sun across the sky and scorching the earth, Phil steals his Daddy's Harley and ends up in a drag race where he wipes out, careening into a meadow where the gas tank explodes, starting a huge fire.

Now that you have your ideas on paper, choose a partner and take turns telling your new version of the story. Allow yourself the freedom to improvise; change your mind if you like. Telling it first will make it easier to write it. After telling it, *write it*!

Practice, practice, practice. Tell the story several times to anyone who will listen. When you get the story polished, rewritten and rehearsed, ask your teacher if you can tell it to the class.

From *Content Area Reading, Writing, and Storytelling: A Dynamic Tool for Improving Reading and Writing Across the Curriculum through Oral Language Development* by Brian "Fox" Ellis. Westport, CT: Teacher Ideas Press. Copyright © 2008.

RECIPES FOR A STORY AND STORY MENUS

This is a lesson best served near the end of an in-depth study of folklore and storytelling. It is one of the few lesson plans that does not begin with a particular story. Well, okay, here is a story about diversity in story choices.

Today I performed at a small Catholic school in Lawrenceburg, Tennessee. When I was first hired, I asked the teacher what kinds of stories she wanted me to tell. We discussed several programs, including holiday stories, lives of Saints, science, fables, and tall tales. She asked if I could cover all of the possibilities we talked about under the unifying theme of encouraging reading, one of my favorite topics.

I began with "The Ghost with Red Hair," a ghost story from my CD, *River Ghosts*. We discussed discernment; could this story be true? Then I told a tall tale about Davey Crockett, who lived in Lawrenceburg along with my Cherokee great-great-grandma. I then told the Cherokee pourquoi story of "How Groundhog Lost His Tail." I recited a poem about my Cherokee ancestors and my family tree as a transitional piece into a personal narrative, a nonfiction science story about the food web, *The Web at Dragonfly Pond*. Then I ended with a Christmas story from St. Francis of Assisi that I learned when I went to Italy to research his life.

In this one-hour program, the students heard a wide variety of stories. If you have the working repertoire to pull it off, you could begin this lesson with four or five different types of stories linked together through your cultural and family history, like mine, OR better yet, you could invite a storyteller to your school to kick off the unit!

Grade Levels: 3–8

Time Estimate: Two 50- to 60-minute class periods

Objectives:

- Students will demonstrate an ability to differentiate between genres of literature.

- Students will write a story that blends their favorite genres.

- Students will create a story menu that will allow them to write many stories over time.

National Standards:

- NCTE 1—Students read a wide range of print and non-print texts to build an understanding of texts, of themselves, and of the world; to acquire new information; and for personal fulfillment. Among these texts are fiction and nonfiction, classic and contemporary works.

- NCTE 2—Students read a wide range of literature from many periods in many genres to build an understanding of the many dimensions (e.g., philosophical, ethical, aesthetic) of human experience.

- NCTE 6—Students apply knowledge of language structure, language conventions, media techniques, figurative language, and genre to create, critique, and discuss print and non-print texts.

- NCTE 7—Students conduct research on issues and interests by generating ideas and questions, and by posing problems. They gather, evaluate, and synthesize data from a variety of sources to communicate their discoveries in ways that suit their purpose and audience.

- NCTE 11—Students participate as knowledgeable, reflective, creative, and critical members of a variety of literacy communities.

Materials:

- Paper and pencil

- Handout "A Recipe for a Story"

Background Information: This is the kind of lesson that can work with first or second graders who have exposure to a wealth of folklore, and it can be the basis of a post graduate doctorial thesis on folklore. I originally wrote this lesson plan for my third- and fourth-grade class and was pleasantly surprised when several students created several more rows of boxes and filled them in with information for all of the genres we had covered throughout the year. The important thing is that students have an understanding of the differences between fables and pourquoi stories, between tall tales and myths, and so on.

Instructional Procedures

Introduction: As a class, begin with a brief discussion of their favorite types of stories. Whenever a student says, "I like fantasy!" or "I like mysteries!" ask the child what kind of characters we find in fantasy, or what usually happens in a mystery that makes it mysterious? These kinds of follow-up questions provide a segue into the lesson.

Activity: At this point you can then tell them several stories that model these different genres. Or if it is late in a semester full of stories, you can plunge right in and pass out the chart "A Recipe for a Story." Ask the class to think about what makes each type of story unique. We know that all stories have characters, setting, and plot, but how does a different type of character or setting change the story type?

As a class, begin to fill out the form. Jump around a little by discussing the parts that have already been filled in for them. Choose a type of story the entire class is familiar with and fill in all four boxes in the row through Socratic questioning.

This next activity works best with a small group of four. Give each group about 10 minutes to complete the chart. I always give incentive to turn the paper over and add to the chart. If they fill in all of these boxes on the front correctly, they get a C; if they add two rows, they can get a B; if they add four rows, they can get an A. If they want insurance or bonus points, maybe they want to add more than four rows!

At the end of the allotted time, inform them that finishing the chart is homework. They will be collected the next day, and it is perfectly acceptable to share their notes with friends from other groups; it is not cheating to share, it is a chance to ring up a lot of bonus points while learning from each other!

Inform students that the instructions at the bottom of the chart are all they need to write an original story. Before they begin, emphasize number five. This lesson can lead to a formulaic tale unless they are creative in the creation of their characters, use a specific place in time, and add some unusual twists to the plot. With older students, you may wish to discuss how movies often blur these lines. Action movies use a mix of humor and pathos, romantic comedies blend romance and comedy, and even a simple cartoon fable can have the animals solve a mystery.

Using information from the chart, walk students through the writing process. Ask them to choose a category and write it at the top of their page. Using "A Recipe for a Story," the first thing they have to do is to go shopping for ingredients. Every story has the same ingredients, character, setting, and plot, but what makes a story unique is the blend of spices—the details. Maybe you use corn instead of wheat, a white sauce instead of marinara, a blend of Romano and blue cheese instead of mozzarella!

Allow them a few minutes to write two sentences about each character. Remind them to make three-dimensional—3-D—characters: Description, Dynamic action, and Dialogue. Describe the characters in Detail: what they look like, what they wear, how they part their hair. Provide Dynamic action, what they do tells more than words. Include Dialogue that allows us to look into their heads and hearts so we know what they are thinking and feeling.

Invite the students to close their eyes for a moment and imagine the time and place in rich imagery. Ask them to write three sentences about the setting of the story.

Skipping lines, ask students to number 1 to 5 down the side of their page and make an outline. With the following list of questions, assist them in making a sketch of their story. The most important question being: "If you were this character in this setting, what would you do?"

1. Beginning, how do you want to start the story?

2. Problem, what is the crisis that makes it compelling?

3. Middle, maybe they try, fail, and try again; what is the climax of the story?

4. Solution, how do they finally succeed in solving the problem?

5. And how does the story end?

Using this information as the raw ingredients, now it is time to shake and bake, to put the ingredients in a pan and stir them up, put it in the oven and let it rise. At this point, you can invite students to close their eyes and daydream before turning to a partner and telling their story. If they tell it first, their writing will be clearer. Or you could ask them to turn directly to a clean sheet of paper and reorganize the information from the worksheet into the rough draft of their story.

If time allows, they can write their rough draft in class, or it can be a homework assignment. You might also ask them to make a quick story map to help them remember their outline.

Begin the second day with a brief review of their story. Give students five minutes to read over their story and begin to ask themselves the question, "How can I make this a better story?" Using the ideas found later in this chapter, "Storytelling as a Rewriting Tool," invite students to rehearse as a way of rewriting their story. Ask them to tell the story to themselves, using the vocal elements of storytelling to help the story find its voice, adding drama, dialogue, and sound effects. Ask them to stand up and tell the story to themselves focusing on the body language and action of the story. Invite students to turn to a partner and tell their rough draft of their story.

Give students the rest of the period to rewrite and edit their stories, incorporating the ideas they garnished from retelling the tale. These stories can then be collected for a grade. As time allows, invite students to take turns telling their stories to the class. Create an opportunity for several students to travel to other classrooms to tell their stories!

Students should be required to keep the chart in their portfolio to help them write future stories.

Assessment: The chart itself can be collected for a grade with points given based on both the number of categories they added to the chart as well as the accuracy of its completion.

Both the rough draft and final draft of their original stories can be collected for grades. As always, I encourage you to give two grades, one for mechanics and one for style.

Follow-up Activities: Encourage students to keep this chart beyond your class. This tool can be used to help them write stories for the rest of their academic career.

Comments: Whereas some of the lessons in this book request a very specific type of story, students respond really well to the freedom they have with this type of lesson. They are given a constructive frame to ensure a high-quality writing experience, yet they are given lots of room to experiment and follow their passion.

A Recipe for a Story

Fill in the following chart. List your favorite stories, and fill in the types of characters, settings, and plots that fit each category. Use this chart to help you write a variety of stories.

Stories	Characters (People, Animals, etc.)	Settings (Time & Place)	Plots (Problem & Solution)
Tall Tales			Impossible feats and superhuman solutions
Myths	Gods, Goddesses, and Mortals		
Ghost Stories		Haunted houses and cemeteries at midnight	

Make a larger chart to include other types of stories, characters, settings, and plots.

I. Choose which type of story you would like to write.

II. Write two sentences about each character. Include a description, dynamic action and dialogue.

III. Write at least three sentences about the setting including a specific place, time of day, season, and time in history. Also use all your senses; include smells, sounds, flavors, and feelings as well as sights.

IV. Outline your plot (What happens first, second, third, fourth, fifth, and so on?)

    1. A Captivating Beginning   Introduction

    2. Problem   Build Suspense

    3. An Exciting Middle   Climax

    4. Solution   Introduce Irony, a surprising twist

    5. A Satisfying End   Resolution

V. Use these notes to write a story. Admittedly, this method creates a formula tale. To make an original story, use your creativity to make an unusual character, a unique setting, and a surprising plot.

VI. After you finish your rough draft, turn to a partner and tell your story before rewriting your story. As you rewrite, look for ways to add drama, suspense, dialogue, action, and other elements to make your story more exciting or funnier.

VII. Edit and then type your story.

From *Content Area Reading, Writing, and Storytelling: A Dynamic Tool for Improving Reading and Writing Across the Curriculum through Oral Language Development* by Brian "Fox" Ellis. Westport, CT: Teacher Ideas Press. Copyright © 2008.

"BUZZARD BAKED BEANS": STORYTELLING AS A PREWRITING TOOL—THE PERSONAL NARRATIVE

Buzzard Baked Beans

When I was a little boy, I loved my Aunt Dorothy's baked beans. You know how everyone has a favorite dish and whenever you have a potluck or family picnic you can count on that aunt or cousin to bring his or her specialty. My grandma made the best potato salad. It was an old German family recipe with celery seeds, vinegar, and oil instead of that thick mayonnaise dressing that most people know as potato salad. My sister-in-law is an incredible baker who can make sweet, rich cakes from scratch, cakes that put Betty Crocker and her kin to shame.

But it was Aunt Dorothy's delicious baked beans that I pined for. My Aunt Dorothy made the best baked beans in the world. She used big chunks of bacon, not those fatty little scraps that you find in the cans. She used just the right amount of brown sugar, so it was plenty sweet but not too sweet. The beans were well cooked so they melted in your mouth. She baked them for hours so all the flavors melded together. When I was a little boy I loved my Aunt Dorothy's delicious delectable baked beans.

When we had a potluck, I would heap a big pile on my plate. I remember one family gathering where beans were all that I ate. I won't tell you about the effect this had on my digestive system. I will let you imagine how my brothers reacted to the digestive difficulties caused by a heaping plate of my Aunt Dorothy's delicious, delectable, desirable baked beans.

When I was five years old, I asked my Aunt Dorothy for the recipe. I begged. I pleaded. At first she refused, saying it was a secret recipe. "It won't be a secret if I tell you." Then she snapped, "You don't know how to read. What will you do with it?"

I pleaded, "Please, Aunt Dorothy, I will give it to my mom and she can bake them for me."

A sly smile came over her face, though at the time I did not recognize it as such. I was five years old. I did not know what she was smiling about or why she changed her mind.

She patiently wrote the recipe in very elaborate script. Big curling letters rolled off her pen as a Cheshire grin rolled across her face.

From Content Area Reading, Writing, and Storytelling: A Dynamic Tool for Improving Reading and Writing Across the Curriculum through Oral Language Development by Brian "Fox" Ellis. Westport, CT: Teacher Ideas Press. Copyright © 2008.

As soon as she was done I ran upstairs to my mother. We lived in a duplex. My family was in the upstairs apartment. My aunt, uncle, and four cousins lived downstairs.

I excitedly told my mother that Aunt Dorothy gave me her secret recipe for baked beans. My mom looked surprised because she had asked Aunt Dorothy for me, and she knew it was a closely guarded secret. My mom asked for the piece of paper. I handed it to her. She began to read quietly to herself. Almost immediately she began to snicker. The more she read the more she laughed. By the end she was laughing so hard her eyes were literally wet with tears!

I kept asking, "What's so funny Mommy? What's so funny?"

After she caught her breath, she read it out loud. At first I did not understand it. When she got to the end, I realized that my Aunt Dorothy was making fun of me. I cried, but not tears of joy. At the time I did not think it was a very funny joke.

But my mom thought it was hilarious. She read the recipe to everyone who would listen. My dad had a good laugh. My brothers laughed. Even my stiff old uncle had a good belly laugh. After I heard it several times and heard the peals of laughter I began to lighten up. My Aunt Dorothy has a great sense of humor, I've always known that, and eventually the story became a family classic that was often brought up at family reunions and potluck suppers. As I grew older I relished being the center of attention.

In her infinite wisdom my mother saved the recipe so I can share it with you today:

BUZZARD BAKED BEANS

- 2 buzzard brains
- 1 rotten egg
- 1 crushed toad

- Cow poop
- 3 horse turds
- Mix well and bake

Feed only to Brian.

Aunt Dorothy's Baked Beans
Aug. 28, 1967

Storytelling As a Prewriting Tool—The Personal Narrative

Grade Levels: K–12

Time Estimate: Two 50- to 60-minute class periods

Objectives:

- Students will gain a clearer understanding of the writing process.

- Students will use oral language skills to write a personal narrative.

- Students will develop listening skills, while learning from their partner.

National Standards:

- NCTE 4—Students adjust their use of spoken, written, and visual language to communicate effectively with a variety of audiences and for different purposes.

- NCTE 11—Students participate as knowledgeable, reflective, creative, and critical members of a variety of literacy communities.

- NCTE 12—Students use spoken, written, and visual language to accomplish their own purposes (e.g., for learning, enjoyment, persuasion, and the exchange of information).

- NCSS 4—Individual Development and Identity

Materials:

- Paper and pencil

Background Information: One complaint that many children have when they face a blank piece of paper is that they don't know what to write about. Every teacher has heard the whining and forlorn chorus of voices; they have seen the fidgeting and lack of work. I call it the blank paper syndrome, "I don't know what to write, I don't know what to write."

Yet every child's life is filled with stories waiting to be told. Each day is an adventure if viewed through the correct lens. (If Alexander Solzhenitsyn can write a full-length novel about one day in the life of Ivan Denisovitch, it seems that each child should be able to fill a few pages from their life!)

The trick is finding a way to mine the rich life that every human experiences. How do you inspire kids to want to tell their story? How do you help them to see the miracles and tragedies hidden in everyday existence?

The truth is that everyone wants to be heard, everyone wants to tell their stories. Who we are, are the stories we tell. We are telling stories constantly—to ourselves, to our family, to everyone we meet. Every time we open our mouths, we are telling stories. By using oral language development as a step toward reading and writing, we play to our students' strengths.

The following lesson plans are guaranteed to motivate most every child to write, even the hard-to-reach student. Early elementary and adult education classes have all produced excellent work, beyond the required number of pages, when properly stimulated.

Based on the model of the writing process, first take some time with a deep memory and oral presentation. If students can think it through and talk about it before they come to the printed page, then their thoughts and ideas are much clearer. This oral process is an extended form of prewriting that produces amazing results. Tell it before you write it.

Instructional Procedures

Introduction: Start by modeling what you are asking them to produce. Tell a personal story or read aloud an exciting passage from your favorite autobiography. Discuss autobiographies and how other people's lives can inspire and inform our own. Who are your heroes and role models?

This is of the utmost importance! I am asking every teacher who uses this lesson plan to first tell a story from your own life. It is important that students have good models of what makes a good story. Universal themes such as food, pets, vacations, older relatives, and sports are sure to spark similar stories from your students.

Activity: After students have heard a few personal narratives, ask them to briefly discuss what they liked about the stories, if they reminded them of any of their personal experiences, and what worked for them with these stories.

Next, ask students to choose a partner and to sit in front of him or her. Students are then given prompts to spark vivid images and asked to take turns telling each other stories.

The way it works is this: Ask one student to be the listener and the other to be the speaker. They will switch roles about halfway through. Ask the listener to repeat after you when you read the prompt. This way the speaker hears the prompt twice and has more time to formulate a response. Ask the speaker to respond to the prompt with whatever comes to mind. They should simply begin speaking, telling the listener any tidbit of information or story that comes to mind. At this point, they do not need complete stories; the goal is just to spark their memory. Give them only one or two minutes to respond, then ask for silence (or ring a bell or clap twice or flick the lights—somehow signal the end). The idea here is to simply open the floodgates of vivid memory. Read a second prompt. The same listener repeats the prompt, and the same speaker responds. Give each speaker four to seven prompts before asking them to switch roles. Repeat the process for the new speaker and listener.

Following are two sets of prompts, but feel free to write your own. Make sure they are general enough to elicit a response from everyone, yet specific enough to get vivid images. Knowing your class and their common experiences, create prompts that will elicit a variety of responses.

- *Tell me about your favorite aunt or uncle or other relative.*

- *Tell me about a pet that you loved or other animal you knew.*

- *Tell me about a family vacation, where you went and what you did.*

- *Tell me about your first day of school or some early school memory.*

- *Tell me about your favorite food and the last time that you ate it.*

- *Tell me about your grandma, grandpa, or other older person that you have known.*

- *Tell me about your favorite teacher and why you liked him or her.*

- *Tell me about a family holiday (Christmas, Hanukah, or the like) and what you do that is special.*

- *Tell me about your favorite game and how to play it; describe the last time you played it.*

- *Tell me about your favorite smell and the last time that you smelled it.*

After each student has had a chance to participate, ask them to free-write about their memories. Give them a limited amount of time and ask them simply to jot down a few sentences about each memory. They could also respond to their partners' memories if they reminded them of similar stories. Tell the students, "Do not write down what your partner said. But if your partner's story about his or her pet reminded you of your own pet, jot down a few notes about your pet." Next time they say, "I don't know what to write about," remind them that they have five or ten ideas on one sheet! If your class is a writing workshop, ask the students to keep these notes in their writing folders for future projects.

The next step is to ask them to choose their favorite short memory and to expand on it through a process I call a "deep memory." Have the students move so they are near their partner again. After they remember their story, they will tell it to their partner, but this time with more detail.

Explain to them the process of deep memory and how you will use this technique to help them recall important events and characters from their chosen life story. Deep memory is simply a tool for unlocking long-forgotten details from the past using deep breathing and relaxation to clear the mind.

Before you begin the process, ask all participants to sit up straight, close their eyes, and begin to breathe deep, quiet breaths. Tell them, "Breathe in as much air as you can, quietly, hold your breath for one second, and then breathe out all of your air. Empty your lungs without a sound and hold the out breath for one second. Continue to breathe like this at your own pace, breathe in and hold, breathe out and hold. Take ten deep breaths like this, in and hold, out and hold. With each breath, relax a little more. Feel the breath breathing you. Clear your mind. Think only about your breathing. And relax, relax." (Be quiet for a moment.)

After they are fully relaxed, ask them to enter into their chosen memory.

"Go back into that time. [Pause] First, I want you to be inside your body at that time. What were you wearing? What were your feelings? [Pause] Look at the other characters in your story. Who else was there? Look them over one at a time. See each of the characters for a moment in your mind's eye. Think about all the things you know about them. [Pause] Now, be inside that place. Where did that story take place? Look around you. What do you see? What does it feel like? Is it warm or cool? Light or dark? Moist or dry? Are there any unusual smells or sounds? Be in this place. [Pause] Now let the events unfold. Where does this story begin? Build toward the most important point. Where is a good place to end this story? For the next few minutes of silence, relive this story. [Long pause] If you are finished, begin to attach words to these feelings and images, but stay with the feelings and images. Create a clear beginning, middle, and end. [Pause] Remember the story again, run through it in more detail. [Pause] This time imagine yourself telling the story, hold onto the images but focus on the words. [Long pause] If you need more time take it, keep your eyes closed. But, when you have the story locked in, come back into the present and open your eyes. [Pause] Take another minute and finish up. When you are finished, open your eyes so we know when to go on. [Pause] Okay, open your eyes." [Clap twice.]

Ask students to turn to their partners and tell their stories, taking turns.

When each person is finished, their partner should give them one compliment. "My favorite part was _____, because _____." And ask one question: "Could you tell me more about _____?" You may wish to write these sentences on the board.

Next, give them a sizable block of time to make a rough draft of their story. Remind them that at this point spelling, grammar and punctuation are not as important as they will be later. They should be trying to get their ideas down on paper. If they seem to finish early, ask them to reread it and add details, elaborate. If they get stuck, invite them to close their eyes and briefly review their memory.

When they finish their first draft, ask them to trade papers with a new partner. As they read their new partner's paper, they should focus only on the strengths. They are not editing yet but only looking at the clarity of ideas. Ask them to fill in the blanks on two of the following sentences:

"When I read _____, I felt _____, because _____."
"I would like to know more about _____."
"I knew _____ was changing when _____."

These are only sample questions that are geared toward measuring emotional impact, encouraging elaboration, and noting plot development. Carefully worded questions can be written to encourage any aspect of story writing from setting and character development to foreshadowing and resolution. Students can also fill in the blanks on their own stories.

Remind students that the writing process is circular and not linear; at any point, they can go back to deep memory (prewriting), or free writing or rewriting. But now is a good time to move ahead to editing.

The editing process can be done individually, in pairs, or in cooperative groups. It is usually best to get at least one other person to proofread a piece of writing.

If done with a partner, they should simply trade papers, look over their partner's paper, and circle each mistake. If the students have been taught proofreaders' symbols, they should be encouraged to use them. Or they could make notes in the margins on recommendations for corrections. It should be left up to the writer to actually correct the mistakes so they learn not to repeat them. Editors should focus on spelling, grammar, and punctuation.

If done in small cooperative groups, the papers could be passed to the left three separate times with each round of editing given a certain focus: The first paper received should be checked for spelling (with plenty of dictionaries available); the second paper received should be checked for errors in punctuation; and the third paper received should be checked for grammatical errors with emphasis on run-ons, fragments, verb tense, and other common mistakes. This way three people review each paper, and each student checks three different papers. It also helps students learn what kinds of mistakes to look for in their own work.

Allow students one last chance to make any revisions in their story, before making a final draft. Ask them to check and double-check their paper one last time before turning it in for a grade.

The next step could be an oral presentation of their work. Because so much emphasis has been put on the writing process, students could be encouraged to read aloud from their papers. Or the teacher can read aloud a couple of the better works and ask the students to guess who wrote them. Another option is to allow students to tell, not read, their stories with dramatic interpretation.

Assessment: Because of the personal nature of these stories, teachers should be sensitive about evaluating content and focus instead more on mechanics. If the fill-in-the-blank questions emphasized character development or foreshadowing, then this aspect of style should be evaluated.

Follow-up Activities: This lesson can be collected into a class book, be an introduction to a literature unit on autobiographies and biographies, or introduce a unit on family stories and oral histories. This same set of prompts can be used for a family literacy night (see page 232) or in training students to interview elders at a senior citizen center or retirement home.

Comments: I am always pleased with the stories students write through this kind of exercise. I especially love the bubbly conversations as the students tell each other stories and their reluctance to stop writing when we are out of time! Also, this same kind of deep-memory experience can be used to help students write about their adventures in nature for science class (see the "Cottonwood," page 135), or with a little imagination they can write historical fiction (see page 105).

STORYTELLING AS A REWRITING TOOL

This is one lesson that can be used with every story in this book!

Grade Levels: K–12

Time Estimate: One hour if you spend fifteen minutes on each of four phases; four class periods if you allow an hour for each segment.

Objectives:

- Students will strengthen their performance skills through repeated rehearsals.

- They will learn to use rehearsal skills to improve their rewriting skills.

- Students will learn to be self-critical in a constructive fashion that improves their ability to rewrite their stories.

National Standards:

- NCTE 3—Students apply a wide range of strategies to comprehend, interpret, evaluate, and appreciate texts.

- NCTE 4—Students adjust their use of spoken, written, and visual language to communicate effectively with a variety of audiences and for different purposes.

- NCTE 5—Students employ a wide range of strategies as they write and use different writing process elements appropriately to communicate with different audiences for a variety of purposes.

- NCTE 6—Students apply knowledge of language structure, language conventions, media techniques, figurative language, and genre to create, critique, and discuss print and non-print texts.

- NCTE 11—Students participate as knowledgeable, reflective, creative, and critical members of a variety of literacy communities.

Materials:

- Paper and pencil

- A rough draft of one of their stories

Background Information: Most teachers will agree and most writers will confirm that rewriting is one of the most difficult things to teach and one of the hardest parts of the writing process, but it is also the most important part of the writing process. Rewriting is the difference between a good idea and a great story. When students say, "It is done. There is nothing I want to change." I challenge them to go over it again and again, telling them that rewriting means rethinking, reworking, and recreating, not simply copying it over.

Every time storytellers stand up and perform a story, they are carefully recrafting the work. Storytelling is one of the most potent ways to teach students the art of rewriting. It is also a lot of fun and removes the drudgery of rewriting.

Storytelling is already acknowledged as an effective tool in teaching prewriting (see the previous lesson on personal narratives). It can also be a powerful tool when it comes to rewriting. I often tell and retell a story a dozen times before I write it down. I then retell the story to a dozen more audiences to get feedback before I rewrite the story. The act of telling and retelling allows me to rewrite and edit the story midstream in response to the audience's appreciation or consternation.

After students have written a rough draft of their story, invite them to tell their story aloud several times, each time asking them to focus on different aspects of the story. By doing this piecemeal and taking the story apart, one part at a time, they learn the rewriting skills that real writers and publishers use. Storytelling is the tool that allows them to see each part clearly. They can focus in turn on dialogue, verbs, imaginative detail, and audience response.

Instructional Procedures

Introduction: I often speak of rewriting as being similar to math. It is simple addition, subtraction, and regrouping. Add details, images, sentences, verbs, adverbs, dialogue, a plot twist, or irony. Subtract the distractions, tangents, unnecessary detail, and cloudy elements. Sometimes you can regroup an idea and move it to another place in the story where it makes more sense. Instead of a straight chronological timeline, discuss foreshadowing or a flashback.

Remind students that before word processors were invented, the phrase "clip and paste" meant literally to cut out a sentence or paragraph and glue it down someplace else. Just as we teach computational skills in the classroom before we give them calculators, it might be helpful for them to at least once have the physical experience with scissors and glue, so when they click and drag on a computer screen, they know what it means to clip and paste.

By asking students to retell their story several times, they can clean up and embellish their stories. Each time they tell it, ask them to ask themselves, "How can I make this a better story? How can I make this a better story? How can I make this a better story?" I even ask students to chant this sentence with me at the beginning of the lesson and then sing it out several times in the middle to remind them of the task at hand!

Activity: The Tools of Storytelling Become the Tools of Rewriting

Begin with a brief review of the tools of the storyteller: voice, body, imagination, and the audience.

VOICE—The voice is the most important tool of the storyteller. You must be loud and clear: articulate, enunciate, express clear feelings, change voices, and make sounds.

BODY—Stand up and act the story out. Use facial expression and gesture, pantomime and body language to tell your story.

IMAGINATION—Tell the story silently in your imagination. Close your eyes and be inside the story. I believe that the better I can imagine it, the easier it is for the audience to be in the story with me. Use all of your senses. Describe smells, sounds, feelings, and tastes as well as what you see. Relive the story as you tell it.

AUDIENCE—Tell your story to a partner and watch your audience watch the story. Involve the audience with rhetorical questions, similes, and metaphors. Compare your ideas and experiences to things they can relate to, and ask them to join in with sing-a-long songs!

Finding Your Voice

Talk about the ways we use our voice in telling stories. It is important that students are loud and clear. Ask them to listen and repeat: *Enunciation.* I want to hear every syllable, listen and repeat: *Articulation.* I love these words. By saying them we are doing it. *Elocution.* These words are an exercise for your teeth and tongue, an exercise in speaking clearly. Listen and repeat: *enunciation, articulation,* and *elocution.* Singing is also a good way to warm up your voice. Listen and repeat: MA-MAY-ME-MO-MOO. Loud and clear: MA-MAY-ME-MO-MOO.

Challenge students to tell, not read, their story out loud. As they tell it, what question are they asking themselves? "How can I make this a better story? How can I make this a better story? How can I make this a better story?"

The first time through, they should focus on the vocal elements. Ask students to ignore everyone else and tell their story to themselves. The room will get noisy, and that is okay.

As they tell it out loud, ask them to experiment with dialogue, add feeling, and add sound effects. If they do not like the way it sounds, hit rewind and replay and try something else. Rewrite these changes in the margins. At some point brainstorm a list of synonyms for words that have more emotional impact. Keep this list on the chalkboard or on chart paper for future reference. Use the insert mark, ∧, to add a sound effect, an onomatopoeia. Use an asterisk, *, to mark the place where you want to add dialogue. Rewrite conversations to add detail, add feelings, and make it sound more natural, like something real people really say.

After telling it to themselves, give the students several minutes to rewrite the vocal elements of their story.

Lights, Camera, Action!

Another way to convey your story is through body language; your body language can add to the written version of your story.

As they tell it ask them to act out the action words. Celebrate the verbs. Instead of a boring sentence such as, "He *walked* across the meadow," how can they expand this sentence so they have more to act out? Ask several students to help you. Change the verb. Add some adverbs. Add some explanatory clauses or sentences. Better yet, insert a whole new paragraph that gives the actor more to act out.

I often discuss a few examples with Socratic questioning. How can we act out and expand this verb? Instead of, "He *walked* across the meadow," they could rewrite the sentence to say, "The fox silently slipped along the edge of the meadow. He looked left and right, above and behind to be sure no one had seen him. When the coast was clear, he dashed across the meadow, leaping over rocks, ducking under the branches of bushes, and swerving around the clumps of tall grasses."

Instead of, "We *played* baseball," it could be, "I was on deck, hoping my best friend would get on base so I would get a turn this inning. As I was stretching out and taking a few swings, Bernie hit a foul ball that bounced in the dirt between my feet, scaring the bejeebers out of me." I often ask, "Which is better, this one verb 'played' or these several sentences?"

Ask the students to take just one minute and underline as many of the verbs in their story as they can find. Ask one student to share a verb. Ask her to recite the sentence. Ask her to stand up and act it out. What does that look like? As a class, discuss ways of making that one verb a whole new paragraph. It is always helpful to model this process with a few examples from their writing to help them expand the details in their stories.

Invite all participants to stand up and simultaneously tell their story to themselves, focusing on the action. Ask students to "Stand up and stretch, reach for the ceiling, touch your toes, twist and yawn, shake your left arm, shake your right arm, shake your left leg, shake your right leg, do the hokey-pokey, and turn yourself about. That is what it's all about!" Storytelling is a dance. Ask them to act out their story. Use their voice and rehearse the vocal elements that they just rewrote, but this time they should focus on facial expression, gesture, and body language. What question are they to ask themselves? "How can I make this a better story? How can I make this a better story? How can I make this a better story?" After they are finished telling the story with body language they can sit down. This lets you know they are done.

Give them time to rewrite their verbs and add action. Turn at least three or four individual verbs into three or four new sentences!

Imaginative Details

The third time through the story, ask them to tell the story silently in their imagination. (See the "deep memory" exercise on page 67.) Close their eyes and be inside the story. I usually walk them through a guided daydream in which they close their eyes, breathe deep, and re-imagine their story—beginning, middle, and end. I ask them to use all of their senses. Describe smells, sounds, feelings, and tastes as well as what they see. If it is a personal experience story, this imaginative journey—revisiting the scene—will allow them to remember more detail and then add that detail to the story. I believe that the better I can imagine it, the easier it is for the audience to be in the story with me. Again, what question are they asking? "How can I make this a better story? How can I make this a better story? How can I make this a better story?"

Give students several minutes to rewrite the imaginative details of their story.

Knowing Your Audience

Finally, allow them to tell the story to an audience of one. Ask them to tell their story to a partner and watch their partner watch the story. If they are not reading aloud but telling the story, they get immediate feedback from their partner about what works and what doesn't work. Where it is clear or cloudy is visible in their eyes. If the listener laughs out loud or smiles, keep that part because it is truly funny. If the listener looks confused or bored, change that part because it isn't clear or interesting. Watch the audience watch the story, and they will help you to be a better writer.

This is also a chance for the partner to practice listening. The better job they do listening, the better job their partner will do telling the story. They can honor each other with the quality of their listening. They can also learn peer editing. As they listen, ask them to focus on what they like about the story. What can they learn about writing from their partner's story? When their partner is done, they should offer one or two compliments—*no criticism*—at this point.

Only later when they learn the difficult art of constructive questioning can they comment on the weaknesses. To help focus their comments, you may write a few sentences like these on the board:

My favorite part was _____ because _____ .

I want to know more about _____ .

I knew the character had changed when _____ because
_____ .

I could really see the setting of _____ when you described
_____ .

I knew _____ was coming when you gave me the clue _____ .

As you can see, each of these sentences focuses on a different aspect of the story. Ask students to comment using two of these sentences. Better yet, write some of your own sentences on the board to focus on the elements of writing that you are trying to teach.

Ready for a Final Draft

Now students are ready to rewrite their final draft of their story. Ask them to go over it one last time with a fine-tooth comb and focus on each of the elements that we have discussed. They should double-check the dialogue and sound effects they added the first time. They can underline all of their verbs and adverbs and rethink the action of the story. They can recreate the scene through their imagination using all of their senses. They can use the feedback from their partners to tighten up the stronger parts of their story.

As a storyteller-in-residence, I often walk students through all four steps in one class period. A classroom teacher who has more time may want to focus on one element with one story, another element with another story, and so on. But by breaking it down into its component parts, students can be more objective and therefore more constructive in working with their own writing. Once they develop this insight, rewriting becomes as natural as writing.

Assessment: If you walk your class through all four steps, then the paper could get four grades, or at least four sets of comments in four colors of ink: one on the vocal elements, another on action, a third on imaginative detail, and the fourth on awareness of their audience's response.

Follow-up Activities: If in this process you have not yet typed the stories into a word processor, now would be a good time to use technology to teach editing. Spell check. Click-and-drag, clipping and pasting. Playing with fonts and adding headlines and graphics can enhance the writing by giving students increased opportunity to publish their stories as a classroom collection.

Comments: This leads to one final note: There is no doubt that technology has changed writing and rewriting. With desktop publishing, Web page applications, e-mail, chat rooms, blogs, and bulletin boards, it is more important than ever that students learn to think and write well. Rewriting—the ability to critically self-analyze—is the cornerstone of good writing. Good writing is also one of the most complex skills in education. It requires higher-level thinking as well as an ability to fully integrate, digest, and comprehend the content. But writing is still basically a human endeavor. In this increasingly technological world, it is important that students learn storytelling and writing by working with other writers and storytellers one on one, in small groups, and with flesh-and-blood teachers. Oral language development is the most important step toward better reading and writing. Meaning is so much more than black squiggly lines on a computer screen. Without these steps of telling and hearing good stories, students as writers are less able to add or anticipate a lot of the subtle elements of good literature that are required for clear understanding.

To quote an information technology consultant I recently met at the airport as we were both flying off to our next consulting jobs, companies are hungry for people who understand computers but speak and write in plain English, not "geek speak."

Writing is a human endeavor, but technology also opens worlds to which writers of the past had no access. Students can explore story ideas on the Web. Rewriting can include Internet research. Students' stories can easily be collected into manuscripts for desktop publishing. Students can build Web pages and share their writing with Internet pen pals. These high-tech extensions not only add meaning and purpose to their writing, increasing motivation, but they also allow students to learn the technology skills so necessary to future employment.

As I write these lesson plans on my laptop in an airport on my way home from another artist-in-residence program, there is no doubt that technology has changed my writing and rewriting. Click and drag is so much easier than clip and paste. Before spell check was invented, I used to hire a proofreader to double-check my spelling. I often e-mail a rough draft to a friend for feedback before I attempt to publish a story or poem. Actually, these inventions help with the mechanics of editing; rewriting will always require rethinking and recreating, reworking and the feedback from human beings on the other side of the page or stage or computer screen.

A Day at the Zoo: Playing with Genre or Using Oral Language Skills to Improve Writing Tests Scores

This is a lesson in which the students' stories stand well on their own. Through storytelling, discussion, and debate, they will model for each other the various genres of creative writing.

Grade Levels: 3–12

Time Estimate: Three class periods

Objectives:

- Students will tell and then write a personal narrative.

- Students will discuss and then write an expository essay.

- Students will debate and then write a persuasive essay.

- Most important, students will develop thinking skills that lead to better writing skills and an improved understanding of the diverse forms of writing.

National Standards:

- NCTE 3—Students apply a wide range of strategies to comprehend, interpret, evaluate, and appreciate texts.

- NCTE 4—Students adjust their use of spoken, written, and visual language to communicate effectively with a variety of audiences and for different purposes.

- NCTE 5—Students employ a wide range of strategies as they write and use different writing process elements appropriately to communicate with different audiences for a variety of purposes.

- NCTE 6—Students apply knowledge of language structure, language conventions, media techniques, figurative language, and genre to create, critique, and discuss print and non-print texts.

- NCTE 11—Students participate as knowledgeable, reflective, creative, and critical members of a variety of literacy communities.

- National Academy of Sciences (NAS) 3—Life Science: Populations and ecosystems; Diversity and adaptations of organisms.

- NAS 6—Science in Personal and Social Perspectives: Populations, resources, and environments; Risks and benefits

Materials:

- Paper and pencil

Background Information: As discussed in more detail in the preface to this chapter, teaching writing is about teaching thinking. Allowing students to think out loud, to tell stories, and to discuss and debate allows them to clarify and organize their thoughts. This translates directly to clearer writing. I like to joke with students and scientists that if you give me a list of 10 facts on the same subject, I can use those facts to create poetry, tell a story, write an essay, or carry on a debate.

Through this process of helping students to use the same information to write in different genres, students will gain a better understanding of each genre as well as the mental acuity to organize their thoughts and their writing into the form that best suits the material at hand.

Instructional Procedures

Activity: With virtually no introduction, engage students in a rambling classroom discussion about zoos. Which zoos have they been to visit? What are their favorite zoo animals that they have seen? With whom did they go to the zoo, and what did they do there? What do they like or not like about zoos? The idea here is that you want your students engaged in a friendly dialogue about zoos. Within this classroom conversation, some students will share a piece of a story, others might share facts about the animals or the enclosures, while others might express opinions. Within an engaging conversation humans naturally narrate, essay, and debate. This is all part of the fine art of conversation.

After about ten minutes of this freeform discussion of zoos, highlight through compliments who told a story, shared ideas, or expressed an opinion. For example, "Joey, I like the story you told about the goat eating your name tag." "Jolanda, thank you for all of the information you shared about pandas!" "Jackie, you seem to have strong opinions about why people should not throw things into the animal cages."

Introduce this idea that the same set of facts, the same information can be shared in different forms. On the board or overhead projector, in three columns, review the differences and similarities among narrative, expository, and persuasive writing.

A Personal Narrative Is a Story

Invite students to turn to a partner and take turns telling stories about a trip to the zoo. Remind them that a good story is about characters, setting, and plot; beginning, middle, and end. They might want to start with a description of the friends and family who went with them or the animals they saw, then describe the zoo, taking us on a little tour, all the while going through the details of what they did first, second, and third. Encourage them to focus on a few of their favorite animals.

You may want to invite them to close their eyes and day dream using the deep memory exercise found on page 67.

After they are done telling their stories, give them the rest of the period to write a rough draft of their personal narrative.

For homework, they are to learn all they can about their favorite animals. Their assignment is to find at least 10 facts about the animal and its natural habitat and behavior.

An Expository Essay Is a Lecture

On the second day, inform students that they are going to take what they learned about their favorite animals at the zoo and write an expository essay. Review with the class the differences and similarities between expository and narrative writing. Remind them that an expository essay has a theme, a big idea, and then at least three points or sets of facts that support the theme. It then ends by restating the theme in different words.

Based on their research, ask students to look for a thesis, a theme, a big, overarching question that they would want to answer in their essay. Invite them to turn to a partner and help each other. One student shares her facts about a favorite animal, and then they both discuss what the theme might be. Then the second student shares his facts, and both students discuss a possible theme for his paper.

With some prompting students can explore ideas about endangered animals and a zoo's role in preservation; zoos as an educational facility and what they learned about their animal; the larger issue of their animal's role in its ecosystem; or the simple idea about their animal being a carnivore, herbivore, or omnivore, its eating habits, the food served at the zoo, and its relationship to its habitat. Although there is more risk involved, it is usually better if students are engaged in true inquiry and exploring ideas important to them.

If you want your entire class to write to the same prompt, you can put something like this on the board: What are the habitat requirements of your favorite zoo animal and how well does your zoo meet its needs?

In either case, time to discuss their ideas with a partner is an important step in improving the clarity of their thinking process.

Give the students the rest of the period to finish their expository essay. As they are working independently, encourage them to use as many of their facts that fit in the context of their theme. Also encourage them to stretch, noting that each of the supportive paragraphs need elaboration. "Tell me more . . . tell me more . . ." is something I often whisper over their shoulder as they are writing!

If you want to emulate the test-taking scenario, you can give them a time limit after they have discussed their ideas with a partner, and then collect their essays at the end of the period.

A Persuasive Essay Is a Debate

100%	In Favor	50/50	Against	100%
	————————————————————	————————————————————	

Draw a number line on the board. One end of the scale is 100 percent in favor of the issue. The other end of the scale is 100 percent against the issue. Ask students to copy this number line at the top of their paper. The important thing here is that the teacher never states an opinion in introducing the issue. Use a number of questions that hint at both sides of the issue.

Without talking to their neighbors, ask students to think for themselves: "Are zoos good or bad? Are you in favor of zoos or against them?"

Before you make up your mind, listen to these questions: "Are animals treated well in a zoo? Would they rather be free in the wild? Do zoos perform a useful or needed service? If so, what kind of service do they provide? Do the people who catch animals for zoos harm them? Is it okay to put animals in a cage for us to enjoy? Do you enjoy seeing animals in a cage? Are some zoos better than others? What should we do about zoos that are not up to standard? Do you like going to the zoo? Do animals like going to the zoo? Do zoos help breed endangered animals to set free? Are zoos a good place to learn about endangered animals?"

Now make your mark on your number line. If you think a zoo is 100 percent wonderful, put a mark at the left end of your line. If you think a zoo is 100 percent bad, put a mark on the right end of the line. If you think a zoo is 75 percent good and 25 percent bad, your mark is three-quarters of an inch toward the left. If you think a zoo is 35 percent good and 65 percent, bad your mark is toward the right of center. Students cannot sit on the fence; no one is 50/50! Ask students to make a mark on their number line and write two numbers above the mark, for example: 35/65 or 75/25.

Give students a moment to put a number on the top of their page.

Without discussing their answer with their neighbors, ask students to line up against the wall where they think they fit in. No talking. One hundred percent for toward this end; one hundred percent against toward that end. If they are somewhere in the middle, ask them to move to the place along the line that best represents their opinion. The only talking should be the trading of numbers so they are lined up in order. If two or more students have the same number, they stand next to each other so there is one long line across the front of the room.

Next, ask students to count off A, B, A, B. A is B's partner on down the line. Give them three to five minutes to talk to someone they agree with, someone next to them in line. Allow them a chance to trade ideas and discuss why they hold this opinion. The emphasis should be on discussing the reasons they hold this opinion. What are the facts, or statistics, or life experiences that lead them to this opinion? Come up with a least three reasons why they chose this position.

After they have had a chance to affirm their beliefs, you have two choices: fold the line in half or cut it in two and slide the line so the middles meet their opposite end. Which way you divide the students depends on the issue and their opinions. If your class is polarized, fold the line. Usually they are clustered toward the middle, so splitting the line and sliding it down ensures that students now have a partner who disagrees with them. One line faces the front of the room, the other half faces the back. They are now facing an opponent.

Lay down the ground rules for a civil debate. Students facing south have to be silent listeners, while the students facing north have two minutes to expound on their point of view without interruption. Then they switch roles. Students facing south have two minutes to express their opinion while students facing north are quiet. After they have expressed their opinions they can trade questions and take turns answering their opponent's concerns. Each can ask the other just two questions. Then give them two minutes to politely exchange ideas.

At this point I always ask: "How many of you changed your point of view even a little? If your hand is in the air, give yourselves a pat on the back for having an open mind! How many of you now understand your opinion and this issue more clearly? Now it is time to put your opinion on paper. Remember, when you answer your question on a writing exam, you need to be 100 percent for or 100 percent against and give three good reasons to support your answer. No one can be wishy-washy!"

If necessary, spend a few minutes reviewing what makes a good persuasive essay. Basically, you start with an opening statement that clarifies your point of view on the issue. In three paragraphs or more give three or more reasons why you have this opinion; give facts, evidence, statistics, and life experience to support your point of view. Then close with a statement that expresses your point of view with a different vocabulary.

With paper and pencil in hand, ask students to put on paper what they just discussed with their first partner. "What is your point of view? Give at least three reasons why you believe this. As you write, keep in mind the arguments of your second partner." A good editorial takes into account the counterpoint.

When they are finished with their rough draft, they can trade papers and critique each other's essay before they rewrite and edit their final drafts.

Assessment: The stories can be graded on the basis of the conventions of a good personal narrative: descriptive detail, character development, a well-defined setting and overall flow.

The expository essays can be evaluated for their use of facts to support their thesis.

The persuasive essays can be reviewed by the same standards used to assess the state writing sample, but with an emphasis on a clear opening and closing statement and well-thought-out and articulated reasons.

Follow-up Activities: This same set of lesson plans can be used to cover a variety of themes. Students love to talk about food and almost everyone has a favorite recipe or a story about a pizza party. Writing out the directions for cooking their favorite food is another genre of writing using the same information. Students can then have a debate about whether their favorite food is a healthy choice.

Also note that each of these three lessons stands well on its own. In particular, this last lesson on debate is one you will want to bookmark and use often. Talk about a hot topic, an issue ripped from today's headlines, or choose an eternal issue that your students should have strong opinions about—like homework or school lunch. When I taught seventh grade, we talked about Anita Hill and Judge Clarence Thomas. When I taught Adult Basic Education and helped young adults prepare for their GEDs, we had a debate about what age parents are no longer responsible for the crimes committed by their children. My favorite debate of late uses the Emancipation Proclamation to teach document-based questioning. I ask students to pick apart the original document and then write their own position paper: Is it one of the greatest documents in American history? Or is it a convoluted piece of political jargon filled with compromise and empty promises?

Comments: Remind students that they cannot have an open debate while taking the state test, but if they keep this process in mind while writing their persuasive essay, they will write better essays. Ask them to put a gauge on where they stand, think through their opinion, come up with three reasons, make an outline, and then write their essay, keeping in mind the opposite point of view and how their opponents might respond to the essay.

YOUNG AUTHOR PROJECTS: BOOK IN A DAY, INSTANT MINIBOOKS, AND STRATEGIES FOR SIMPLIFYING THE PUBLISHING PROCESS

As a published author, I love the virtually universal Young Authors program. I have had the honor of keynoting several state conferences, and every year several school districts invite me to help kick off their program, or I tell stories at their award ceremony. As evidenced with every lesson plan in this book, I am all about encouraging students to publish or otherwise share their work.

I have also had firsthand experience with the stress of meeting a deadline, writing and rewriting, rewriting, rewriting. My first children's picture book, *The Web at Dragonfly Pond*, went through about twenty rewrites and was rejected several times, twice by the company who later published it. Then the publisher said, "Now the rewriting begins!" We went through sixteen more edits! If you do the math, this means more than thirty-six rewrites!

I am also the proud father of a state Young Author's award winner (Congratulations, Laurel!). So I have seen the pressure put on children to work hard and do their best. It is all well intentioned and has produced some great results.

With that said, I also think it is important for students to publish more than one big project a year. I think the process can be fun, efficient and completed start to finish in one period.

In the following pages are several ideas for constructing simple books. Every student can build a library of original books. As a class, you can exchange handmade books as gifts, build a classroom library, and, most important, make writing more vital. By providing an audience for your writers and allowing students to read each other's book, both reading and writing become more meaningful.

Starting with the most simple and adding layers of complexity, here are several book designs. All of them can be used with almost any of the lessons in this book.

An Instant Minibook

Using the sequential picture story map from the first lesson in this chapter (see page 31), students can simply cut along the folds, arrange the pages in order, and staple them together for a wordless picture book. If you give them a piece of colorful construction paper that is twice as large as the rectangular pages of the book, they can fold it in half to make a cover. Two holes punched near the margin and a piece of string allow them to bind the book rather than staple it. With pictures on one side only, the back of each picture provides a place for the corresponding text if you have students write out the story.

The Field Notebook, Journal, or Poetry Chapbook

Probably the easiest book to make and the most useful is a simple chapbook. If each student is given several sheets of unlined copy paper and a piece of stiff construction paper, they can make a simple book. It is helpful if each page is folded individually and then they are each nested inside the other. The center fold can be stapled. My preference is to make three holes with a hole punch in the center fold. Then use a long piece of string, or three strings braided together, or some raffia, and by threading in and out you can bind the book with these strings. Students can then use the loose ends to add a few beads or feathers or something meaningful to them.

You can use this type of book as a field journal when you take your class outside. They can make sketches of their bird, take notes, write poems, and make a rough draft of their story for "Bird is the Word." Through the course of the year, you can make books about mammals, trees, insects, and so on until each student has his or her personal library of field guides to local wildlife!

It is also an instant chapbook for collecting poetry. Students can come back to it again and again to add additional poems. It can also be constructed in a way that pages can be added later by untying the string. If you are using it for collecting stories, students can add folktales throughout the year.

A fun yet frustrating exercise is the process of pagination. If students are typing a story over multiple pages and want to print the book from their computer, they need to make a mock-up to figure out this one complicated idea—pagination. If it is a sixteen-page book with each page taking up half a sheet of paper, how many sheets of paper do you need if you print front and back? This translates to four sheets of folded paper, because there are actually four pages on each sheet of paper. When you format the pages, what is on the back of page 1, 2, 3, and so on? This requires students to think spatially in three dimensions. On the back of page 1 is 2, but facing page 2 on the same side of the paper is page 15! On the back of page 3 is 4, but facing 3 on the same side of the paper is page 14, and facing 4 is 13! Confusing? Make a mock-up of your book and it all becomes clear!

Because I work so much with Young Author programs, I went through the effort to self-publish two chapbooks of poetry, *Frog Songs* and *Song of the Red Fox*. I also wanted to have the experience of taking a book from idea to press. Pagination is tricky. The only way to figure out pagination is to make a mock-up with scrap paper.

The Three-Ring Binder

As a class, collect all of the student's work from many of the lesson plans, each into its own three-ring binder. Office supply stores sell one-inch binders in bulk, so you can buy a case inexpensively. Ask the PTA nicely, and maybe they will buy you two or three cases! These binders come with a clear plastic sleeve so you can print a cover with a title, author, date, and a nice graphic, then slide the cover into the sleeve. They have a clear plastic sleeve on the spine too, so once you build a set they will look good on a bookshelf.

Mr. Smith's Fables, Classic Myths for Modern Times, and *Bird Is the Word* are just three titles of classroom collections your students can write and add to your library from lessons already discussed. When students know their work is to be collected into an anthology, there is more incentive for them to get it right. Each student can make a title page for their story with an illustration, type and print their story, and then add a short "About the Author." One student can be responsible for a table of contents and collecting the final drafts of the stories, punching holes and putting them into the three-ring binder.

Simultaneously, each student can have his or her own three-ring binder for a "collected works of." As the year progresses, they can keep adding stories and poems, pictures and essays. This gives the teacher a great way to monitor progress, and, more important, it gives each student a source of pride in their accomplishments!

The Accordion Fold

Another easy book to make, but one that is more of a fine art book, is the accordion fold. It works best with those large rolls of butcher paper or bulletin board paper. Cut a strip 4 inches wide and as long as you want it; 24 inches will give you 8 pages; 48 inches will give you 16 pages. Give each student one long strip of paper, two 5-inch squares of fiber board or cardboard, and two pieces of ribbon. Instruct students to take their time and fold the paper carefully, measuring the first fold so it is a 4-inch square, then folding over, under, over, under until the entire strip of paper is a 4-inch square.

Students will then lay a piece of ribbon across the cardboard and then glue one end of the paper over it. Lay the second piece of ribbon over the other piece of cardboard and glue the other end of the paper strip to it. The two ribbons allow you to tie the book closed. If you untie one ribbon, you can turn the pages like a normal book. Retie the ribbon and untie the other side to read the other side of the paper. This other side of the paper can be a second book, or on one side you can have the text and the other side the pictures. So when you read the book you have a wordless series of pictures on one side or a set of paragraphs with no pictures on the other side.

A One-Page Book Inside Out

Practice this on your own several times before you attempt to teach this to your students. It is very tricky at first, but once you get it, it is very simple!

Take a plain piece of paper and fold it three times, so that when you open it you have eight rectangles. First fold it the long way, like a hotdog bun. Then fold the long ends together. Then fold the long ends together a second time. Unfold it. It helps if you refold it on the same creases, but fold it in the other direction so each fold is well creased.

Now comes the tricky part. You want to cut the middle of the fold, the long way, between the second and third pages. (Look carefully at the diagram on the next page to make sure you cut the correct line.) Pull the middle pages apart to open this cut. Crease it. Fold the cover over to make an eight-page book. When students get to this point, they can then copy their favorite haiku, one to a page, and add illustrations. For the adventurous, you can attempt to format this on a computer with a landscaped page and inverted text boxes, but this is more difficult.

Please visit **www.foxtalesint.com** to download a free mini-book (in PDF format) that includes illustrations and text for "The Stonecutter." The model you will find there is carefully marked to help you and your students create your own mini-books.

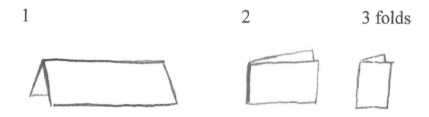

1   2   3 folds

Unfold and cut on the line between the middle pages

Pull on the middle pages and make an accordion fold

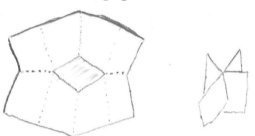

CHAPTER 3

STORYTELLING AND SOCIAL STUDIES

"HUMMINGBIRD AND CRANE": CULTURAL VARIANTS OF THE GREAT RACE

Hummingbird and Crane

She was hot! She was a long, tall, cool drink of water, and one look at her made you thirsty! Part of her charm was that she was also clever; she exuded strength and confidence in the way she walked, the way she noticed you notice her and gave you a wink, just to pique your interest. She was the kind of woman who knew what she wanted and knew how to get it. She would not settle for second best.

Most of the birds knew she was out of their league and did not even try. Most birds found someone of their temperament, their temperature, and they were happy to daydream, happy to settle down with a good woman who knew how to be good to them. The suitors, one by one, faded away.

Finally, her parents said, "It is time to find a partner. You cannot let life pass you by."

Oh, she had trouble deciding. The two who showed the most interest in her, the two who would not give up, were Whooping Crane and Ruby-Throated Hummingbird.

Whooping Crane was gawky. He was tall and lanky, awkward, with big feet and a big heart. He was also a great dancer. In the Council circle, on the powwow grounds, all of his angular limbs seemed to melt into waving grasses. Whoop! Whoop! Whoop! He was an amazing, fancy dancer. She also knew he was a great hunter. He could catch frogs and snakes like nobody's business.

But hummingbird, Ruby-Throated Hummingbird, oh, he was a whole 'nother matter. He was handsome with his ruby-red throat, his emerald-green back, and his buff-white chest. She was reluctant to admit it, but he was almost as gorgeous as she was. *What?* She was just admitting what everyone knew. He was also fast! He could zip around here and there and be back in an instant, with an insect he had just caught and coated in nectar for a sweet tasty treat. He was always bringing her presents.

Humpf, she had trouble deciding.

So one evening early in the summer, after the corn planting was done, she announced at the Council circle to all who were listening that there would be a race, a race to the distant mountains and back and whoever won would be her man. She would let them decide, though of course, she was hoping it would be hummingbird who won.

The next morning at dawn all of the bird tribe gathered at the Council grounds in the center of the village. Hummingbird rested on a twig. Whooping Crane just stood there flat footed. As the signal was given, Hummingbird zipped up, flew once around the crowd for sport and then disappeared. Everyone cheered!

Whooping Crane took a few awkward steps, flapped his wings, and began flying off—in the wrong direction? The others tried not to laugh. He began making big circles. Other birds wondered if he knew which way to go, but he knew what he was doing. He was looking for a thermal, a place where the sun had begun to warm the earth and warm air would lift him higher and higher. Soon he appeared to be smaller than hummingbird, and he disappeared into the clouds. Other birds shook their heads and wondered how far ahead Hummingbird must be by now.

But those who knew crane knew he had the greatest stamina and endurance; no, not the fastest bird, but he could fly all night and all day and that is what he did.

Hummingbird stopped near dusk. He fed on a few flowers and munched a few insects to keep his strength up. He had been to the mountains and figured it would take six or seven days. In the morning he fed again. Shortly after he zipped off toward the mountains, he was shocked to find Crane wading in a stream catching fish for his breakfast. How had Crane caught up? Hummingbird pushed himself and flew faster and farther than he had ever flown before.

Crane just smiled and nodded as Hummingbird flew past. After a little rest he found another thermal and let the warmth of the earth lift him; from this height he could glide for miles with hardly a flap, saving his strength for the long night.

The next morning, Hummingbird flew for some time without seeing any sign of Crane. Mid-morning, can you imagine his surprise when he found that Crane was finishing his breakfast and already looking for a sun-warmed meadow?

And so it went each day, Crane was a little farther ahead. Though most days Hummingbird passed him, each day it was later and later in the afternoon. On the fourth day, as Hummingbird approached the top of the sacred mountain, high above the village of Wayah, he passed Crane—who was already on his way home! On the fifth day, Hummingbird passed Crane near supper time. On the sixth day he did not see Crane at all. He became frantic. On the seventh day Crane did take a little rest; he bathed and groomed himself in the stream nearest his village. He came into the Council grounds well before the sun reached its apex.

84 *From Content Area Reading, Writing, and Storytelling: A Dynamic Tool for Improving Reading and Writing Across the Curriculum through Oral Language Development* by Brian "Fox" Ellis. Westport, CT: Teacher Ideas Press. Copyright © 2008.

The whole village was there waiting. Most were surprised, except those who knew Crane. Most said he looked handsome, regal even, but no one said anything about the disappointment in her eyes. Hummingbird came into the Council circle late in the evening, just before sunset, and he looked bedraggled, beaten, and confused.

And so her choice was made . . . or was it?

Though she did not marry him—she never married—she did whisper something into Whooping Crane's ear. And though he never told, it made him grin, a grin wider than his long beak, even years later when he was an old bird, happily married to another crane, he always smiled when he remembered that day, and then he would look at his wife, and she would blush like a young hen when he looked at her that way.

From Content Area Reading, Writing, and Storytelling: A Dynamic Tool for Improving Reading and Writing Across the Curriculum through Oral Language Development by Brian "Fox" Ellis. Westport, CT: Teacher Ideas Press. Copyright © 2008.

"Hummingbird and Crane": Cultural Variants of the Great Race

Grade Levels: 4–12

Time Estimate: Two hours

Objectives:

- Students will compare two cultural variants of the same story.
- They will learn to see cultural motifs within a story.
- Students will rewrite a traditional story using their modern cultural details or their traditional cultural roots.

National Standards:

- NCTE 1—Students read a wide range of print and non-print texts to build an understanding of texts, of themselves, and of the world; to acquire new information; and for personal fulfillment. Among these texts are fiction and nonfiction, classic and contemporary works.
- NCTE 2—Students read a wide range of literature from many periods in many genres to build an understanding of the many dimensions (e.g., philosophical, ethical, aesthetic) of human experience.
- NCTE 3—Students apply a wide range of strategies to comprehend, interpret, evaluate, and appreciate texts.
- NCTE 4—Students adjust their use of spoken, written, and visual language to communicate effectively with a variety of audiences and for different purposes.
- NCTE 5—Students employ a wide range of strategies as they write and use different writing process elements appropriately to communicate with different audiences for a variety of purposes.
- NCTE 6—Students apply knowledge of language structure, language conventions, media techniques, figurative language, and genre to create, critique, and discuss print and non-print texts.
- NCTE 7—Students conduct research on issues and interests by generating ideas and questions, and by posing problems. They gather, evaluate, and synthesize data from a variety of sources to communicate their discoveries in ways that suit their purpose and audience.
- NCTE 8—Students use a variety of technological and information resources to gather and synthesize information and to create and communicate knowledge.
- NCSS 1—Culture
- NCSS 9—Global Connections
- NAS 3—Life Science: Structure and function in living systems; Reproduction and heredity; Regulation and behavior; Populations and ecosystems; Diversity and adaptations of organisms

Materials:

- Paper and pencil
- Access to a library of folklore from around the world

Background Information: Teachers should begin this lesson with their own research into three or more cultural variations on a story. "Cinderella" in France is "Ashenputtel" in Germany and "The Rough-Faced Girl" among American Indians; all three stories are about coming of age for teenage girls. "Little Red Riding Hood" is an Anglicization of Germany's "Rotcapchen"; she appears in China as "Lon Po Po," and all three are important tales about stranger danger. Because I believe this kind of work is so vital to an understanding of storytelling, our deeper selves, and our relationships to the world around us, this is a lesson in which every student should participate, and teachers who use storytelling in the classroom should feel confident in their ability to lead this kind of discussion.

Though we are attempting to dig into this rich topic in just two class periods, one could make their career in this field and barely begin to get at a handful of the jewels that could be unearthed. I do believe that there are several universal stories that we as humans keep acting out, and the better we understand these universal stories, the better we understand ourselves. I also believe that seeing these stories through the lens of another culture adds another facet to our understanding. By understanding these similarities and celebrating our differences, we could end a lot of the strife in the world and gain a deeper self-knowledge. These are tall orders for a simple lesson plan, but world peace and inner peace do begin with small steps.

Instructional Procedures

Introduction: Ask students if they have heard of the race between the tortoise and the hare. Who won and why? Discuss the idea that many cultures tell different versions of the same stories, and with a little digging they can find a story about a great race in almost every culture in the world. Ask them to listen carefully to this Cherokee version of the story.

Tell the story of Whooping Crane and Hummingbird.

Activity: Lead a classroom discussion of how this story is like *The Tortoise and the Hare* and how it is different. The two pivotal questions are: "What is the same in each story, and how does this relate to ways in which all people are alike?" and "What is different in each story and how does this relate to the cultural differences?" Make a Venn diagram to discuss the similarities and differences between these stories. (If it is helpful, tell or read a traditional version of "The Tortoise and the Hare.") In your conversation, highlight the cultural differences; what can we learn about Cherokee culture from this story? Namely, they live in villages with a central council grounds; women seem to have much more power and say than in other cultures, and, though only hinted at, they have historically been both a hunting-gathering and farming culture.

Based on the teacher's research topic, discuss variations on "Cinderella" versus "The Rough-Faced Girl" or "Little Red Riding Hood" versus "Lon Po Po." With younger students, discuss the basic concept of culture and cultural differences. With all ages, you may want to share a copy of the worksheet "Storytelling and Multicultural Understanding" found on page 208.

With a lot of support from your librarian, set your class loose in the library with the goal of finding two or three versions of the same basic story concept, not two translations of the same story. For example, we do not want two translations of the Grimm's Brothers story "Hansel and Gretel," but two different stories from different countries that have some core idea—lost children who have to make it on their own. While some are combing through 398.2, others could be looking at children's picture books or searching the Internet. Yes, it is okay if several students are working on variants of the same tale, and you may even want to go a step further and search in advance for several copies of the three or four core stories or enlist your librarian's help in finding enough samples beforehand.

Their assignment for this first day is to simply make a Venn diagram comparing the stories with an emphasis on cultural details. How are they alike? How are they different? They are to bring these to class the next day.

The next day, give your students two choices. Using these stories as models, they can write their own version of the story, either updating it with modern cultural motifs or immersing the plot in the student's cultural heritage.

With the first option remind them of the five Ws and the H in the earlier lesson plan. How can they use modern language, modern technology, and today's cultural details to update the story?

If they would like to rewrite it as a traditional story from their culture of origin, maybe they would like to make a list of cultural details such as foods, clothing, tools, lifestyles, values, and the like. Then think about how they can weave these details into the story so that it has the rich flavor of their grandma's favorite recipe.

Remembering the idea of storytelling as a prewriting or rewriting strategy, after the students have had about fifteen minutes to work independently on their rough draft, ask each student to find a partner, preferably one working on a variation of the same story, and allow them time to take turns telling their version of the story to each other. With a compliment and a question, structure the feedback they give each other.

Give them the rest of the period to finish their version of the story.

If time allows, ask one or two students to tell their story to the class.

Assessment: Their Venn diagram comparing the two versions of the story can be evaluated on the number of differences and similarities they identified.

Their stories can earn three grades, one for grammar and mechanics, one for stylistic issues regarding character development and plot, and a social studies grade for how well they maintained the cultural tone and the number of cultural details they included.

The students can also be given a chance to perform the stories for the class and their performances can be evaluated based on the rubric at the end of Chapter 1.

Follow-up Activities: Although it would require some careful choreography on the part of the teacher, it might be a hoot if three students who wrote three very different versions of the same story could weave them together in a unique multicultural performance. It might be something like this:

"A long time ago there was a rabbit and turtle."

"Wait a minute, I heard it was hedgehog and a hare."

"No, I have it on good authority this story is about a hummingbird and a crane."

Then each student could describe their main characters. In turn they could describe the three different settings, the beginning, the middle, and at the end they could all say the same moral of the story together. "At least we agree on one thing!"

This same lesson plan can also be used for a very specific type of story. For example, students can be asked to compare Greek and Norse mythology, or American Indian and African Star stories, or Tall Tale heroes like the American Pecos Bill, the English Jack, and the Yiddish Hershel of Ostropol.

Comments: Storytellers love these kinds of conversations. This is what gives a seasoned storyteller depth and breadth in their telling. Your students will instantly grow both a deeper and a broader understanding of storytelling through this simple lesson plan.

"PRAIRIE FIRE!" AND THE ORAL HISTORY INTERVIEW

Prairie Fire!

My sister and I were playing in the yard out by the well. My sister had some of them little cornhusk dolls; maybe you've seen them?

Now I don't want you to get the wrong idea thinking a little boy would be playing with a doll. But back then we didn't have electronic gadgets—shucks, we didn't even have electricity. We had to entertain ourselves, make our own fun. Anyhow, I was playing with my sister in the front yard with those little cornhusk dolls, when our father came racing over the hill.

I knew something was wrong by the way he was whipping that horse. Our father loved his horse. Sometimes we thought he loved his horse more than he loved his kids. He never whipped his horses, so I knew something was wrong.

Our father was yelling, but we couldn't make out his words because he was too far away and the wind was whipping his voice around. But finally he was close enough and we could understand. He said, "There's a fire coming, a prairie fire coming, run in the house and tell your ma!"

Back in those days we always did what our father told us, especially when he spoke in that tone of voice. So we ran in the house and my sister said, "Ma, Ma there's a fire coming, a prairie fire coming!"

Now I almost forgot to tell you, we lived in a sod house. On the prairie there weren't many trees. Most people think sod houses are made out of grass—that's not exactly right. The truth is they cut off the grass to use the roots and dirt. The top couple inches of grass and the bottom couple inches of roots are cut into bricks, like the brick homes you might live in. So our house was like a brick house except for one important difference: In the spring when it rained, the grass would sprout and our house would turn green. In the summer, that grass would turn brown and dry. It was perfect kindling for a fire. So we ran in the house and I echoed my sister, "Ma, Ma there's a fire coming, a prairie fire coming!"

Ma was kneading the dough, baking the bread as she did most every day. When Ma heard those words, her jaw dropped nearly to the floor. After she picked it up she wiped the flour from her hands onto her apron. Peeling off her apron she said, "Go round up your brothers and sisters, get all of the buckets you can find and meet me outside by the well."

Well, I ran out behind the barn where my older brother was working in the garden.

I ran back through the barn where my older sister was milking a cow. My sister dumped the bucket—we didn't want to cry over spilled milk . . .

But we rounded up all of the buckets we could find and met Ma out by the well. By the time we arrived Ma had already pulled up the first bucket of water. She dumped it into my bucket. I handed it to my little sister, who handed it to my older brother, who handed it to my older sister, who took the bucket and dumped it on the house. We passed the empty bucket back.

Back and forth we were passing buckets and dumping them on the house. This makes sense, right? When it was hot and dry we knew that one spark and this old soddy would burst into flames. This makes sense, right? While we were getting the house wet, Pa started to do the strangest thing. I couldn't understand it, Pa took the horse out to the barn and he hitched up the plow.

Summer is not plowing season; you plow the fields in the spring, not the summer.

But Pa wasn't plowing the fields. No, he started plowing a circle around the house and the barn. Not once, but twice, three times, four times, five times. Then Pa moved the plow about ten or fifteen yards out, and he started plowing a bigger circle around the first ones.

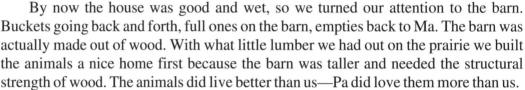 By now the house was good and wet, so we turned our attention to the barn. Buckets going back and forth, full ones on the barn, empties back to Ma. The barn was actually made out of wood. With what little lumber we had out on the prairie we built the animals a nice home first because the barn was taller and needed the structural strength of wood. The animals did live better than us—Pa did love them more than us.

We were dumping water onto the barn, that makes sense, right? But I thought for sure that Pa had plum lost his mind. He went into the house with a shovel and he took a shovel of red hot coals . . . .

We always kept a fire going even in the heat of the summer for cooking and such. Pa took the red hot coals out to the front yard, and he started a fire. I thought, "Pa! There is already a fire coming; why are you starting another one?" But Pa knew what he was doing! Pa was burning the grass between the circles where he had plowed to make a fire break.

Good thing he did, because it was just about then that we could smell the fire coming. Like some distant campfire, ribs bar-b-queing on the grill!

It was just about then that we could feel the temperature rise. Within about five minutes the temperature climbed ten, fifteen, twenty degrees. It felt like your skin was going to boil and drip off the bone!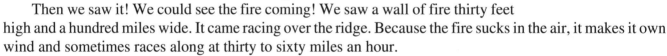

It was just about then that we could hear the fire coming. At first it sounded like a freight train, but I knew that the freight train hadn't made it this far west quite yet. Then it sounded like a dozen freight trains, and then it sounded like a tornado, and then a dozen tornados! It was the loudest thing that I'd ever heard!

Then we saw it! We could see the fire coming! We saw a wall of fire thirty feet high and a hundred miles wide. It came racing over the ridge. Because the fire sucks in the air, it makes it own wind and sometimes races along at thirty to sixty miles an hour.

As quick as it came, it was gone again.

Because it rained sparks and ashes, Ma had taken the last bucket of water and dumped it on us kids. The sparks that fell on the house and barn didn't catch because the house and barn were good and wet. And because Pa had made the fire break, that fire burned around, not through, our lives.

 Come Sunday morning, when I heard the preacher talk about fire and brimstones I knew what he was talking about, because I had seen the fire falling from the sky. And Lord knows we went to church come Sunday, to give thanks 'cause we survived. We survived the prairie fire 'cause we had worked together, and I knew, if we could survive a prairie fire, we could survive anything!

From *Content Area Reading, Writing, and Storytelling: A Dynamic Tool for Improving Reading and Writing Across the Curriculum through Oral Language Development* by Brian "Fox" Ellis. Westport, CT: Teacher Ideas Press. Copyright © 2008.

"Prairie Fire!" and the Oral History Interview

Grade Levels: 3–12

Time Estimate: Three class periods of 50 to 60 minutes

Objectives:

- Students will immerse themselves in their family history.

- Students will learn to write good questions and conduct an interview.

- Students will demonstrate an ability to turn rough notes into a tellable tale.

National Standards:

- NCTE 2—Students read a wide range of literature from many periods in many genres to build an understanding of the many dimensions (e.g., philosophical, ethical, aesthetic) of human experience.

- NCTE 3—Students apply a wide range of strategies to comprehend, interpret, evaluate, and appreciate texts.

- NCTE 4—Students adjust their use of spoken, written, and visual language to communicate effectively with a variety of audiences and for different purposes.

- NCTE 6—Students apply knowledge of language structure, language conventions, media techniques, figurative language, and genre to create, critique, and discuss print and non-print texts.

- NCTE 7—Students conduct research on issues and interests by generating ideas and questions, and by posing problems. They gather, evaluate, and synthesize data from a variety of sources to communicate their discoveries in ways that suit their purpose and audience.

- NCTE 11—Students participate as knowledgeable, reflective, creative, and critical members of a variety of literacy communities.

- NCTE 12—Students use spoken, written, and visual language to accomplish their own purposes (e.g., for learning, enjoyment, persuasion, and the exchange of information).

- NCSS 1—Culture

- NCSS 2—Time, Continuity, and Change

- NCSS 4—Individual Development and Identity

- NAS 3—Life Science: Structure and function in living systems; Reproduction and heredity; Regulation and behavior; Populations and ecosystems; Diversity and adaptations of organisms.

- NAS 6—Science in Personal and Social Perspectives: Personal health; Populations, resources, and environments; Natural hazards; Risks and benefits; Science and technology in society

Materials:

- Paper and pencil

- Handout "The Oral History Interview"

- Optional: recording device, batteries, tape

Background Information: After a performance at a Prairie Nature Center in Toledo, Ohio, an elderly woman came up to me to thank me for my stories, and then she asked me my favorite question: "I have a story, would you like to hear it?" and the story of the prairie fire fell into my lap. I did have the sense to take good notes, ask a few follow-up questions, and thank her graciously. Since I have been telling this story throughout the Midwestern prairie states, I have had several folks tell me versions of this story. My wife actually interviewed her grandmother, who told her a piece of a similar story. This is my favorite story that I collected from the oral tradition, and over time I have embellished it with details from several sources.

If who we are are the stories we hear and tell, then collecting oral histories will give students an empathically larger sense of self and connection to their local history. I love to tease audiences with the following question: "Have you ever talked to your grandma about her grandma? If so you have travelled back one hundred to two hundred years in time!"

Stories let you travel back in time and meet these people. It was not so long ago, nor so far away. It was right here yesterday. Oral history helps students connect with the past in a way that is personal and meaningful.

This lesson works best as a follow-up to the autobiographical stories students wrote in Chapter 2. Within a unit on American history, challenge students to think about ripples on a pond when a stone is dropped into it—concentric circles of personal stories, family history, local history, regional, state and national history. Stories are the threads that tie together these various layers of history. Oral histories can help students make the connections between how World War II affected their grandfather and how his choices affected them. Also, the process of interviewing a student partner is good training for an oral history project.

This process of collecting history also helps students to feel like they are players and not just witnesses. They can meet people who were there and had a voice in the Civil Rights movement or helped the flood victims after Katrina. This kind of listening is an empowering experience—yes, we *can* make a difference.

Instructional Procedures

Introduction: With virtually no introduction, other than an invitation to travel back in time, plunge right in and tell the story of "Prairie Fire!" Or, better yet, tell a story that you have collected using this process, a story that models the types of stories you are hoping they will find.

Activity: Briefly discuss what the students liked and what they learned from the story. Pass out the handout and walk students through the instructions.

First, challenge them to make a list of three or four people they might interview. Encourage them to choose someone who is a good talker, maybe someone who has already told them stories, someone who will do their homework for them. An older neighbor, a grandma or uncle, every community has a village elder who is the keeper of lore. It is their job to find that person in their extended family

Set a deadline for students to conduct their interview. A long weekend or vacation when they are likely to visit with distant relatives is a good time frame. Emphasize that a personal interview is always more productive than a phone interview. And though a parent would be acceptable, offer an incentive for students to interview an elder: bonus points for every year older they are.

Or as a class you can plan to visit a neighborhood senior center. Work with the activity director so students can work in pairs to interview an elder; this is a little less daunting than interviewing a stranger alone, but make it clear that each student is to write his or her own story.

Lead a classroom discussion of what makes a good question. Discuss the difference between fact questions and story questions. Although both fact and story questions are useful, why should you avoid yes/no questions? Write the five Ws and H on the board: who, what, when, where, why, and how. Ask each student to get out a piece of paper and write three questions for each of the six categories. Invite them to share their best examples and to write down the ones they hear their classmates share. As a class, brainstorm story questions and take notes on the board.

Emphasize the idea that whom you plan to interview will determine what questions you might ask. For example, your mother was not alive during the Depression, but your grandpa might remember World War II. One good question is all you really need if you know whom you are planning to talk to and what they like to talk about! Ask the right question and they will talk for hours, doing your assignment for you. All you have to do is take good notes!

For homework their assignment is this: Tomorrow each student will turn in a list of at least ten questions—bonus points for twenty or more. At the top of the sheet they need to have the name of the person they will interview, the time and date of the scheduled interview, and at least two sentences about this person. The idea here is that their homework is to actually schedule the interview.

Spend the next few minutes briefly discussing etiquette, equipment, note taking, and follow-up questions.

Save time at the end of the first class period, the last fifteen or twenty minutes, so you can have students conduct a practice interview. You can have the entire class interview you, or schedule to have the principal, janitor, nurse, librarian, or a special guest arrive to be interviewed, or students can turn to a partner and practice interviewing each other. Set up the next lesson at the very end of the class by briefly discussing what story might come out of the practice interview.

On the preappointed day, each student is to bring the notes from their interview to class. These rough notes can be collected for a grade. Using the second side of the handout as a guide, walk the students through the process of "Turning Notes into a Story." If they took good notes and interviewed a natural-born storyteller, then this should be easy, a matter of shaping and editing. If not, then they will have a little more work ahead of them.

The first two points are the most important: What is the pivotal moment; what is the story about? And who is telling the story? Do students want to tackle it first person or as an omniscient narrator? Students may need an explanation of these points.

First-person or outside observer is more of an aesthetic question, but as a creative writing exercise you can ask students at some point in the middle of the assignment to write just one paragraph in the opposite voice to see how it feels. Allow them to choose which works better for them.

Maybe the person talked about five or six different topics; all we need is one good story, beginning, middle, and end. Choose the one that will make the best story.

Walk students through the handout. Ask them to write a few sentences about each character and the setting of their tale, emphasize three-dimensional characters and using all of your senses to bring readers/listeners into the setting. Help them make an outline of the plot. If they think of a question that they cannot answer but the answer is vital to the story, encourage them to write down the question and ask it later. A couple of follow-up questions can make or break their story, and it is okay to do these over the phone. There might be other historical or contextual questions best answered at the library or online. Encourage students to write two or three of these questions in the margin as they work on their story, and offer bonus points for the inclusion of these facts in their final draft.

Most of the second class period should be spent organizing their notes. Occasionally interrupt the class to share ideas from a fellow student's paper or answer one student's question out loud for the entire class. By the end of the period, they should have the notes from their interview organized into an outline; some may go ahead and get started on the rough draft of their story. Their homework is to ask and answer a few follow-up questions and tell the story to anyone who will listen—the dog, stuffed animals, the mirror.

In the third class period, students should finish their rough draft and get a solid start on the rewriting process through rehearsal. Allow the first fifteen minutes for students to get a solid start on their rough draft. Then ask students to take turns telling their stories to a partner using the "retelling is rewriting" concepts on page 120. Allow students the final fifteen minutes to work on their final draft of the story.

These stories can then be collected into a classroom collection of local history.

Assessment: When grading the interview preparation notes, if students simply copied ten questions from the board, this deserves a C. If they have 20 or more questions, including several original and thought-provoking questions, an A is in order.

The notes from the interview should be evaluated based on the quality and quantity of information recorded. If follow-up questions and thinking-on-your-feet questions were emphasized in the practice interview, then this could be highlighted in the teacher's comments and bonus points given.

Their final assignment should read like a short story, not a journalistic question-and-answer interview. Did the students do their job of translating the notes into a tellable tale? Having the notes in hand to compare to the story will help make this assessment.

Follow-up Activities: The culminating activity should be a performance in which the elders who were interviewed are invited to listen.

Comments: Once students are familiar with the process of collecting oral histories, your class can then complete a series of projects. They can work with the local historical society to collect stories of the town's history. Students can research the history of their school, focus on World War II, or focus on some recent aspect of history related to their community. In these specific topical studies, teachers may want to help students find the right people to interview and work together as a class to build the right set of questions. They can explore a range of issues or themes and participate in the work of real historians. This kind of community dialogue can also effect real change in a community by getting the community to talk openly about an issue; people are then motivated to be more participatory in our democracy.

The Oral History Interview

I.   Choose an interviewee who is interesting, "a good talker."

II.   Arrange an appointment at a time and place that is comfortable and convenient to them.

III. Write questions before the interview.

     A. Fact Questions: Five Ws and H

     B. Story Questions: Tell me about _____ .

IV. Double-check equipment and materials.

     A. Pen and paper

     B. Tapes, batteries, and recorder

     C. Camera

V.   Be prompt and courteous, and relax.

VI.   Start with fact questions, then introduce story questions.

VII. Take good notes, occasionally asking for spelling and further clarification. Do not ask the interviewees to repeat themselves too often.

VIII. Make up questions as you go: Tell me more about _____ .

IX.   Thank the interviewee graciously.

X.   Review your notes and take more notes *immediately* after the interview.

XI.   Piece together a story (see reverse side):

     A. Characters—Allow the readers to get to know three-dimensional people

     B. Setting—Create a clear picture in a distinct time period

     C. Plot—Build the sequence of events around one key happening

XII. You may need to do a follow-up interview to clarify a few details.

XIII. Send your interviewee a copy of your story with your thank-you note.

From *Content Area Reading, Writing, and Storytelling: A Dynamic Tool for Improving Reading and Writing Across the Curriculum through Oral Language Development* by Brian "Fox" Ellis. Westport, CT: Teacher Ideas Press. Copyright © 2008.

TURNING NOTES INTO A STORY

I.   What is the key event?
Choose one key event, climactic happening, and build the story around it.

II.   Who is telling the story?
Choose point of view—first, second, or third person?

Find a voice, a distinct persona.

III.   Who is in the story?
Write a least two sentences defining each character:

   A.   Description—You can tell a lot about a person by what they wear, what they look like, their makeup, haircut, eye color. Focus on details.

   B.   Action—You can tell a lot about a person by what they do. How do they treat others? Don't tell me they are nice or mean, show me. Actions speak louder than words.

   C.   Dialogue—You can tell a lot about a person by what they say and how they say it. What is their vocabulary? Tone of Voice? Use quotation marks: He said, "Oh, Please don't . . . ."

IV.   Where does the story take place?
Write three sentences about the setting.

   A.   Place—In the world, in the country, in the house. Be specific. Not just any apartment, but the third floor of an old brownstone building with a spiral staircase that squeaked about every fourth step so you always knew when someone was coming.

   B.   Time—of day, of year, in history. Midnight when the wind howled and the sky was glowing with strange lights behind the clouds is very different from a sunny spring morning with birdsongs and the fragrance of wildflowers mingling in the air.

   C.   Use all of your senses—Sounds, smells, tastes, textures and sights are what bring the setting to life!

V.   What happens in this story?
Outline your plot:

1. Beginning	Introduction
2. Problem	Clues, but don't give it away
3. Middle	Climax
4. Solution	Twists and turns
5. End	Resolution

(Teacher can introduce concepts of foreshadowing, suspense, and irony.)

VI.   What did /could you/we learn from this story?
Make the personal universal. Put the story into historical perspective. Look at the big picture. Don't teach us something; write the story in a way that allows us to discover something. Create hooks that we as readers/listeners can relate to—an "Ah, yes, I know" experience.

VII.   Use the sentences you have written in response to these questions as the outline of your story. Rewrite your notes into a historically accurate adventurous tale!

From *Content Area Reading, Writing, and Storytelling: A Dynamic Tool for Improving Reading and Writing Across the Curriculum through Oral Language Development* by Brian "Fox" Ellis. Westport, CT: Teacher Ideas Press. Copyright © 2008.

"ROWING THE OHIO" AND FIRST-PERSON HISTORICAL NARRATIVES

Rowing the Ohio

1850 Northern Kentucky

I never had no reason to expect to be doing what I was doing, but I was in love. There was a fine young woman who lived down the road—she was sweet—and I was in love.

You see, I was a slave in northern Kentucky in 1850, and my master, he was kinder than most. He let me come and go as I please, as long as I put in a hard day's work. Now a hard day's work for a slave was sixteen hours. And guess how much I was paid for my work? Nothing! Not one red cent! He barely gave me a roof over my head and that I had to build for myself. If I slacked up, the overseer took a whip to my back.

But my master was kinder than most masters. As long as I put in a hard day's work, he let me come and go as I please, as long as he didn't catch me with a book in my hand. Learning to read and write was against the law for a slave. If he caught me with a book in my hand, he'd take a whip to my back. Maybe he figured if I'd learned to read and write, I might get smarter. I wouldn't accept his slavery. It was against the law for a slave to read and write. But as long as I put in a hard day's work, he let me come and go as I please.

And sometimes in the evening, I used to like to head on down the road and visit this fine young woman. She was sweet. And I was in love. I'd do anything for this girl. If she'd tell me to jump, I'd say, "How high, Honey?"

One night I was sitting on her front porch, and we were talking, if you know what I mean. She asked me if I would do her a favor. I said, "For you girl, I would do anything." She said that she had a friend who was a runaway slave. You see, my friend knew that I had a boat—that my master had a boat. She wanted to know if I would take this slave across the river in my boat.

Now I know what they do if they catch you helping a runaway [*Draw your finger across your throat*], but I was in love. I said, "Girl, for you, I will do this thing."

My friend made all of the arrangements. I never saw the young woman's face. That way, if somebody came to me with a poster or a picture and said, "Have you ever seen this young woman?" I wouldn't have to lie. I never saw her face.

But she knew the password, "Manarai." I'm not sure what it means. I think it was a word from the Bible, but like I said, I couldn't read nor write. I met her in the dark of the swamp. I didn't have no lantern or torch. It was a dark night. The clouds were so thick you couldn't see the moon nor stars. I never saw her face, but she knew the password. So I took her on down to the river where I had my master's boat hiding under the bushes. I pulled the branches aside and pushed the boat on into the water. I helped the young woman aboard. I climbed in myself, pushed the boat out and began rowing, rowing the Ohio. The Ohio River is muddy and

From *Content Area Reading, Writing, and Storytelling: A Dynamic Tool for Improving Reading and Writing Across the Curriculum through Oral Language Development* by Brian "Fox" Ellis. Westport, CT: Teacher Ideas Press. Copyright © 2008.

wide. The Ohio River is deep and cold. A shiver went up my spine, goose bumps on the back of my neck. But the goose bumps weren't because of the cold. It was because of what they would do if they caught me helping the runaway [*Draw your finger across your throat again*].

Finally, I pulled the boat onto the Ohio shore. Just as the boat touched the shore, two men came out of the bushes! They grabbed us and dragged us ashore.

I said, "Please don't kill me, Master."

They said, "Kill ya? We're here to help you."

I said, "What are these two white boys here to help me for?"

They said, "We're conductors on the Underground Railroad. Come with us, and you'll be a free man."

I said, "I can't go with you. I got to go back. Take the young woman, but I got to go!"

They said, "Man, you're a fool! Why would you choose to go back; why would you choose to be a slave?"

I said, "I ain't got no choice. You think I would choose this life? If I ain't there in the morning, my master will send out the hounds and come looking for me. I got to go."

They took the young woman and I climbed back in my boat. Let me tell you, if I was afraid rowing over, I was doubly afraid coming back . . . by myself. No telling who might be waiting on that Kentucky shore.

Finally I pulled the boat onto the shore. There was no one there. I pushed the boat up under the bushes and covered it with branches. The coast was clear.

I started heading back toward my cabin. I crawled into bed that night and I had trouble getting to sleep. Tossing and turning. No telling when any minute they might come looking for me! I was scared. But I guess eventually I fell asleep because next morning, I woke up.

Nobody asked no questions; I didn't tell no lies.

That's how it started. Over the next few nights, and weeks, and months, and years, I helped hundreds of slaves to freedom by rowing, rowing the Ohio.

Some nights there would be so many my boat would be filled to overflowing. It would only hold six souls.

Some nights there would be so many I had to make two or three trips. But no matter how many times I crossed that river, I was always afraid, especially coming back by myself. No telling who would be waiting on that Kentucky shore.

By now I knew I could leave any time, but my master was kinder than most, so I keep coming back, 'cause I knew there were many souls who wished to cross that river Jordan.

One night I made three trips. I helped eighteen men and women to freedom. I know that I'd been out late that night. By the time I made that last trip across by myself, the sun was starting to rise. The first fingers of light were creeping over the land. I pulled the boat onto the shore. There was no one there. I pushed it up under the bushes and covered it with branches. The coast was clear.

I started heading on back toward . . . *Bang! Bang!* Gun shots! *Ruff! Ruff*! and hound dogs! I started running. Bullets whizzing by my head. Hound dogs on my trail. I thought that if I ran into the swamp, the dogs couldn't follow my scent. I dove into the mud. I grabbed a reed from the shore. I lay there under the water, under the mud [*pant, pant*], breathing through this reed. I heard the hound dogs come on by, *Ruff! Ruff!* but, they went on by. I heard the men on horseback with rifles saying things—I won't repeat 'em in public—but they went on by. I waited until things got calm and quiet, and I poked my head out of that swamp.

No telling when they might come back looking for me. So I lay back down under the water, under the mud, breathing through that reed all day long. I waited until night, under the cover of darkness, until I felt safe to come on up out of that swamp.

I washed off the mud and started looking for a place to hide. During the night I would move about; and during the day I would sleep in the old haystack or broken down barn. Every night I moved, because I know they was looking for me. I tried to avoid the road, but one night I couldn't help myself.

As I crossed the road, on a tree, I saw a poster. Now I told you I couldn't read nor write, but I know what that poster said. WANTED: DEAD OR ALIVE. Because on that poster there was a man's face, and that face was mine. I tried to avoid the road.

Do you remember that woman I was telling you about at the beginning of this story? Well, eventually we got married. But her master wouldn't let us get married.

He said, "You ain't people; you're property. You do what I say!"

Telling us what we can and can't do. Well, we showed him. We had our own secret ceremony. Late one night we jumped over a broom, like they used to do in the old country. That made us husband and wife. But we couldn't live in the same house, because "you ain't people; you're property." We showed him.

Well, I wanted to escape. I wanted to get out of there, but I didn't want to leave without my wife. So I waited for one cycle of the moon. Do you pay attention to the cycles of the moon? Do you know what phase the moon is in tonight? In the old days we always paid attention to the moon. You had to know the cycles of the moon for planting and harvesting. I waited for the new moon. Funny, they call it the new moon; that's the night when there's no moon at all. I waited until the darkest night.

Then I headed on down the road. I didn't go in her front door, no. I climbed in through her window in case they was watching for me. My wife was asleep. I put my hand on her mouth so she wouldn't scream when I woke her up. And I woke her up.

She took one look at me, she said, "Fool, what are you doing here? If you value your life, you'd better get out of here right now. They come looking for you every night!"

I said, "I'm going. I'm leaving, but I'm not leaving without you."

She said, "I packed my bags a month ago. Been waiting for you, every night." She reached under the bed and grabbed her few belongings—we didn't own much. We were slaves.

We crawled out the window and started heading on down towards the river. And I tell you, if I have ever seen a miracle in all my born days it was that night. The Lord was smiling on me. I swear it was a miracle! Somehow the men on horseback, with rifles and hounds, when they were chasing me, they never stopped to look for my boat. My boat was still there. I swear it was a miracle. I pulled the branches aside and pushed the boat into the water. I helped my wife climb aboard. I climbed in myself and pushed the boat out. I began rowing, rowing the Ohio.

The Ohio River is muddy and wide. The Ohio River is deep and cold, but the goose bumps that night were because of the cold. I wasn't afraid. I was going to be a free man. I pulled the boat onto the Ohio shore. Those same two white boys were there to greet us. They were sons of Reverend Rankin. Reverend Rankin was a white Presbyterian minister. This man risked his life to help the slaves. For this there was a price on his head. The bounty hunters were looking for him so he was in hiding. But his wife and children conducted the station on the Underground Railroad while he was gone. So we climbed the stairs.

A hundred steps to the top of the hill. A hundred steps to freedom. In the Rankin household, down in the basement, they had a secret compartment. My wife and I crawled in underneath. And we went to sleep; slept through the night.

The next day a farmer came. I remember it was autumn because he had a cart and his cart was filled with baskets. And the baskets were filled with apples. He pulled the baskets aside, and there was a place for my wife and I to crawl in underneath.

He put the baskets back and you couldn't tell we was there. And this farmer took us on north to a small town called Wilmington—Wilmington, Ohio. Did you ever hear of Wilmington, Ohio? There is a Quaker college there. The Quakers were some of the first abolitionists. One of the professors at the college had one of those secret bookshelves. Maybe you've seen this in them moving picture shows—if you pull on a little blue book, the whole bookshelf slides aside. There was a secret place for my wife and I to hide in behind.

This Quaker professor said they risked their lives to help the slaves because they knew slavery was not a black versus white thing; it wasn't a North versus South thing; it was a right versus wrong thing. Racism is not a black and white thing; no, it's a right versus wrong thing.

We slept through the night at this professor's home. The next day another farmer came. He had a cart filled with hay. We crawled in underneath the hay, and this farmer took us further north to a small town called Yellow Springs, Ohio. Lots of folks took risks to help us along our way, to feed us and give us shelter. Then we went on to Dayton, Lima, and Toledo, Ohio. You ever hear of Toledo, Ohio? And Detroit, Michigan?

Now a lot of freed slaves settled in Toledo and Detroit. All you had to do was go fifty miles from the river, and you was a free man. But Congress passed the fugitive slave act of 1850. Meant the bounty hunters could come looking for me, because there was a price on my head.

So my wife and I went on to Windsor, into Canada. Now in Canada it is against the law for one man to own another, so I could get a job and get paid for my work. I could own property.

My wife and I, we both got jobs. We bought a house and we had children. And you know 'bout children. They grew up and they had children.

And to this day, I love to gather my grandchildren on my knee, and tell them this story—how I helped hundreds of slaves to freedom, rowing, rowing the Ohio.

From *Content Area Reading, Writing, and Storytelling: A Dynamic Tool for Improving Reading and Writing Across the Curriculum through Oral Language Development* by Brian "Fox" Ellis. Westport, CT: Teacher Ideas Press. Copyright © 2008.

"Rowing the Ohio" and First-Person Historical Narratives

Grade Levels: 3–12

Time Estimate: Three 50- to 60-minute periods

Objectives:

- Students will develop an insider's eye on history through first-person reenactment.

- Students will demonstrate both library and Internet research skills.

- Students will learn to turn diaries, letters, and newspaper accounts into tellable short stories.

National Standards:

- NCTE 1—Students read a wide range of print and non-print texts to build an understanding of texts, of themselves, and of the world; to acquire new information; and for personal fulfillment. Among these texts are fiction and nonfiction, classic and contemporary works.

- NCTE 3—Students apply a wide range of strategies to comprehend, interpret, evaluate, and appreciate texts.

- NCTE 4—Students adjust their use of spoken, written, and visual language to communicate effectively with a variety of audiences and for different purposes.

- NCTE 7—Students conduct research on issues and interests by generating ideas and questions, and by posing problems. They gather, evaluate, and synthesize data from a variety of sources to communicate their discoveries in ways that suit their purpose and audience.

- NCTE 8—Students use a variety of technological and information resources to gather and synthesize information and to create and communicate knowledge.

- NCTE 9—Students develop an understanding of and respect for diversity in language use, patterns, and dialects across cultures, ethnic groups, geographic regions, and social roles.

- NCTE 12—Students use spoken, written, and visual language to accomplish their own purposes (e.g., for learning, enjoyment, persuasion, and the exchange of information).

- NCSS 1—Culture

- NCSS 2—Time, Continuity, and Change

Materials:

- Paper and pencil

- Access to the library, Internet, or local Historical Society archives

Background Information: Although this lesson plan is outlined with a broad sweep, it often works best if your class can focus in on a specific period of history; slave narratives, the American Revolution, Westward migration, Lewis and Clark, and the Civil War are popular topics, and there is a wealth of raw material available.

This key concept that history is made of stories is the foundation to an understanding of history. Through the stories, the first-person accounts, history comes to life; it is meaningful, has both academic and emotional appeal, and gives students that insider's perspective. Students will gain a much deeper appreciation for history if they can read what Abraham Lincoln thought about the Emancipation Proclamation; read Benjamin Franklin's letters to and from Thomas Jefferson; hear the words of a Vietnam veteran who spent several months as a prisoner of war; or read the diary of a pioneer sod-busting farmer. If each student becomes an expert on one moment in history, then the entire class begins to piece together the big picture; the connections between yesterday's news and tomorrow's headlines become palpable.

These documents are easier to find than one might think. Most local historical societies have diaries, letters, old newspaper accounts, and journals waiting for a scholar to decode them and translate them into stories. Most librarians who love their work are eager to help students dig through the microfilm or special collections department and supervise a student's access to these goldmines of significant moments from the lives of our forebears. The Library of Congress, The Abraham Lincoln Presidential Library, The Smithsonian Institution and countless smaller museums are digitizing their collections of primary source documents and posting this material online. A simple search will reveal a Fort Knox of information preserved in our museums. But unlike Fort Knox the ingots of gold are free for the taking! Here are a few places to start:

Library of Congress: http://www.loc.gov/families/

Abraham Lincoln: http://www.papersofabrahamlincoln.org/

The Smithsonian Institution Encyclopedia: http://www.si.edu/Encyclopedia_SI/ History_and_Culture/

Instructional Procedures

Introduction: Begin with a brief conversation about His-Story and Her-Story, too. Introduce the idea that His-Story is really about the stories of everyday people. What are primary source documents? Why is an eyewitness account more meaningful? Invite students to be detectives, real historians. Like an episode of *Cold Case,* they will conduct real historical research looking for the clues in a whodunit, who actually did what most historians just talk about.

If emphasizing a specific period in history, talk about some of the major players, but also ask students how they think this event affected average folks.

Tell the story "Rowing the Ohio."

Activity: Discuss the story in some detail: What did students learn from the story, both big picture historical facts and the personal details? What made this story work both as a piece of entertainment and as a teaching tool?

Invite students to step into the shoes of an actual person from history and to immerse themselves in that moment in time through a first-person narrative. Their goal this first class period is to find a character and begin the research. By the end of the class, they need to have the raw material in hand so that they can begin shaping the story they will tell the next day. By the end of the week, allowing a few days for research and a few more for rewriting, their goal is to develop a five-minute story about an important moment in history from the point of view of someone who was there.

If students are allowed a broad sweep, ask them to choose a time period or a historical event that they already know something about, maybe even a person they have already studied for another project earlier in the year. Research is always easier if one has a sense of where to look and some knowledge of the context.

If the class is exploring a specific historical event—for example, slave narratives—then it is important that students hear a story from that time period to model the type of story you are hoping they will tell. It is also helpful if some advance research is done for them to point them in the right direction, a list of Web pages on the board and a shelf of books from the local library.

If students are willing to do a little digging and not just grab the first thing they come across, their character will do a lot of their homework for them. For example: I perform as John James Audubon in part because his writing is very tellable. Audubon was a storyteller, which makes my job easy. If students choose a character who left no record, it is a lot more difficult to tell a story about them, unless they are doing historical fiction (see the next lesson plan).

By the end of the first period, they should all have found a character and have a sense of the story they plan to tell. If the lesson begins on Monday, give students until Wednesday to complete their research, allowing them time to surf the Internet at home or go to the local library or historical society. Spend Tuesday discussing the big picture, contextual details, and working out of the social studies textbook.

Once they have chosen a character and found the primary source document, the development of their material should be fairly straightforward. It will be helpful if they have already completed the "Oral History" project in the previous section. Whether or not they have, however, the second side of the handout for that lesson, "Turning Notes into a Story," is a useful guide.

For students who need more guidance, use the story "Rowing the Ohio" as a template. Ask them to write two or three sentences of background to foreshadow the crises to come. Allow the characters to introduce themselves and their situation by writing two or three sentences, first-person, describing themselves. Set the stage by writing two or three sentences about the setting. Use the plot outline near the bottom of the handout to outline the story. Please note that I added the facts about the Fugitive Slave act of 1850, the African wedding ritual of jumping over the broom, and some of the detail about how Canada had a different set of laws with more opportunity for people of color. Of course this is all true, and a slave in 1850 would know these facts. Highlight the idea that students are being asked to teach us something and additional contextual research will help them score more points in social studies.

Challenge students to use quotes as much as possible, allow the characters to tell their story in their words. Again, if students have chosen a character they know a lot about and who left a good record of primary source documents, then they are actually being asked to edit and reorganize the text, writing segue and filler to stitch the story together. A good rule of thumb is that the story should be nearly 70 percent of the character's words and 100 percent their perspective and experience. Most of the second class period should be spent writing their story.

Allow a few minutes at the end of the second period for students to discuss costuming. Sometimes a hat or bonnet, a pair of their grandmother's glasses, or grandfather's old bow tie is enough to convey the character. Students do not need to be decked-out to the nines to pull it off; the story should be enough to convey authenticity, but one simple prop, an old straw broom or handkerchief on a stick, is enough to create the illusion. Allow students an extra day to finish their final draft and rehearse to anyone who will listen. Their homework is to go home and tell their story to their family and friends. Whoever they tell the story to should sign a piece of paper, and students need to get at least three signatures.

In the third class period, students should spend the first ten or fifteen minutes reading over their story one last time and then taking turns telling their stories to a partner, rehearsing and refining their story.

The culminating activity is a historical hall of fame in which students dress and portray characters from history. Within the class you can simply have students take turns standing up and performing for their peers. It is highly recommended that teachers give students a chance to perform for a wider audience. The easiest way is to line up the historical characters along the hallway with plenty of space between them so they are not intruding on each other's stories. Invite other classes, in small groups of eight or ten students, to tour the hall of fame. Each small group can hear five or more historical speeches, and each historian can have several chances to perform his or her story. If they are waiting for the next speech before bumping along, a short Q & A can be used as filler. You can even have the students make a button on the floor so the people can push the button to hear the story—like a wax museum!

Assessment: Students can turn in copies of their research, both for a grade and for a standard to help teachers evaluate the writing. The signatures from listeners at home the second night can be used as bonus points. The final draft of the story can be evaluated for two grades, language arts and social studies. Teachers should look for historical accuracy with points added for the wealth of facts students should be encouraged to add.

Follow-up Activities: This same set of lesson plans could also be used for students to explore the lives of important scientists, mathematicians, artists, authors, or saints, or even to host a presidential hall of fame. Feel encouraged to talk to your colleagues and plan an interdisciplinary unit in which the language arts teacher helps with the writing and the content area teacher helps with the research.

I have worked with dozens of local historical societies and museums to train volunteer docents. These organizations are always looking for eager, bright, talented volunteers to portray historical characters and act as a tour guide. Historical villages regularly hire youth in period clothing to people the village. This kind of research could lead to a summer internship or even a paying job.

Comments: As a working historian, I cannot begin to express the rapture of discovering an original primary source document, of holding in my hands the actual riverboat captain's log of Henry Detweiller, or receiving as a gift the typewritten letters of a young farm girl from Iowa who helped organize the labor movement in America.

Just as I light up at these kinds of discoveries, teachers will see history come to life in the eyes of their students when they hear the unfiltered truth. History is more fun—warts and all!

"GEORGE ROGERS CLARK AND THE DOUBLING OF AMERICA"—WRITING HISTORICAL FICTION

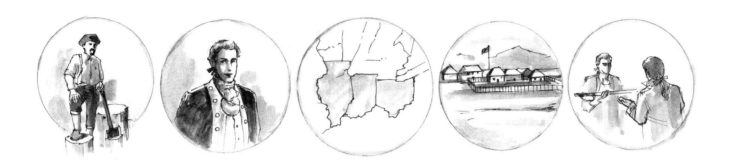

(With a heavy French accent, imagine Gérard Depardieu, and a conversational tone, like yesterday's news.)

Bon Jour. My name is LaBeche. I am uh French fur trader, a trapper, courier du bois. I carry furs through the woods, a courier, I carry, du bois, the woods. I was a young man—a boy—when the war between the French and British was fought. Do you know of the French and Indian Wars? Funny, no? They call them French and Indian wars. Who were we fighting? The British hired Indians as mercenaries. The wars in the old world spilled over to the new world.

Well, as an old man, when I heard about this American Revolution, of course I sided with the Revolutionaries. I never liked the British. But I was too old to fight, and I had seen the horrors of war with my own two eyes. Maybe you have heard the phrase, "Those who live by the sword, die by the sword." Mon ami, this is all too true.

But I heard that the General George Rogers Clark was recruiting men to attack the Hair Buyer. Do you know this hair buyer? This scoundrel, a British general, Lieutenant-Governor Hamilton, he hired Indians to do his dirty work. Just as the British bought beaver pelts, he bought scalps so he knew how many settlers the Indians had killed. Most people think scalping was an Indian tradition; yes and no. It was actually something encouraged by the Hair Buyer, Hamilton. He did not care if these scalps came from women or children. He encouraged the Indians to kill as many of these Americans as they could. The Hair Buyer was a cruel and vicious man. I could not sit on my hands and do nothing in the face of such evil. No.

I knew General Clark only by his reputation. He was a rare breed. He tried to befriend the Indians and only fought when provoked. He respected the French claims and wanted to build a life for his family that was safe, secure. Maybe you know his little brother, no? You have heard of William Clark, and his friend Meriwether Lewis, Lewis and Clark? Yes, it was in part because of George sending letters to President Jefferson that Jefferson bought a huge swath of land—the Louisiana Purchase—from Napoleon. Jefferson invited young William Clark to go with his secretary Lewis, but this came many years later.

Now, in the first years of the revolution it was not going well for these Americans. The British had more men, better arms, and some of the best generals in the world. They also controlled the seas. They brought

From *Content Area Reading, Writing, and Storytelling: A Dynamic Tool for Improving Reading and Writing Across the Curriculum through Oral Language Development* by Brian "Fox" Ellis. Westport, CT: Teacher Ideas Press. Copyright © 2008.

troops and supplies up the Mississippi and Ohio Rivers to attack the Americans from both sides. The Americans suffered one terrible defeat after another, including losses at Long Island and Fort Ticonderoga. The British trampled over Washington at Brandywine and Germantown.

General George Rogers Clark was friends with Jefferson. He had an older brother fighting with General Washington in New York and Clark wanted to do something. He saw his chance.

If he could cut off the supplies coming up the rivers, he might turn the tide. He might help win this war. In the summer of 1788, he traveled down the Ohio River and he began to recruit men. This is where I met George Rogers Clark. He had long red-blonde hair and broad shoulders. In his voice, even in the way he stood, he knew how to lead men. He would accept almost anyone who would join his rag-tag bunch of fur trappers, traders, pioneers, frontiersmen, and courier du bois, like me. We were not trained soldiers. We did not like to take orders! But we were men who knew how to shoot, paddle a canoe, move quietly through the woods.

With barely a hundred men, he was ready to challenge one of the mightiest armies in the world. Either he was foolish . . . or he was brave beyond measure, no? Or maybe, just maybe he was a little of both.

Clark knew he must keep his plan a secret for it to succeed. He did not even tell us, his men.

We floated down the Ohio River toward the Mississippi, but if we attacked the Fort at Kaskaskia by water, they would see us coming. So we pulled ashore and hid our canoes in the woods near Fort Massac on the Ohio River. We hiked overland several days and crept up on the fort late at night. They never knew we were there until it was too late. The fates were with us. There was a party at the fort that night, and many of the men had too much to drink. They had no guards to speak of, and we entered the fort with no real resistance.

I know it not to be true, but one story tells us the commander was in bed. Clark pulls his pistol on this man and says, "Surrender or die!" What would you do? He surrendered.

We do know this to be true: Clark captured the fort without killing a man!

He sent men up the Mississippi to capture the old French Forts of Chartres and Cahokia. Since there were few British soldiers in these towns and most of the inhabitants were French, they were glad to be under American rule! Many of them—no, many of us—were happy to become American citizens and offered to join Clark in his campaign.

But the British General, Hamilton, who was in De-twah, no, you say Detroit? Hamilton was enraged! He organized a troop of several hundred men to crush Clark. His men floated down Lac St. Claire and Lac Erie to the river Maumee. They headed up the Maumee and overland to the Wabash, which led them to the Fort at Vincennes on the Ohio River.

But this took time. Clark watched and waited. He held treaties with the Indians; some of them acted as spies and told Clark of the Hair Buyer's journey. General Hamilton arrived on the Ohio River just as winter settled in. Foolishly, he waited for the ice to melt to make his attack. This was the chance Clark wished for.

Clark took a huge risk. He marched his men across the southern end of the Illinois Country in the dead of winter. We marched one hundred miles through the snow-covered prairies, crossing frozen streams. The ice was too thin to hold us so we waded in icy cold water up to our chest. Could you imagine the cold? We were lucky, so lucky, no one froze. We arrived at Vincennes in the middle of winter when Hamilton did not expect us. The French men who still lived here helped us with food and gun powder.

Oui, Clark was a genius!

He arranged us in a circle around the perimeter of the fort. He told us to fire constantly for as long as it would take to smoke them out. We tried to conserve our lead and gunpowder by firing at irregular intervals. We took turns sleeping and shooting, shooting and sleeping. Hamilton must have thought there were a thousand men out there firing on him and we must have a limitless supply of lead and gun powder, for he surrendered. He sent up the white flag and the battle was over!

Once again Clark won without killing a man! Well, maybe a few were injured as we shot so many times into the fort.

When Hamilton gave up his sword, looking like the wounded puppy, he looked at us, a ragged bunch of trappers, and he said, "Where are the other men?" Clark took the sword and laughed, he laughed in the Hair Buyer's face, and said, "This is it, sir! You have been outfoxed!"

On the morning of February 25, 1789, George Rogers Clark put Lieutenant-Governor Hamilton in shackles and treated him like the dog that he was. He also arrested the top officers. But then Clark turned to the troops and scolded them for serving this criminal. He threatened them, saying he will track them down if they rejoin the British troops. He let the enlisted men go and encouraged them to join the Revolution! Fight against tyranny and claim a piece of America for yourselves! Clark was a genius. He knew he could not hold several hundred prisoners with just a few men, but he could hold their officers. Without officers to order them about, most men will not fight.

By winning two important battles, *without killing a man,* General George Rogers Clark doubled the size of America. He claimed all of the territory of the Northwest, all of the land that eventually became five states, Ohio, Indiana, Illinois, Michigan, and Wisconsin. Ah, if only more battles could be fought this way.

I am LaBeche. A French fur trapper, and I am honored to have served with General George Rogers Clark. I am honored to have done my small part to win freedom for my new nation, to win liberty for you.

Merci. Thank you for listening to the ramblings of an old man, merci beaucoup.

From *Content Area Reading, Writing, and Storytelling: A Dynamic Tool for Improving Reading and Writing Across the Curriculum through Oral Language Development* by Brian "Fox" Ellis. Westport, CT: Teacher Ideas Press. Copyright © 2008.

"George Rogers Clark and the Doubling of America": Writing Historical Fiction

Grade Levels: 3–12

Time Estimate: One or two 50- to 60-minute periods

Objectives:

- Students will blend fact and fiction to create historical fiction.

- Students will learn research skills by learning to ask questions and look for answers.

- Students will model that history is about the stories by performing original historical fiction.

National Standards:

- NCTE 1—Students read a wide range of print and non-print texts to build an understanding of texts, of themselves, and of the world; to acquire new information; and for personal fulfillment. Among these texts are fiction and nonfiction, classic and contemporary works.

- NCTE 3—Students apply a wide range of strategies to comprehend, interpret, evaluate, and appreciate texts.

- NCTE 4—Students adjust their use of spoken, written, and visual language to communicate effectively with a variety of audiences and for different purposes.

- NCTE 7—Students conduct research on issues and interests by generating ideas and questions, and by posing problems. They gather, evaluate, and synthesize data from a variety of sources to communicate their discoveries in ways that suit their purpose and audience.

- NCTE 8—Students use a variety of technological and information resources to gather and synthesize information and to create and communicate knowledge.

- NCTE 9—Students develop an understanding of and respect for diversity in language use, patterns, and dialects across cultures, ethnic groups, geographic regions, and social roles.

- NCTE 12—Students use spoken, written, and visual language to accomplish their own purposes (e.g., for learning, enjoyment, persuasion, and the exchange of information).

- NCSS 2—Time, Continuity, and Change

- NCSS 3—People, Places, and Environments

Materials:

- Paper and pencil

Background Information: Again, history is about stories. Whereas in the previous lesson students were asked to work with primary source documents and write fully accurate stories, this lesson emphasizes historical fiction, coloring in the details we can only imagine.

It is helpful if they have read some of the Dear America or American Girls series of books. *Red Badge of Courage* by Stephen Crane (1917), *Number the Stars* by Lois Lowry (1989), or *M. C. Higgens the Great* by Virginia Hamilton (2002) are a few of my favorite historical novels. The more good historical fiction students read, the better models they will have for writing their own stories.

Also, this particular story is one that has haunted me since I discovered it. I am fascinated by the idea that Clark could outfox one of the best British Generals, capture several forts, and double the size of the country by winning two battles with virtually no casualties (there is some dispute about Vincennes). Yet in high school and college history classes, Clark was never mentioned. I originally found the story in a historical novel, *From Sea to Shining Sea* by James Alexander Thom (1986), my favorite historical novelist. I then read George Rogers Clark's version of the story in his book *The Conquest of the Illinois* (republished by Shawnee Classics in 2001). Both books are breathtaking and highly recommended. If I could travel back in time and meet anybody, George Rogers Clark would be near the top of my list.

Instructional Procedures

Introduction: Plunge right in and tell the story of George Rogers Clark, or one of your favorite pieces of historical fiction.

Activity: Introduce the idea that stories can be like a time machine and allow students to travel back in time. Ask students, "If you could travel back in history, who would you like to meet? Where would you like to go? And what would you like to do? In a few moments this room is going to become a time machine, and we will travel back in time!"

Write "Historical Fiction" on the board. Ask what is fiction? It is made up, not real. What does historical mean? It is true, not made up. In a few moments students will be asked to use both true facts about history and their imagination to make stuff up. Discuss some of your favorite historical fiction and discern what is true and what is made up.

Ask students to take out a piece of paper. At the top of the page, they are to set the gauge for the time machine, writing a date and a short phrase such as "1775 and the Boston Tea Party." If the class is focused on a specific historical period, like the Revolution, then students might be given a moment to get out their textbook and write a specific date, such as "July 4, 1776, and the Continental Congress" or "February 25, 1789, and the Capture of Fort Vincennes." Make sure it is a time and place they know something about. This lesson works best near the end of a unit, because it is hard to write creatively about a subject they do not know well.

Warn students that you are about to pick their brain with a prior knowledge quiz. You want to know what they know. Encourage them to use their imagination to fill in the blanks; remember, this is historical fiction, a blend of facts and imagination. It is okay if they cannot answer all of these questions. Actually, it is impossible to answer all of these questions because they will come too fast and there are almost a hundred questions. Short answers are fine. Complete sentences are not needed at this point. We are just collecting ideas. If you think about this as a recipe for a story, we are shopping for ingredients.

Ask one hundred questions to help them imagine characters, setting, and plot (see page 111).

Now that you have the ingredients you need to write a story, it is time to daydream, to use the imagination and float back in time. Invite students to close their eyes and imagine the room becoming an actual time machine. "Imagine fog rising from the floor and falling from the ceiling. Imagine the fog so thick that everyone and everything around you disappears. Now imagine traveling back in time. As you travel, your clothes change, maybe you grow older or younger; who is telling this story? As the time machine stops, the first thing you notice are the people; who is in the story? What are they wearing; what do they look like? Imagine them talking. What do they talk about? What do they say? Begin to look around. Where are you? What do you see, hear, smell, feel? Use all of your senses to be in this place. Now, I am going to be quiet and so will you, but imagine watching the story unfold around you, like watching a movie inside your head, only better because you are in it! What happens? And then what happens? [Pause.] What problems do you encounter . . . and how do you solve them? [Long pause.] Now you might have to fast forward a little but it is time to wrap it up. How does your story end?"

Assign students a partner and then let them take turns telling their story. Allow them to tell it before they write it, and their writing will improve. Give students time to write their rough draft. As a final task, ask students to write at least three historical fact-based questions they would like to answer to help make the story more historically accurate. Their homework is twofold: (1) answer their research questions and (2) tell the story to anyone who will listen!

If the class spends fifteen minutes listening to the story and discussing it and fifteen minutes with one hundred questions and the deep memory, then students should have thirty minutes to finish their rough draft. So it could be done in one period. With more time, you usually get better work.

In the second class, students can use the rehearsal as rewriting strategies on page 71. Encourage students to work on the vocal elements of the story by telling it out loud. Give them a chance to stand up and act it out as a way of rewriting verbs and adverbs, the action of the story. Ask them to turn to a new partner and retell the story, watching their partner's reaction to the story as a way to understand their clarity, the rough patches, and anticipating their audience's reaction. Assist students as they complete their final draft.

Assessment: A student's answers to the Prior Knowledge quiz should not be graded but can be collected for bonus points. The rough draft of the story can be collected along with the final draft and the two compared as a way of evaluating their willingness and ability to rethink, rework, and rewrite their story. The final draft can be graded for language arts based on mechanics and style, as well as a social studies grade based on historical accuracy.

Follow-up Activities: These stories can be collected chronologically into a three-ring binder so the entire class can read each other's work. They can be shared with future classes as examples of this type of historical fiction. With or without costuming, the students can perform for their peers or for other classes.

Comments: Of the several types of historical storytelling in this chapter, these are probably the easiest to do. Because of the creativity involved, students also tend to respond well to the assignment. If a similar lesson is done several times in various historical periods over the course of the year, students can collect their individual stories into an in-depth tour of historical storytelling.

100 Questions: Who? When? Where? What Happened? The Prior Knowledge Quiz

by Brian "Fox" Ellis from *Green Teacher Magazine* (Winter 2000; used with permission.)

Every story needs three main ingredients: characters, setting, and plot. The following questions will help your students gather their thoughts and collect the information they need to bring their stories to life. You can use these questions to help students write a wide range of stories, from ecological adventures to historical fiction, ghost stories to fables.

Warn students that the questions will be asked at a rapid-fire pace and you do not expect them to answer all of them. (It's a good idea to repeat the most important questions two or three times to be sure they are answered.) Many of the questions can be answered in one or two words, and some will need a brief phrase or two, but complete sentences are not needed at this point. For questions they cannot answer, ask students to make up an answer or do a little research to find the correct answer. Together, these answers will become the raw materials for building their stories.

Characters: At the top of your page write WHO?

The big question is, who is in the story? Answer many of these questions for all of the characters:

What are their names? What do they look like? Are they male or female? Are they black or white or Asian or American Indian? How old are they? How tall are they? Are they skinny or not skinny? What kind of clothes do they wear? What type of boots or moccasins, pants or skirt, blouse or shirt, hat or bonnet? What color of skin, hair, and eyes do they have? How do they wear their hair? Are there any scars, deformities, or unusual characteristics?

You can tell a lot about people by what they look like, but don't stop there. How do they talk? What do they talk about? What tone of voice? You can tell a lot about people by what they say and how they say it. Take a minute and imagine a dialogue between two characters. What do they talk about? What do they love? What do they fear?

What do they do? What kind of job do they have? How do they earn a living? What do they eat? How do they put bread on the table? What do they do for fun? What kinds of games do they play? What kinds of songs do they sing? Don't say they are nice or evil; show this through their behavior. You can tell a lot about people by what they do. What do they do in the morning, afternoon, evening? What does a typical day look like? What kinds of problems do they face? How do they solve them?

Setting: Draw a line under your answers so far and then write WHERE? and WHEN?

The big questions are where and when does the story take place? What country, what part of the country, what city? What do their houses look like? Of what are they made? What other kinds of buildings are around? What kind of environment or ecosystem? What plants and animals live there? Which plants or animals are useful? Which might be harmful? What type of weather do they have? If they are traveling, where are they coming from and going to? What do you see each day of the journey? How do you travel? What does the landscape look like? Are there any mountains, rivers, hills, or valleys? What are their names? How does the landscape change? What does their home look like? Of what is it made?

What time of day is it? What time of year? What time in history? Don't just say it was 10 o'clock on a winter morning; show this in the details. How do you know what season or time of day it is? Use all of your senses. What do you smell? Hear? Feel? Is it moist or dry? Cold or hot? What is the emotional feeling of the place? Do the characters feel safe? Is it tense? Scary? Relaxed? How does this feeling change as the story changes? What causes the changes in feelings?

Imagine looking around. What do you see beside, behind, and on the other side? What do you see far away and right underneath you? If you are inside, what is on the walls or floor? If you are outside, what do you see above or way off in the distance? Make a picture with your words and bring your readers into this time and place.

Plot: Draw a line under what you have written so far and then write: WHAT HAPPENS?

The big question is what happens? The little question is: and then what happens, and then what happens, and then what happens?

What problems do people face in this environment? What problems do people have with the weather, storms, droughts, floods, or blizzards? What problems do people have with the plants, animals, or insects? What are the universal problems that people have always had, such as loneliness, jealousy, head-over-heels love, rage, rudeness, birth, death, separation? Make a list of possible problems, not just war or weather—War with whom? What kind of weather and why was it a problem? Place a star next to the problem that you think will make the best story.

Next to that problem, make a short list of possible solutions. If you were that person in that situation, what would you try to do to solve the problem? If that didn't work, what would you do? If that didn't work, what would you try next? How do you finally succeed? What do you learn from this experience? How does your character change because of this success or failure?

Make an outline of your plot. What happens first? Where is a good place to start? And then what happens? What problem do your characters face? How do they respond? Maybe they try but fail the first time. What happens next? How do they succeed? How does your story end?

Use your answers to these questions as the raw material for writing your story.

"THE STORY OF A FLINT ARROWHEAD": HISTORIC ARTIFACTS ARE DOORWAYS INTO THE STORIES OF THE PAST

The Story of a Flint Arrowhead

(The First Story: What is it? And how I found it.)

Several years ago I was working in my garden, weeding my asparagus patch, when I struck something hard with the hoe. I cleared away the dirt and a glimmer of sunlight reflected from a pearly white stone. I reached down and picked up the rock to toss it away. But when I picked it up, I saw that it was a worked stone. I brushed away the dirt and saw the careful fluting of a craftsman. It was aerodynamic, a perfect razor-sharp edge. Shimmering in the sun, it seemed illuminated from within. I could tell from the size, shape, and design it was not a spear point, but an arrowhead, probably a Plains Indian point made in the historic period three to five hundred years ago. It is about an inch and a half long with a beautifully worked point and fluted ends. There is even a shallow depression on each side where the shaft of the arrow would attach.

As I turned the stone in my hand, my mind reeled on the possibilities. My imagination traveled back through the centuries, back through millions of years as the garden disappeared in the mists of time . . . .

The Ancient Sea

(The Second Story: What is it made from, or what is the raw material? The raw material is fossilized sea sponge, known as "chert" or "flint.")

Three hundred and fifty million years ago most of the Midwest was a shallow sea. During the Devonian and Ordovician periods, a hundred million years before dinosaurs, an ocean covered the land that is now Ohio, Indiana, Illinois, Iowa, Kansas, and Nebraska. This "land" under the sea was actually down near the equator.

Imagine a warm tropical coral reef. There were sea lilies, snails, clams, and an amazing variety of coral. Lime-green brain corals and bright purple fan corals provided hiding places for the trilobites that feasted on unsuspecting prey.

On the sandy bottom of this shallow sea, there was a huge colony of sea sponges. They thrived here for thousands of years. But every year some of these sponges would die and decompose. Their skeleton, what we use to scrub with, would collapse and pile up on the bottom of the ocean. All of this coral and millions of sea shells piled up over the millennia and slowly hardened into limestone. But the sponges themselves formed a harder material, chert, flint.

From *Content Area Reading, Writing, and Storytelling: A Dynamic Tool for Improving Reading and Writing Across the Curriculum through Oral Language Development* by Brian "Fox" Ellis. Westport, CT: Teacher Ideas Press. Copyright © 2008.

Over the course of a hundred million years the land slowly rose above the sea to form the plains of North America. An Ice Age came and went, with mountains of ice adding pressure to the ground below, further compacting the bedrock. When the ice melted back, about 12,000 years ago, the melt water eroded the land, carving deep ravines that exposed the ancient sea bed below.

The Arrow Smith

(The Third Story: Who made it? Step by step, how was it made?)

A thousand years ago, an arrow smith, a man who makes arrows, was traveling down the river, a river carved by the melting glaciers 12,000 years before he came paddling his canoe. He had traveled more than a

hundred miles to this bluff above the river for one reason only: For generations his people had gathered their flint for arrowheads from this cliff. It was a deep rich vein of chert, some of the best flint in the region. This flint was highly prized for its pure white color, with a hint of pink. It was also prized for its hardness. The way it flaked made it easy to shape into tools. The arrowheads, spear points, awls, and knife blades he made from this flint he could trade with other tribes. Some of these tools might travel thousands of miles on the rivers of America, traded from one village to another.

When he had filled his canoe with all of the flint he felt he could safely carry, he began to paddle home, but before he left, he said a silent prayer of thanksgiving and left a small bundle of blue cornmeal as an offering to the river and to the land.

When he arrived home it was three days later, paddling upstream with a full load took longer than going downstream. First he greeted his family, and then he unloaded the precious cargo. His children helped to carry the rough stones up to their lodge. For the next several days he heated the stones in the fire to harden them. He sat in the sun, carefully chipping away at the small flakes to shape them into the tools he needed for survival. He made awls, small points for his wife to poke holes in the buffalo hides so that she could sew hides together to make moccasins and clothing. He made a knife blade and attached it to a piece of deer antler for his son to butcher the meat for dinner. He made dozens of arrowheads for himself and his family and to trade with his neighbors for other things that they made, like clay pots and porcupine-quill jewelry.

He also gathered the straight sticks and the turkey feathers to fashion the arrows. He would slice a small crack into one end of the straightest stick and slide this crack over the bottom of the arrowhead. He would wrap this with sinew from a buffalo to hold it together. He cut grooves in the back of the arrow and attached a piece of turkey feather, also tied with sinew, so the arrow would fly straight and true.

These arrows filled his quiver so he could hunt the food that fed his family.

The Hunter's Tale

(The Fourth Story: Why was it made? How did people use it?)

Early one morning, before the sun rose, a hunter rose from his bed. He quietly slipped on his moccasins, leggings, and his buckskin shirt. He moved silently, so he did not wake his family. He took his bow off of a hook and picked up his quiver full of arrows. The hunter ducked out of the lodge, stood and stretched, then greeted the first rays of morning light. Next, he pulled each arrow out of the quiver. One by one he carefully checked to see that they were straight, that the arrowhead was firmly attached and that the fletching was true.

He flung the quiver over his shoulder and set off down the trail at a trot. After the sun was two fingers above the horizon and he had traveled far from the village, he slowed, moving more quietly toward the river's

From Content Area Reading, Writing, and Storytelling: A Dynamic Tool for Improving Reading and Writing Across the Curriculum through Oral Language Development by Brian "Fox" Ellis. Westport, CT: Teacher Ideas Press. Copyright © 2008.

edge. He entered a copse of willow. He followed a game trail until he saw the fresh tracks and scat of a deer. He bent to feel the mud. He poked a stick into the steaming scat. The deer was near.

The hunter pulled an arrow from his quiver and notched it into his bow. Instead of following the deer tracks, he angled off toward the east so he would be downwind and the deer would be approaching him. On the bank of the river, he hid behind a fallen cottonwood tree. He waited. The deer often crossed the river here to spend the day sleeping in the cottonwood forest on the other shore.

The hunter heard a twig snap. He pulled back on the bow string. He slowly moved the bow and arrow so they were pointing in the direction of the sound. His heart thumped in his chest. He offered a silent prayer to the spirit of the deer, asking if it would offer its life so the people could live. A huge buck came down the trail, cautiously, as if it sensed he was there. The hunter had anticipated the movement of the deer so well, he was already aiming in its direction when it stepped into the clearing. Before he shot, he looked the deer in the eye and asked forgiveness with another silent prayer. The deer stepped forward and turned, as if to give him a better shot. When it felt right, the hunter let the arrow sail. It pierced the shoulder of the deer, through the lungs and into the heart. The deer jumped once . . . snorted . . . staggered . . . and fell.

The hunter sprang and raced toward the deer almost as swiftly as his arrow. He pushed the arrow on through so it did not break. Then he took some blue corn and sprinkled it on the mouth of the deer. Though the deer was gone, he offered a gift to the spirit of the deer so it would return again next year. He sprinkled cornmeal on the hooves of the deer to speed its journey to the other world and back again. He sprinkled cornmeal on the mouth of the deer to nourish it before its journey and so it would speak kindly of him in the other world. He then took out a stone knife and removed the heart of the deer. While it was still dripping, he ate a bite of it, so the heart of the deer would nourish him, their hearts would beat together, and he could feel compassion for the deer.

When this ceremony was complete, he field dressed the game, leaving some of the guts for the buzzards and coyotes. Nothing goes to waste. The hunter put the deer over his shoulder and returned to his village. As he butchered the deer, he offered one flank to his neighbor, another to his mother-in-law, and a third to his elderly father. Most of the deer he gave away. Of course his neighbor would invite him over for dinner and he would later eat with his father, but he wanted to be sure they were fed first. The deer was a gift to him; it was his duty to give it away.

This arrow was used for several more successful hunts.

Until one day, his son, while hunting in the same cottonwood forest, missed the deer and the arrow broke off inside the trunk of a tree. The tree eventually died and slowly returned to the earth.

The Farmer Who Found It

(Another Story: Where was it found, and how did it get here?)

Many years later, but not so long ago, not so far away, I was working in my garden, weeding my asparagus patch. I struck something hard with the hoe. I cleared away the dirt, and a glimmer of sunlight reflected from a pearly white stone. I reached down and picked up the rock to toss it away. But when I picked it up, I saw that it was a worked stone. I brushed away the dirt and saw the careful fluting of a craftsman. It was aerodynamic, a perfect razor-sharp edge. Shimmering in the sun it seemed illuminated from within. I could tell from the size, shape, and design it was not a spear point, but an arrowhead, probably a Plains Indian point made in the historic period three to five hundred years ago. It is about an inch and a half long with a beautifully worked point and fluted ends. There is even a shallow depression on each side where the shaft of the arrow would attach.

As I turned the stone in my hand, my mind reeled on the possibilities. My imagination traveled back through the ages as the garden disappeared in the mists of time . . . .

The Archeologist Who Studied It

(Another Possible Story: Who studied it? Who did the research and created the museum exhibit? What was their process for researching? How did they build the exhibit?)

The Arrowhead

(A second example, a simpler story that answers several questions at once.)

My uncle Mickey is a flint knapper. He is always looking for the perfect piece of rock. When he finds one he flakes off little chips to make arrowheads and spear points, knives, and other stone tools.

Last fall he gave me an arrowhead made from a beautiful piece of Brazilian agate. I carefully tied a piece of sinew to the notch where you are supposed to tie the stick. Then I strung some beads of buffalo horn and bone. I put on one white bone bead and then one black horn bead. In the middle I put a hematite bead. I wear it as a necklace.

People are always asking me about it. They say things like, "That is a beautiful arrowhead; what is it made out of?" Or they will say, "That is such a beautiful stone; what type of rock is that?" I always answer, "It is Brazilian agate," but I really did not know what that meant, so I went to the library to find out.

I already knew that if you learn the language of stones—geology—the stones will tell you their story. When I got to the library, the librarian helped me to find a book about rocks and minerals. I found a really cool picture of Brazilian agate. It did not look exactly like mine; it was different colors and was not carved into an arrowhead.

My stone is smooth. It is shaped like a triangle with notches on the back. It is mostly purple with two yellow streaks. The tip is white. So are the notches. It is very hard, so hard I could not scratch it with my fingernail. I could not scratch it with a nail. But my rock will scratch a penny. Other than the colorful stripes it does not appear to have any layers, like a sedimentary stone. I am guessing that it is igneous, melted by fires deep in the earth.

I started to think about how my stone was made. I began to learn its language and it told me this story.

Two hundred million years ago, the continents of the earth—Africa and the Americas, Asia and Antarctica, Europe and Australia/Oceanaia—all crashed into each other. When this happened, huge volcanoes erupted. The crust of the earth smashed together. The friction of stone rubbing on stone actually melted rocks. Mountains were pushed up. Old sedimentary stones were melted down. Metamorphosis took place, stones were transformed, changed. My stone was melted by fire, making it an igneous rock, an agate. Some of the molten magma cooled to form crystals. Some of it cooled too fast or too slow and became a fiery agate. This rock lay buried under the surface of the earth for millions of years.

A few years ago a mining company began to dig up many of the rich minerals buried in the mountains of Brazil. They clear cut the rainforest, stripping the land so they could get at the minerals underneath. They drilled holes into the side of the mountain and put dynamite into those holes. They exploded the mountains layer by layer. A huge bulldozer began to scoop up the rubble and put it into a big dump truck. The dump truck loaded it into a train car which carried it down to the sea. A big boat sailed up the coast through the Gulf of Mexico and took the minerals to the United States. The agates were loaded into smaller trucks and sold to rock shops across the country.

My Uncle Mickey went to a Knap-in. This is big festival where lots of people who make arrowheads, flint-knappers, get together to share ideas, show off their craft, and buy rocks. One guy from Ohio sold my Uncle Mickey a beautiful piece of Brazilian agate. My Uncle Mickey chipped off this piece. He worked the stone, carefully chip, chip, chipping until he made it into the shape that you see. And then he gave it to me. I put it on a string with beads made of bone and buffalo horn.

And now I have more than an arrowhead necklace. I have a story to go with it!

"The Story of a Flint Arrowhead": Historic Artifacts Are Doorways into the Stories of the Past

Grade Levels: 3–12

Time Estimate: One hour

Objectives:

- Students will learn to write historically accurate historical fiction.

- They will be introduced to basic research skills.

- Students will demonstrate an understanding of anthropology and archeology through hands-on experiences with artifacts.

- Students will learn storytelling and how to use storytelling to improve both their writing and rewriting skills.

- Students will learn strategies for reworking, rethinking, reimaging, and rewriting their stories.

National Standards:

- NCTE 4—Students adjust their use of spoken, written, and visual language to communicate effectively with a variety of audiences and for different purposes.

- NCTE 5—Students employ a wide range of strategies as they write and use different writing process elements appropriately to communicate with different audiences for a variety of purposes.

- NCTE 6—Students apply knowledge of language structure, language conventions, media techniques, figurative language, and genre to create, critique, and discuss print and non-print texts.

- NCTE 11—Students participate as knowledgeable, reflective, creative, and critical members of a variety of literacy communities.

- NCSS 2—Time, Continuity, and Change

- NCSS 3—People, Places, and Environments

- NCSS 7—Production, Distribution, and Consumption

- NCSS 8—Science, Technology, and Society

Materials:

- Paper and pencil or computer

- A suitcase, trunk, box, or trade blanket of historical artifacts, beads, arrowheads, furs, spoons, old glasses, tools and assorted historical brick-a-brack. These are easily acquired from a local historical society, museum, library or nature center that has an educational loan program. It could even be a collection of old junk from your grandma's attic or grandpa's garage.

Background Information: A museum is a large box full of stories. Archeologists, paleontologists, and anthropologists are all professional storytellers at heart. In this hands-on object lesson you will learn to turn historic artifacts into a dynamic writing exercise and an exciting performance opportunity.

I have used this lesson often and always get an enthusiastic response from students. Historical objects are vessels for stories—doorways into tales of the past. Students' intrinsic curiosity and excitement are easily sparked when they have a really cool object to talk about. The stories flow naturally and are easily shaped into both solid writing and the most entertaining storytelling.

Instructional Procedures

Introduction: Whether you are teaching about the French explorers, Lewis and Clark, or sod-busting prairie farmers following the Oregon Trail, World War II, the Civil War, or the poverty of the Great Depression, it is always important that you begin with stories. Read aloud, or better yet, dramatically tell stories of the type that you want students to write and tell. These stories give them solid models of good historical fiction and build a foundation of knowledge from which they can draw information; it is hard to write creatively about a subject you do not know.

During an artist-in-residence program, I always begin with a large assembly. After my performance, I then visit each classroom and help the students write their own historical fiction. I spread out a fur trapper's trade blanket filled with accurate reproductions of historical artifacts. Many of them I have made. Most of them can be borrowed from a local museum or historical society. (I recently put together a Harris Loan Exhibit Box for Chicago's Field Museum that explores the Lewis and Clark Expedition. With the recent 200th anniversary of the Corps of Discovery, many Midwest and Western communities have access to this kind of material.)

The students' eyes light up when I tell them that in a minute they get to pick one item from the table and tell its story. But first, model the process. Pick up an object, hold it to your ear, and in a comic fashion move it away saying, "No," hold it back to your ear and then say, "Really, you don't say? Listen, this artifact just told me this wonderful story . . ." and then tell them the tale. Please see "The Story of the Arrowhead" for an example. It is best if the teacher invents a story based on an artifact she has in her hands.

After the story discuss the questions. They should ask them out loud and answer them in their stories. Every artifact actually tells several stories about the materials, how it was made, how it was used, and how it got here.

Ask students to line up and walk past a table strewn with arrowheads, beads, furs, antique toys, cattail dolls, bark rattles, miniature canoes, claw necklaces, musket balls, horn spoons, Jefferson Peace Medals, and other historic artifacts. These should be things students are familiar with, not strange, weird, or hard-to-identify things. As they walk by, they pick up one object that catches their attention. If they pause or take too long, the line pushes them forward, and their chance is missed. They are not to linger at the table. Grab something and go!

Discuss It with a Partner before You Write It Down!

Back at their seats, ask students to choose a partner and discuss their artifacts. In a conversation discuss the following questions as a way of laying the foundation for writing their story. Partners take turns helping each other focus on one artifact at a time. Put the following questions on the board. Each question could be the basis for a different story.

What is it?

What is it made from or what is the raw material?

How was this material acquired?

Who made it?

Step by step, how was it made?

Why did they make it? How did they use it?

Where was it found? And how did it get here?

Because this is historical fiction, it is okay to guess, to imagine, to make up part of the story, but the more "true facts" they have in their story, the more points they can get in social studies. Offer students two As for the price of one: They can get an A in language arts for writing a good story, with well-defined characters, a clear setting imagined with rich multi-sensory detail, and a solid sequential plot with a beginning, middle, and end. They can also get an A in social studies. The more facts they have, *cha-ching!* The more points they get! But if their facts are grossly wrong or exaggerated, they can lose points, so encourage them to double-check facts they are not sure about.

After they tell it to a partner they write it like a story. All they really need to answer is one question, but answer it well, not with a short phrase or a strictly factual answer. The answer should turn into a story. Allow approximately fifteen minutes for students to write their rough draft.

Using the rough draft as a starting point, allow students time to do a little research to add to the historic accuracy of their story. They can surf the Internet, visit the library, or ask an expert. If there are facts they are unsure of, they can look them up. Reading general information about the culture or historical period is also helpful and encouraged.

Retelling Is Rewriting

Next students choose a new partner and retell the story, taking turns practicing good listening and telling their stories. Retelling is a way of reshaping, reworking, and rewriting their story. Challenge them to watch their partner watch the story. If they look confused, explain it. If they look excited or scared, stretch this part out and build on the strengths.

Their homework is to finish their final draft and double check some of their facts.

Assessment: The final draft of the story is potentially graded three ways:

First, a careful reading of the story for grammar, spelling, and stylistic elements. The most important question: Is the information conveyed in a dramatic narrative fashion?

For a social studies grade, reread the story and keep points in the margin, 5 to 10 points for each fact, 20 or more points if they illuminate some important historic concept, minus 2 to 4 points for blatant inaccuracies. Admittedly, I am both generous and forgiving.

A third grade can be given for the performance. Over the next few weeks, allow a few students each day to tell their story to the class. These performances can be graded using the rubric at the end of Chapter 1.

Exceptional stories, well told, can be allowed to travel. Students can perform for other classes. Student can even host a school-wide assembly or parent night.

Comments: I am often amazed at the imaginative quality of the writing, the evocative nature of the performance. At a recent residency, the fifth-grade students who performed at the end of the week were confident and engaging. A visiting scholar from a local museum asked about recruiting students to interpret at the museum.

Having an object in hand to talk about, motivate research, and share with their friends makes it easy for students to see themselves as storytellers. The artifact invites a story. Simply telling stories makes it easy to write. The whole process makes history visceral and alive!

"WATKAWES: THE NEZ PERCE WOMAN WHO SAVED LEWIS AND CLARK": PROS AND CONS OF LEWIS AND CLARK—AN EXERCISE IN PERSUASIVE DEBATE

Watkawes: The Nez Perce Woman Who Saved Lewis and Clark

The following story has been passed down through the Nez Perce oral tradition.

Nearly sixty years before Lewis and Clark came over the Rocky Mountains to the village of the Nez Perce Indians, a young girl headed down the Columbia River to the bay with her parents. At this time there were Russian and British traders who sailed up the Pacific coast to purchase beaver pelts and otter furs. The tribes of this region valued the metal tools, beads, mirrors, and other beautiful and odd things these white men had to trade. The cheap muskets, knives, and hatchets were traded far up the rivers into the mountains.

Here is where the story gets blurry. Some say this girl became lost. Others say she was stolen and possibly sold into another tribe. Both stories could be true. In either case she was scared and alone. She was afraid for her life and afraid she would never see her people again.

A white man came to her aid. He helped her to find her way home. He helped her to find her people.

Years slowly swam by. This young girl grew to be an elder. Watkawes was her name.

In the late autumn of 1805, Lewis and Clark came over the Rocky Mountains. They traveled down the Snake River to find the village of the Nez Perce Indians. The Nez Perce had never seen a white man come over the mountains that way. These strange men seemed weak and hungry. They had beautiful things to trade, but they were not generous with their gifts. They had muskets that seemed much more powerful than the cheap trade guns bought from the coast. There were not many of them. Though they were well armed, they traveled with a young woman and her child, so they could not be a war party.

That night the Nez Perce had a Council about these strange visitors. They debated when and where they should kill them. The village would be much stronger than their enemies with these new guns. We should kill them and take their guns was the decision the Council recommended. Clearly the Nez Perce outnumbered them. It would be easy. It was not a debate about if or maybe; it was a debate about when the Corps of Discovery should be killed in their sleep.

But then Watkawes stepped forward. In Council everyone has the right to speak and the people would listen, but as an elder, her words had weight. She told them the story of when she was a young girl and a white man was kind to her. Because of this kindness, she said, we should be kind to them. Clearly they are far from home and lost. We should help them because a white man once helped me.

And so it was decided.

The Nez Perce did not kill Lewis and Clark. They helped to feed the Corps of Discovery. Helped them make canoes and head down the Columbia River to the coast. Watched their horses through the winter and helped them back over the mountains the next spring. Without the help of the Nez Perce, Lewis and Clark may not have survived. Without the word of Watkawes, they may not have lived through the night. And Lewis and Clark never even knew of this Council meeting.

Without the kindness of that stranger so many years ago, this story would have had a very different ending. Who knows what fruit shall be born of some small kindness that you or I might perform this day?

From *Content Area Reading, Writing, and Storytelling: A Dynamic Tool for Improving Reading and Writing Across the Curriculum through Oral Language Development* by Brian "Fox" Ellis. Westport, CT: Teacher Ideas Press. Copyright © 2008.

Pros and Cons of Lewis and Clark: An Exercise in Persuasive Debate

Grade Levels: 3–12

Time Estimate: One hour

Objectives:

- Students will learn debate skills, most notably how to agree to disagree.

- They will practice persuasive writing.

- Most important, they will see that most events in history can be viewed from two or three distinct perspectives.

National Standards:

- NCTE 4—Students adjust their use of spoken, written, and visual language to communicate effectively with a variety of audiences and for different purposes.

- NCTE 5—Students employ a wide range of strategies as they write and use different writing process elements appropriately to communicate with different audiences for a variety of purposes.

- NCTE 6—Students apply knowledge of language structure, language conventions, media techniques, figurative language, and genre to create, critique, and discuss print and non-print texts.

- NCSS 1—Culture

- NCSS 2—Time, Continuity, and Change

- NCSS 5—Individuals, Groups, and Institutions

- NCSS 6—Power, Authority, and Governance

Materials:

- Paper and pencil

Background Information: Clearly there is room for debate about the significance of the Lewis and Clark expedition. Whereas some organizations wished to celebrate the anniversary, other groups were very pragmatic in calling this a commemoration, not a celebration of the 200th anniversary, while there is also a third vocal group who still feel we should mourn the event. There is no doubt that Lewis and Clark and their hardy crew were brave, courageous, and full of determination. There is also no argument about the fact that the opening of the West meant that disease, destruction, and the attempted genocide of indigenous people followed.

One Lakota woman was quoted as saying, "Why should we celebrate two white guys lost in our neighborhood, too stupid to ask for directions? They discovered *nothing, nothing* that we did not already know."

Many times the American Indians they encountered along the way quite literally saved their lives, gave them food, shelter, horses, and directions. The Indians helped them at most every turn and in exchange they received a few trinkets, demeaning speeches, and empty promises.

This lesson gives students a chance to view the expedition from both points of view and decide for themselves if the Corps of Discovery was more of a corrupting influence that should be mourned or an accomplishment to be celebrated. This type of lesson is always better served near the end of a unit, so the students have some prior knowledge of the content to argue persuasively.

Instructional Procedures

Introduction: Begin this lesson by reading, or better yet, telling the story of Watkawes.

Against   **For**

|—————————————————————|————————————————————————|

100%   50/50   100%

Commemoration   **Celebration**

Ask students to get out a piece of paper and a pencil. In just a moment, they are to make a number line and make a mark on that line. To the left is 100% against Lewis and Clark, and to the right is 100% in favor of the celebration. You cannot be 50/50, sitting on the fence. Maybe they will be 55/45, a little more against than for, or 25/75, much more for than against. Instruct the students to listen carefully to the following questions before they make up their minds, before they make their mark. Teachers should read the following questions:

"Was the Lewis and Clark expedition a great thing for *all* Americans? Why was the Corps of Discovery so important for America? Who benefited from this and why? Who suffered because of their journey? Was this expedition a good thing for the Indians? What makes Lewis and Clark heroes? Were they brave and determined? If you were an Indian and everything you knew changed, would you want to celebrate this anniversary? Was this expedition Jefferson's attempt to expand the United States regardless of the people who lived there? Who was Napoleon to sell land that belonged to the Indians? Can we blame Lewis or Clark for the diseases and destruction that followed them? Or can you blame them for the land grabbing, destruction of the prairie, and extinction of animals? Chances are you are somewhere near the middle. Where do you stand?"

The important point in this kind of questioning is that the teacher tries not to influence students one way or the other but asks two or three questions that might lean one way and then two or three that might lean the other way.

Now ask students to make a mark on their number line; remember, no fence sitting; they must lean for or against. Next, ask students to stand, without talking, and move into a single-file line. Those who are for Lewis and Clark and believe we should celebrate their adventure move to the right, and those against Lewis and Clark and feel that they led to many of the problems we now face move to the left. The only comment should be: "What number are you?" so students can jostle into a single-file line. If they find someone with the same number, they can stand beside each other, but it should be a single-file line.

Once in line, invite students to count off A-B, A-B; A is B's partner so they have a partner who basically agrees with them. Give the students three minutes to discuss why they chose this point in the line, this point of view, with someone who basically agrees with them. Challenge them to come up with three solid reasons and to elaborate on these reasons.

Next, divide the line in half. Slide one half down so they are facing an opponent, someone who disagrees with them. Allow one partner to talk at a time, no arguing. Students facing in one direction have three minutes to express their opinion and to elaborate on three reasons why they chose this opinion. Their partner can only listen. Switch roles after three minutes. If the class is engaged in *civil* debate, the next step is to allow a question-and-answer period during which each partner can ask and answer one question.

Invite students back to their seats to write a persuasive essay. In this piece of persuasive writing they must be 100% for or against. Using the National Standards as a guide, students should be reminded that persuasive writing begins with a solid statement of their opinion with at least three more paragraphs that elaborate on three reasons why they believe what they believe, and then a final paragraph that restates their opinion in new words.

Follow-up Activities: As an exercise in creative writing and flexible thinking, they can also write an essay with the opposite point of view.

Another instructive lesson can be a careful reading of the speech that Meriwether Lewis delivered to tribe after tribe. A detailed outline of this speech is available in Rhoda Blumberg's (1987) book, *The Incredible Journey of Lewis and Clark* on pages 38–39. Before you read the speech to the students, ask them to listen with both ears: From the point of view of Lewis and the United States Government, why would he say these things? And from the point of view of the Indians, how would you feel about his word choice and tone, as well as what is said?

To learn more about some of the negative effects of westward migration, students can be asked to research and write reports about the spread of disease, the outright slaughter of the buffalo, the trail of broken treaties, and life on a reservation.

You may also wish to do a Web search on "Why Lewis and Clark Don't Matter," or "Stop Lewis and Clark," (see http://www.stoplewisandclark.org/stop_expedition.html) for a more radical opinion.

"THE TWIN SISTERS": STORIES MAPS COULD TELL: FOLKLORE AND GEOGRAPHY

The Twin Sisters

North of Chillicothe, Illinois, in the middle of the Illinois River, you will find a pair of islands known as the Twin Sisters. They say these islands are racing down the river. These twins have been racing since a time before time and they are still racing today. If you look at an old map of the river, you will see that these islands have indeed moved several hundred yards since the river was first mapped. How do islands move you might ask? I will tell you.

Many long winters ago, before the Illiniwek moved into this valley, before the Mississipian Mound Builders built the powerful pyramids at Cahokia, nomadic hunters still followed the huge herds of mastodons. When woolly mammoths and saber-toothed cats still roamed this land, these hunter-gatherers began to settle down in this fertile valley, a place where the food was abundant.

In this time before time, there was one born among them that had a gift. Some would call her a shaman or medicine woman. Others would call her a sorceress. Regardless of what she was called, everyone agreed that she was born with a gift.

She could look into the future, and she could talk to the spirits of the past. She could look into you and see what was in your heart. As a young child she went to live with the village elders who shared with her their secrets of magic and medicine. She learned which plants were medicines and which plants were poisonous. She learned the sacred songs and the ways of working with spirit. Soon she became one of the more powerful healers in this valley.

And then for some unknown reason, she began to dabble in dark magic. Maybe her power made her vain. Maybe she healed someone, and that person did not "gift her" what she thought was fair payment for her services. She began to curse people instead of cure them. Inexplicably people became sick with strange diseases. A dark cloud seemed to hang over her, and people began to fear her.

In those days as in these, people did not like this dark magic. She was ostracized. She was forced to leave the village. She moved out into the swamps along the river's edge were she could practice her black magic undisturbed. What the people did not know is that she was pregnant with twins when she left.

From *Content Area Reading, Writing, and Storytelling: A Dynamic Tool for Improving Reading and Writing Across the Curriculum through Oral Language Development* by Brian "Fox" Ellis. Westport, CT: Teacher Ideas Press. Copyright © 2008.

She had helped many children into this world, just as she had helped others enter the next world. When the time came she gave birth to two beautiful girls. But in those days as in these, children inherit the strengths and sins of their parents. Her daughters had her gift for magic, but they also grew up in the shadow of her twisted mind.

As the girls grew, they were always competing. They were always racing. They were constantly arguing.

One would say, "I am faster than you!"

And the other would say, "I am smarter than you, and that is more important!"

One would say, "I am better looking than you."

And the other would say, "You may think you are pretty on the outside, but inside you are wicked."

"I may be wicked, but you are evil!" the one would reply.

One day, one of the girls called her sister out and challenged her to a contest of black magic. The girls began hurling curses at each other. Bolts of lightning flew from their fists. Thunderclouds roared. Tornadoes and twisters whirled up around them. The trees were bending to the ground as stones began dancing into the air. The river's current rose to flood stages!

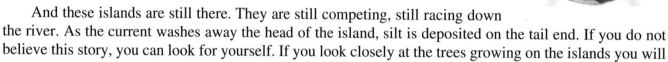

Maybe their black magic backfired, or maybe the Creator took pity on them. In that moment these twin sisters were transformed into islands in the Illinois River.

And these islands are still there. They are still competing, still racing down the river. As the current washes away the head of the island, silt is deposited on the tail end. If you do not believe this story, you can look for yourself. If you look closely at the trees growing on the islands you will

see that trees at the head of the islands are older and taller, whereas trees on the downstream end of the island are shorter and younger. They also say that as one island pulls ahead, the current shifts so that more silt is deposited at the tail of the other island, and it soon catches up to its sister and passes her only to shift the current so the other island catches up and passes.

These twin sisters are still racing down the river. These islands are here to this day to remind us of this story, to remind us of what happens when you dabble in the darker realm.

Stories Maps Could Tell: Folklore and Geography—Helping Students Write and Tell Landform Stories

Grade Levels: 3–12

Time Estimate: Two hours

Objectives:

- Students will gain a hands-on understanding of topographical maps.
- Students will learn basic cartography skills.
- Students will improve their visual-spatial thinking ability.
- They will demonstrate their understanding of geography and geology through the creation of a myth that exemplifies these concepts.

National Standards:

- NCTE 4—Students adjust their use of spoken, written, and visual language to communicate effectively with a variety of audiences and for different purposes.
- NCTE 5—Students employ a wide range of strategies as they write and use different writing process elements appropriately to communicate with different audiences for a variety of purposes.
- NCTE 6—Students apply knowledge of language structure, language conventions, media techniques, figurative language, and genre to create, critique, and discuss print and non-print texts.
- NCTE 7—Students conduct research on issues and interests by generating ideas and questions, and by posing problems. They gather, evaluate, and synthesize data from a variety of sources to communicate their discoveries in ways that suit their purpose and audience.
- NCSS 3—People, Places, and Environments
- NAS 4—Earth and Space Science: Structure of the earth system; Earth's history
- NAS 1—Science as Inquiry: Abilities necessary to do scientific inquiry; Understandings about scientific inquiry

Materials:

- Paper and pencil

Background Information: Throughout the world people tell stories of how things came to be. Mysterious mountains, unusually deep canyons, and precipitous cliffs are pregnant with stories of adventure, failure, and triumph. The Dine, or Navajo, say that the landscape stalks us with stories. These stories remind us of our place in the world; that cliff or this boulder reminds us of our relationship with others, of the right way to walk in this world. The Aborigines of the Australian Outback use stories as a map to help them find their way in that bleak landscape. The stories are told at a walking pace as you cross the land. As features of the landscape come into view, they remind you of the next chapter in the story; as the story unfolds, it reminds you which way to turn so you can get to the next watering hole, the next village, or wherever this chosen story leads you.

These stories can be powerful tools for teachers who want to bring geography to life. Many of these stories, although considered fiction or folklore, contain scientifically accurate interpretations of geological processes. Case in point: In the Shawnee version of the creation of Turtle Island, North America, they say the continent is shaped like a turtle, and it is swimming in the ocean. It takes very little imagination to see Florida and Baja California as legs and Mexico as a tail. Alaska and Nova Scotia are peninsulas; the front legs, and Greenland is the head. The truth is that North America is moving like a turtle, slowly, two to three inches per year. This is why we are having earthquakes in California. Another example: In the Hawaiian creation story, they say that the Earth Goddess belched fire and gave birth to Pele, the Goddess of the Volcano. Indeed, the Hawaiian Islands are volcanic eruptions from the earth's underwater crust.

These stories can make flat maps multidimensional, adding drama and suspense to a better understanding of geography and geology. These stories also add multicultural dimensions to the teaching of geography. Especially if you are teaching a diverse ethnic population, it makes sense to reach out to them by teaching the content area with stories from their culture of origin.

Instructional Procedures

Introduction: Begin this unit with a brief discussion of the basic landforms and how they are made (see the list below). Introduce map vocabulary terms such as *elevation, latitude, longitude,* and *color-coded keys.* There are wonderful charts and graphics available in most textbooks. The state and federal departments of geology also have free charts and maps available for the asking.

This is in no way a complete list and is meant simply as an introduction:

Types of Landforms	Causes
Hills	Erosion—wind or water
Volcanoes	Rifts in the earth's crust; plate tectonics
Mountains	Plate tectonics
Valleys	Glacial carving and moraines
Plateaus	Faults—earthquakes
Rivers	Melt water erosion
Plains	Glacial till
Bays	Continental shelves
Canyons	River erosion
Islands	Volcanic or coral growth or silt deposits

Activity: To make these ideas geographic and to give your kinesthetic learners a hands-on opportunity to create topographical maps, you can invite your class to do one or both of the following lesson plans.

Knuckle Mountain

Several years ago when I took a field course in environmental education, my instructor, Marot Snow, shared a lesson plan that I have used countless times with student groups. First, you ball your hand into a fist and lay it flat on a table or desk. Next you draw concentric circles on your knuckles, moving down in elevation approximately a quarter or half an inch. The first circle is a small irregular oval around your tallest knuckle. Moving down about a quarter inch, draw a second oval that includes two or three knuckles. Draw a third, fourth, and fifth oval, each time moving a quarter inch lower on the topography of your fist. You will notice that steep places have lines that are closer together; less steep places will have lines farther apart; the gaps between fingers will be inverted Vs; and if you have bony hands or large veins, you will see little Us on the back of your hand. After drawing the lines on your fist, flatten your hand on the table, and you will see a two-dimensional topographical map that approximates the three-dimensional Knuckle Mountain. Demonstrate this for the students and then draw your topographical map on the chalkboard or overhead projector. Using Socratic questioning, discuss water drainage, elevation changes, the proximity of lines related to steepness, capturing three dimensions on a flat page, and any questions they may have.

Ask students to draw lines on their fists, flatten their hands, and then copy their topographical map of their Knuckle Mountain on a piece of paper. Students can then color code their topographical maps and make a key to explain their colors. To further their understanding of three-dimensional thinking, students can also draw a mural of Knuckle Mountain based on the reading of their topographical maps. What would this mountain look like from the south? From the northeast?

Underwater Mountains

Materials:

- Water

- Small pointed rocks four to six inches in diameter and four to six inches tall

- A large flat-bottom bowl deep enough to submerge the stone

- Paper and pencil

Activity: This is an activity that students can perform individually or in small cooperative groups of two to four students. The advantage to group work is that they ensure each other's accuracy and you need fewer sets of materials.

Instruct students to carefully measure the depth of the bowl and draw notches every half inch on the inside of their bowl. A flat vertical wall on the bowl works best. Ask them to carefully place the pointed stone in the bottom of the bowl and then fill the bowl with a half inch of water. Each student will then draw the shape of their stone at the waterline. The students will then fill the bowl to the next half-inch increment and again draw the shape of the stone at the waterline. This will be an irregular oval inside the first outline. Ask them to repeat this process until only a small tip of the rock protrudes from the water. Their maps will be a series of irregular concentric circles. Students can then color code their topographical maps and make a key to explain their colors.

Each student now has a topographical map of their stone. This can be a springboard for discussions of scale, volcanoes as underwater mountains, color coding altitudes above and below sea level, ways in which actual mountain maps and seafloor maps are drawn, and the reading of real topographical maps. As a test of the efficacy of their maps, students can trade maps with someone who used a different stone. They could then draw murals of this other stone based on the maps. The stones can be placed on a central table, and students can try to match their drawings and their partner's maps with the correct stone.

Telling and Writing Landform Stories

Now that students have a basic understanding of topographical maps and landforms, this is the time to introduce the landform stories from various cultures. Discuss Paul Bunyon, Pele the Fire Goddess, Turtle Island, Sleeping Bear Dunes, Devil's Tower (from *Close Encounters*), and other land form stories they may know (see the bibliography that follows).

Tell the story of "The Twin Sisters," "Coyote Dances with the Stars," "Grandma Turtle," or one of your favorite stories of landforms.

After telling the story, discuss the fact and fiction within the story. What parts are scientifically accurate? Which are fictional? What can we learn from this story about the creation of landforms? What can we learn from the culture depicted in the story?

Pass out detailed topographical maps of your region, state, country, or the world. Challenge students to choose a favorite landform, an actual landform on the map. Ask them to draw a picture of this landform based on their reading of three dimensions from two. Ask them to hypothesize about the geological processes that created this landform as they draw. They can also begin to daydream about stories in which they explain this formation.

Using the "100 Questions" technique outlined on page 111, assist students as they brainstorm about the details of their creation myth. You may want to begin with the questions about setting and then ask the questions about characters. Also adapt the questions to create superpowers or godlike magical abilities. These are to be mythological stories, rather than the historical fiction students wrote earlier.

Using their answers to the 100 questions as the raw materials for a story, ask the students to close their eyes and daydream a vivid, virtual-reality version of their story. Tell them to make it up as they go along, like watching a movie inside their forehead!

When they open their eyes, ask them to turn to a partner and take turns telling their stories. Writing is always clearer and more succinct if students first tell the story, then write it.

After they have a rough draft, assist them in researching the scientific facts about their landform focusing on the geological process that actually shaped their piece of the earth. Offer bonus points as an incentive for them to weave this scientific information into their story as they rewrite their creation myths. As an example of this, review "The Twin Sisters" and how the author added information about hydrology and erosion near the end of the story.

Finishing the rough draft and doing additional geological research can also be assigned as homework.

Assessment: The Knuckle Mountain and underwater mountains can be collected for a grade in geography, with an emphasis on accuracy, color coding, and their key.

Once again, the stories can be evaluated based on writing mechanics, grammar, spelling, and stylistic elements, and a second grade can be given for use of geographic and geological vocabulary and an explanation of these processes. If emphasized in the instruction, students can also be evaluated for the cultural information embedded in the story.

Follow-up Activities: When the stories are finished, each student can create a topographical map of their landform as well as a mural of their story with the canyon, mountain, or island in the background. These can be bound together as a classroom collection of short stories or mounted on a bulletin board. Students can also perform their stories for the class!

Comments: This lesson was originally created for a seventh-grade social studies class when the teacher told me both her and her class were bored with maps, and the students were just not getting it when it came to keys and geographical terminology. About this same time, the books, *Dear Katie, the Volcano Is a Girl* and *Sleeping Bear Dunes* (see Recommended Reading below) had just been published. It was magical how everything came together. The students loved writing creation myths that involved petty jealousy, double–cross, and the tragic repercussions of bad behavior—all of the ingredients of classic mythology. Yet woven into their stories were the vocabulary words of geography and geology, and most important, the concepts were clearly understood, used correctly, and everyone had a good time doing it.

Recommended Reading

Baylor, B. *The Way to Make Perfect Mountains*. Illus. Leonard F. Chana. Cinco Puntos Press, 1997. ISBN 0-938317-26-1. Beautifully erasing boundaries between science and mythology, Byrd Baylor uses her fine-crafted poetry to illuminate the mountains of the desert Southwest.

George, J. C. *Dear Katie, the Volcano Is a Girl*. Illus. Daniel Powers. Hyperion, 1998. ISBN 0-7868-0314-2. Through a fictional dialogue between a scientific grandmother and a little girl who believes in the mythology of Pele, the Fire Goddess of Hawaii, the reader sees the validity of both points of view. The illustrator even went so far as to include a mystical goddess prompting the scientific schematic drawings of how volcanoes are made.

Wargin, K. J. *The Legend of Sleeping Bear*. Illus. Gijsbert van Frankenhuyzen. Sleeping Bear Press, 1998. ISBN 1-886947-35-X. A forest fire in Wisconsin forces a mother bear and her two cubs to swim across Lake Michigan. The cubs do not make it, leaving the mother to grieve upon the Michigan shore, forming Sleeping Bear Dunes. The cubs become North and South Manitou Islands. It could be a stronger example of a landscape story with just a sentence or two about the sand deposition from glacial times in the formation of these islands and sand dunes.

CHAPTER 4

STORYTELLING AND SCIENCE

"THE COTTONWOOD": HOW I LEARNED THE IMPORTANCE OF STORYTELLING IN TEACHING SCIENCE-PROCESS SKILLS

Most would agree that storytelling is one of the most important tools for teaching science. If you think about it . . . What *is* science? Science is an attempt to understand the story of the universe.

A well-told science story does three important jobs. It brings facts to life. It makes abstract concepts concrete. And through the virtual reality of storytelling, it walks listeners through the process approach to scientific inquiry.

I love all of the amazing tidbits of intriguing information—science facts. And students do too, if those facts are presented in an intriguing way. Did you know that a pronghorn antelope can run fifty-five miles per hour? Cool fact, but if you stop with facts, you are not teaching science. Science should be a verb, an activity, not simply a body of knowledge.

By concepts, I mean theories, the big-picture ideas like the food web, the water cycle, evolution, and animal adaptation. These concepts are critical to the understanding of modern ecology. Usually an animal, like the antelope, develops an incredible speed because it has a predator that chases it. Co-evolution is a cool concept, but if you stop with concepts, you are still not teaching science. You are building a necessary conceptual framework for the ordering and understanding of facts. Again, science is something you do.

Science is about asking good questions and looking for answers. Why do pronghorn antelopes run fifty-five miles per hour when there are no predators that run that fast in North America? By asking good questions, formulating a hypothesis, designing an investigation, collecting data, analyzing and reordering data, and drawing conclusions, you are engaged in scientific inquiry.

A good story involves the listener in many of these same strategies: gathering the facts from the story, making predictions about the outcome, and checking their hypothesis against the unfolding details of the tale. Also, you can employ a story to make abstract concepts personal and tangible. You can convey important facts within a dynamic context so the facts stick; they have more meaning and more impact.

Let me share a short story that will show you what I mean:

When I was a student at Oberlin College, one of my favorite biology professors was a man whom I only remember as George. At ninety-four years of age, he still taught an occasional class. His father, too, had been a biology professor at Oberlin College. He spent his entire life studying the flora and fauna of northeastern Ohio. Botany was his specialty, and he knew every plant on campus on a first-name basis.

On Sunday afternoons, George led a hike in the arboretum. He meandered through the arboretum telling stories about whatever plant caught his fancy. One afternoon as we were walking in the flood plain of Plum Creek, he stopped next to an ancient cottonwood. This huge tree was almost a meter wide and maybe thirty meters tall. He leaned against this giant tree and said, "When I was a little boy, seven years old, my father told me that cottonwood trees had a unique characteristic: If you break off a branch and stick it in the mud, it will sprout. It is called regeneration.

"When my father told me this I thought, Poppycock! If you break off a branch, it is dead. A dead stick will not sprout. Note that I did not say this; I have more respect for my father than to openly dispute him without a bit of evidence, but I did not believe him.

"Well, a few weeks later I was walking through the arboretum when a huge storm blew in. I love those Midwestern summer thunderstorms. As the clouds roll across the Great Lakes, they pick up steam, literally. Most kids might run home, but not me. I love the crack of lightening, the roar of thunder, and the warm rains that pummel the earth.

"As I was walking along Plum Creek a strong gust of wind snapped off a branch from a cottonwood tree, and it stuck in the mud. I thought, Aha! This is my chance to prove my father wrong. I came back each day for five days to gather evidence. Sure enough, after the third hot summer day, the leaves started to wilt. Because of the heat, it was losing more water than it could absorb; "evapo-transpiration" is the scientific word for tree sweat. By the fifth day, the leaves were curled. This branch was dead.

"I went home and told my father he was wrong, and I had the proof. I was a precocious child, and my parents encouraged my inquisitive nature. My father calmly listened to my interpretation of the facts. He said, 'Son, you're jumping to conclusions. You need to collect more data.' He told me to go back to that tree every day for the next ten days, write down what I saw, and then to tell him what I thought. Being a good son and wanting to be a good scientist, I went back to that stick every day for ten days.

From *Content Area Reading, Writing, and Storytelling: A Dynamic Tool for Improving Reading and Writing Across the Curriculum through Oral Language Development* by Brian "Fox" Ellis. Westport, CT: Teacher Ideas Press. Copyright © 2008.

"Sure enough, after five more days the leaves started to uncurl. After seven days, they started to plump up. By the tenth day, the stick was indeed alive. I wanted to know why, so I carefully dug down around one side of the stick. I saw small roots that had begun to grow. So, my father was right. Cottonwood does have a unique characteristic; if you plant a stick in wet earth it will sprout. It's called regeneration. This is why cottonwood and willow are very important in preventing erosion. Streamside stabilization projects use willow posts and cottonwoods to help hold the stream banks in place.

"I'll never forget this idea because, you see, this giant cottonwood tree that we are standing next to is that cottonwood stick I watched wilt more than seventy years ago. Obviously, my father was right because that stick has grown into this huge tree."

And now having heard the tale, you will never forget this concept either.

While the story is still fresh in your mind, make a short list of some of the *facts* you learned from this story. And which major *concepts* stand out for you? What are the *science-process skills* modeled in this study of the cottonwood? (And if you tell this story to your class as an introduction to this lesson, please ask the same questions before continuing.)

Through George's inquiry approach, we have collected data about transpiration, root growth, and regeneration. We have formulated the hypothesis that sticks cannot regenerate and then designed an investigation to prove or disprove our theory. We have drawn an incorrect conclusion and collected more evidence to discover the truth. We have learned about trees, but more important, we have learned the process skills we need to learn about the unfolding drama that is the story of the universe.

Storytelling and Science-Process Skills

Grade Levels: 3–12

Time Estimate: One hour

Objectives:

- Students will demonstrate an understanding of science inquiry by designing an investigation.

- Students will learn to use the personal narrative to model scientific inquiry.

- Students will outline the steps needed to complete an investigation.

National Standards:

- NCTE 4—Students adjust their use of spoken, written, and visual language to communicate effectively with a variety of audiences and for different purposes.

- NCTE 5—Students employ a wide range of strategies as they write and use different writing process elements appropriately to communicate with different audiences for a variety of purposes.

- NCTE 6—Students apply knowledge of language structure, language conventions, media techniques, figurative language, and genre to create, critique, and discuss print and non-print texts.

- NCTE 7—Students conduct research on issues and interests by generating ideas and questions, and by posing problems. They gather, evaluate, and synthesize data from a variety of sources to communicate their discoveries in ways that suit their purpose and audience.

- NAS 1—Science as Inquiry: Abilities necessary to do scientific inquiry; Understandings about scientific inquiry.

- NAS 3—Life Science: Structure and function in living systems; Reproduction and heredity; Regulation and behavior; Populations and ecosystems; Diversity and adaptations of organisms.

- NAS 6—Science in Personal and Social Perspectives: Personal health; Populations, resources, and environments; Natural hazards; Risks and benefits; Science and technology in society

Materials:

- Paper and pencil

Background Information: The most important scientists have all been good storytellers. Think about the scientists who have had the most lasting contributions to our understanding of scientific principles and the way things work. They have all been great writers and storytellers.

I believe that Rachel Carson (1962) changed the world in the first few pages of her landmark book *Silent Spring*. Her modern parable about pesticides and the absence of songbirds in the spring helped to write new laws and radically transformed our relationship with the wild world. Her story took you inside the dilemma of a toxic environment and the long-term implications of what was then acceptable behavior. Her story, like the writings of Charles Darwin, John James Audubon, Madame Curie, and others can give you a front-row seat on scientific discoveries.

Through their stories, you feel like you are looking over their shoulders as they fumble through their mistakes and stumble upon the truth. A good science story needs this sense of immediacy, this in-the-moment, insider's view.

To paraphrase an old proverb, these kinds of stories not only give us fish for supper, but also a net for catching all the fish we desire. Science stories can make abstract theories concrete by bringing the listener into direct experience with the concept. The food web is not just an idea in a textbook; it is what you had for lunch. The water cycle flows through your blood streams.

Storytelling engages listeners in the scientific process through the suspense and virtual reality that a good story creates. Students get to make discoveries along with the author or main character in the tale. You can tell stories from your life experience, or you can dramatize important discoveries in the history of science. Even works of realistic fiction, if grounded in good science, can be written or told to illuminate a concept, introduce a chapter, or prepare students for a science experiment.

In telling these stories, exercise your science vocabulary while defining terms with explanatory clauses. If young kids can memorize the Latin names of dinosaurs, they can certainly learn science vocabulary if they hear the words in a meaningful context. The truth is, they will never learn these words unless they hear them in a meaningful context.

After having said all that, I'll say something more: If you stop here it isn't enough.

It is necessary for students to be energetically *engaged* in the activity of designing investigations and conducting research. After listening to this story about the cottonwood, what questions does it raise for you? How could you design an investigation that would find the answers? Go ahead and conduct this investigation. Remember: Science should be a verb!

Instructional Procedures

Introduction: This story, written with the introduction and follow-up questions embedded, was originally intended as a piece to be used in my school consulting and teacher training. I have found that it works just as well with students if you begin with a brief discussion of the differences between science facts, concepts, and process skills, as outlined in the introduction to the story. Use the pronghorn antelope example provided in the story's introduction; the introduction is a springboard for dialogue, not monologue. Spell out the steps to scientific inquiry: Ask good questions, formulate a hypothesis, design an investigation, collect and analyze the data, and draw a conclusion. The introduction is meant to be a dialogue.

Ask students how they might test my theory about co-evolution. Are there any predators in North America that run fifty-five miles an hour? When they have a solid sense of the scientific process, ask them to listen to how George uses the process. Warn them that after the story, they will be asked to discuss the facts, concepts, and process skills.

Activity: Tell the story of "The Cottonwood."

Immediately following the story ask students to turn to a partner and dissect it, take it apart. Make a list of the science facts, the big-picture concepts, and how George modeled the steps of the inquiry approach.

Tell them it is now their turn to create a science story. Invite students to take a moment and remember some discovery they made, some encounter with a tree or wild animal, a special day in the wilderness. It could have happened several years ago on vacation or at summer camp, or it could have happened last week in the backyard watching a bird at the feeder. What clicked for you in that moment? What did you learn from nature? Think about some passionate moment in your life as a scientist or citizen of the earth. This passion and enthusiasm is important to the writing and telling of the tale.

Invite students to close their eyes and relive that moment. Using the deep memory exercise on page 10, walk them through the process of remembering the details and reconstructing the story. Allow them a few moments to turn to a partner and take turns telling their stories; tell it before you write it. When they are done telling their stories, allow them an extra moment to ask each other questions. What do they want to know more about having heard their partner's story?

Ask them to get out a piece of paper and write a rough draft of their story. Offer bonus points if they use their science vocabulary. As they work, remind them that all good stories need well-defined characters. Who was there? Help us get to know something about these people and their motives. They need a clear setting. Where were they? Describe the place using all of your senses; take us into this unique moment and specific location. They also need a dynamic plot with a sense of mystery or surprise. What happened? What led to your discovery? What did you learn from your mistake or success? Take us step by step through the questions that led to the research, the methods you used, and your "Aha!" moment when things clicked for you. Let the reader or listener share your sense of discovery.

Use these questions to help them build their story.

Invite them to interrupt their own stories to ask questions of their listeners, engage the audience as guinea pigs in their experiment, or have their audience members choose a partner and tell each other their hypothesis.

When they are finished with the rough draft of their story, ask them to turn to a new partner and retell the story, asking the question: "How can I make this a better story?"

When both partners are finished, allow time for them to process the ideas, ask questions about the outcome, and internalize the concepts. Challenge them to help each other design an investigation. First, both partners talk about one story:

What questions come up? Make a list and then choose one open-ended question.

What is their hypothesis? Make an educated guess.

How could they test their hypothesis? Design an investigation.

Now both partners talk about the other person's story.

Create time over the next week or so for them to conduct follow-up studies.

If the story motivates students to be active participants in scientific inquiry, you know you have a great story!

Assessment: This is another assignment in which I often offer two for the price of one: They can get an A in language arts for writing a good story and an A in science if they use their science vocabulary, include some cool facts, explore one concept, and design an investigation. Their investigation can also be given a third A.

Follow-up Activities: Though most of the creative writing and storytelling components of the lesson can be accomplished in one class period, time should be given for them to conduct genuine inquiry. The rough draft can be collected at the end of the hour, and the final draft can be a homework assignment.

If these stories motivate students to want to do science, everything within your power should be done to help them conduct their investigations; realizing that some of the research will have to be done on their own, provide class time, access to the Internet and library, and time to work with peers who might be exploring similar concepts to create a science lab environment.

This simple story can also lead to some dynamic science fair presentations. Students can take turns performing their stories for the class, and in the midst of the performance demonstrate their scientific process in a Mr. Wizard–type scientific demonstration. Please give bonus points if they model the steps of inquiry *and* engage students in genuine inquiry through their performance. These performances can also be graded using the rubric at the end of Chapter 1.

Comments: The first time I told this story to students, one of the students' hands shot into the air just as I was uttering the last few words. Before I could call on him he blurted out, "Is this true of other trees?" Before I could ask what he thought, several other students joined in a spontaneous debate. They discussed regeneration and different trees that might or might not do this. They began to design an investigation before I had a chance to explain what science-process skills were. One child said, "We could plant sticks from different trees and see if it is true." Another student chimed in, "Maybe we should water some and not water others."

This is the other important role of storytelling in science education. A good story can motivate listeners or readers to want to become scientists. Think about it . . . who were the professors or teachers who inspired you to pursue this field? I'll bet they were all good storytellers. What are your stories? How can you share your discoveries in a way that can inspire and instruct your students? What are some of the classic tales of science that you remember from your education?

If you want to invigorate your science classroom, tell your students stories. Then inspire them to add their voice to the chorus to deepen our understanding of science, the story of the universe.

"WALTER THE WATER MOLECULE": THE WATER CYCLE AND CIRCULAR STORYTELLING

High in one of those wispy clouds that looks like strands of horse hair, a cirrus cloud, there was a little droplet of water named Walter. Walter, this molecule of water, was frozen into an ice crystal. The sun's rays sliced through the cloud. The frozen water bent each ray of light to make a small arc of a rainbow, what some folks call a "sun dog." Have you ever seen just a little piece of a rainbow on a sunny day? Then you have seen a sun dog! These cirrus clouds floated high over the Arctic Ocean.

As the endless summer turned to the long night of winter, Walter the drop of water was caught up into a blizzard! The wind howled! The snow fell! Walter—now a snowflake—was blown this way and that, high and low, whipped up by the screeching winds and dropped down, down, down toward the frozen tundra. Soon he blew into a snowbank, a large snowdrift that crusted over with a layer of ice. He was trapped. The snow kept falling and falling. Every year more snow piled up each winter than melted in the summer. Walter became part of a glacier.

Walter the iceberg sat there frozen for more than 10,000 years. Gradually, with the compacted snow piled up on top of him, Walter began to migrate. He was part of a large glacier that grew and grew as more snow piled up each year. More snow fell than melted for several thousand winters, so the glacier began to creep down over North America.

Eventually, almost all of what's now Canada and the northern parts of the United States were covered with a mile-high wall of ice! Walter was part of the Ice Age! The land was locked in with these huge glaciers. Like bulldozers, they flattened everything in their path. They carved the tops off of hills and filled in the valleys. Walter the drop of frozen water slowly churned toward the south.

Finally, the climate changed. The earth warmed. The ice began to melt. To give you an idea of how big these ice cubes were, one ice cube melted and made Lake Michigan. Another ice cube melted and made Lake Erie. A thousand little ice cubes melted in Wisconsin and Minnesota and created the land of a thousand lakes.

As the ice melted, the rushing water pushed sand and gravel and carved many of the rivers in the Midwest. Walter rushed down into Lake Michigan and out the southern end into the Illinois River.

At this time, as the Ice Age ended, there were still big hairy elephants—wooly mammoth and mastodon—roaming this land. A wooly mammoth waded into the river and drank Walter through his big trunk. Walter became part of a wooly mammoth! He flowed through the blood streams of this prehistoric beast. He pounded through the huge heart, almost as big as a basketball. He streamed through the lungs to get oxygen and then went back to the heart. He raced toward the leg to feed the muscles and back to the heart. Then Walter flowed into the wooly mammoth's bladder—and—I am going to skip what happens next in good taste. Let me just say, when the mammoth walked away, Walter was left behind—and please don't eat that yellow snow!

What is waste to one, is fertilizer to another. When the snow melted, Walter trickled down into the ground, and soon a spruce tree's root drank him in . . . *s-s-l-l-u-u-r-r-p-p!* Yes, as the Ice Age ended, much of the Midwest was cloaked in plants from the far north—spruce, willow, blueberry, and sedges. One of these spruce trees drank Walter up and he flowed into the root, up through the trunk and out into a branch. He went into a twig and into a sharp and square spruce needle. It was an unusually hot day for the northern tundra. The tree was losing water through every pore. Walter leaked out of the tree and back into the air. He sailed up, up, up into the upper atmosphere.

He was invisible—vapor—and he evaporated.

Walter floated around for a while, but that night it grew cold. The air condensed. Walter the drop of water realized he was not alone. A little droplet of water stuck to his side, *zoop*, his back, *zoop*, his other side, *zoop*. Can you say "condensation"? When droplets of water come together, they form a cloud. But this time Walter was not a high, wispy cirrus cloud; no, he was huge, dark cumulonimbus, a thunder cloud. *Crack*! Lightning flashed and thunder roared.

Walter passed the dew point. Can you say "precipitation"? When moisture falls from the sky it is called precipitation. Walter started to fall, *ah, ah, a-a-a-h-h-h! Whoosh!* A big gust of wind blew him back up into the upper atmosphere, where he froze.

Walter changed form, from a gas, vapor, to a liquid, rain, to a solid, ice; Walter became sleet. He started to fall once more. *Wah, ah, a-a-a-h-h-h! Whoosh*! Another gust of wind blew him back up into the clouds. He met a drop of rain falling down and it stuck to him and froze. Walter was a ball of hail! He started to fall. *Whoosh*! Another gust of wind blew him back up into the upper atmosphere. (Next time you find a ball of hail, make a prediction. How many times did this ball of hail rise and fall? Take a really sharp knife, a serrated knife for cutting meat, and, with parental supervision, carefully slice through the hail. You can count rings, like the rings of a tree, and you can tell how many times the ball of hail was blown back up. Try it!)

Wha-a-a-a-h-h-h! Walter fell all the way to the earth. *Splat*! He landed in a swamp. Slowly, he melted and seeped into the ground, following a worm tunnel, down, down, down, into an underground aquifer. The glacier had deposited huge piles of sand, silt, and rubble into old creek beds and ancient river bottoms. Though you cannot see them from above, these ancient rivers still flow deep under the surface of the earth. Walter went into the Sankoty Aquifer.

In some of these underground rivers, there are blind salamanders and glass fish that you can see through. There are weird insects and crawfish that live off the bacteria that live off the dead things that fall into the cave. But not the Sankoty—it is too deep. The water is ancient, filtered by limestone, pure and sweet. Walter was trapped again!

Ten thousand years later, cities grew up across the Midwest. Small towns and farmers began to dig wells and sink pipes deep into this aquifer. They use this water to flush toilets, water crops, wash dishes, cook their food, and they drink it.

Peoria, where I live, uses about two-thirds of its water directly from the Illinois River, but about one-third of our water comes from this ancient aquifer. Walter came up through a pipe, through a series of pipes, and eventually he arrived at my faucet. I was cooking up a pot of my famous chili verde. I always soak my beans overnight so they are less, um, tootful. I sautéed my onions and garlic, added the ground turkey to the skillet and let it brown. I put the navy beans, canned tomatillos, green chili peppers, green peppers, celery,

From *Content Area Reading, Writing, and Storytelling: A Dynamic Tool for Improving Reading and Writing Across the Curriculum through Oral Language Development* by Brian "Fox" Ellis. Westport, CT: Teacher Ideas Press. Copyright © 2008.

white hominy and secret spices all into the pot and let it simmer all day long. Now a lot of water evaporated as the chili simmered, but Walter was soaked into a navy been.

My daughter loves my chili. She had two bowls, with grated cheese and organic blue corn chips. M-m-m good! Walter went into her belly, through the stomach wall, into her blood veins. Walter traveled from the heart to the lungs to get oxygen, to the heart and out into the body, heart to the lungs, lungs to the heart, heart to the body, body to the heart, heart to the lungs, lungs to the heart, heart to the body. That's the way the blood flows through *your* body. Can you say this little rap with me? Heart to the lungs, lungs to the heart, heart to the body, body to the heart, heart to the lungs, lungs to the heart, heart to the body—faster and faster racing through your body. That is why we call them blood streams; the blood *streams* through you.

My daughter is also an amazing athlete. The next day after school she was at cross-country practice running, running, running. She worked up a sweat. She began leaking! (If you took a very powerful magnifying glass and looked at your skin, you will see you are full of holes. You are leaking!) Walter came up out of her, soaked into her shirt, and because it was a warm autumn day, he evaporated back into the atmosphere.

Walter the drop of water is still out there somewhere; where he will go next is up to you.

"Walter the Water Molecule": The Water Cycle and Circular Storytelling

Grade Levels: Pre-K–12

Time Estimate: One hour

Objectives:

- Students will demonstrate an understanding of the water cycle by retelling their own versions of "Walter the Water Drop."

- Students will learn both creative ideas and the mechanics of good writing from their peers.

- Students will make a concrete connection between science and storytelling through the telling of their original version of "Walter the Water Drop."

National Standards:

- NCTE 4—Students adjust their use of spoken, written, and visual language to communicate effectively with a variety of audiences and for different purposes.

- NCTE 5—Students employ a wide range of strategies as they write and use different writing process elements appropriately to communicate with different audiences for a variety of purposes.

- NCTE 6—Students apply knowledge of language structure, language conventions, media techniques, figurative language, and genre to create, critique, and discuss print and non-print texts.

- NCTE 11—Students participate as knowledgeable, reflective, creative, and critical members of a variety of literacy communities.

- NCSS 9—Global Connections

- NAS 2—Physical Science: Properties and changes of properties in matter; Motions and forces; Transfer of energy

- NAS 3—Life Science: Structure and function in living systems; Reproduction and heredity; Regulation and behavior; Populations and ecosystems; Diversity and adaptations of organisms

- NAS 6—Science in Personal and Social Perspectives: Personal health; Populations, resources, and environments; Natural hazards; Risks and benefits; Science and technology in society

Materials:

- Paper and pencil

Background Information: This is one of the first stories I created in this genre of creative nonfiction; it came out of a conversation—actually an assignment I gave fellow environmental storyteller Garth Gilchrist. I have since performed Walter for Ph.D. aquatic ecologists at the

National Non-Point Source Pollution Conference and for preschoolers at a local summer camp. The story first appeared on my cassette/CD *Adventures in Nature* (Fox Tales International, 1994). If you would like to read a more in-depth version with more extensive follow-up lesson plans, please find a copy of my first book, *Learning from the Land: Teaching Ecology Through Storytelling and Hands-on Science* (Teacher Ideas Press, 1997). It also appears on my DVD, *Our Planet* (Storywatchers' Club, 2006).

The version you have before you is boiled down to better fit the format of this book and to include some new information I have learned since writing the original story. The beauty of this tale is that it is infinitely adaptable to include your local watershed, aquatic flora and fauna, and the environmental issues you wish to cover. At the National Non-Point Source Pollution Conference, I talked about storm sewers and the gasoline that leaks into rivers from boat engines. In this version, I talk about the chili I made last night for dinner and introduce concepts such as the Ice Age and global warming and the importance of ancient underground water sources and aquifers, a current issue in Peoria, Illinois, environmental politics.

When you tell this story, name local rivers and lakes, and model for your students how the water cycle is not just some vague concept in a book; it flows through their neighborhood and into their blood streams!

Instructional Procedures

Introduction: Begin with a brief introduction or review of the water cycle. I often ask students to chant these four words with me while pantomiming the cycle: Evaporation (wiggle your fingers as you lift your arms); Condensation (bring your fingers together); Precipitation (wiggle your fingers as you lower your arms); and Collection (cup your hands together). I say it, they say it with me, and then they say it twice on their own with gestures. Depending on the age of the class, we might talk about where their drinking water comes from, the types of clouds they have seen, the forms of precipitation, the names of local rivers and lakes, and how water moves through the cycle.

Next, explain to them that you are going to start a story, and then they are going to finish it in the circular storytelling game. Ask each student to choose a partner and each set of partners to find another set of partners, so they are a group of four. When the time comes, they are to turn to this group and pass the story around in the circular storytelling game. When it is their turn, they can add a few words, a few sentences, or a few paragraphs. When they are done they say, "and then . . . ." It is their partner's turn to add to the story. Emphasize that it is important that they listen closely so they know where Walter has been and where he might be going. Also encourage them to use the four key words as a map: "Say it with me one more time, Evaporation [wiggle your fingers as you lift your arms]; Condensation [bring your fingers together]; Precipitation [wiggle your fingers as you lower your arms]; and Collection." Model this in your example.

Tell the story of "Walter the Water Molecule," going at least once around the cycle.

Activity: When you are done, remind students of the importance of listening to their partners. Allow each small group about five minutes to pass the story around. I often interrupt them about halfway through to emphasize the science in the story: "Not just that Walter went into a plant, but what kind of plant, what do you know about the inner workings or parts of this plant?" Ask them to raise their hands if they learned something from your version of the story. Now, it is their job to teach their partners something they know about plants, animals, clouds, weather, or whatever it is that they take Walter into!

After about five minutes of playing the game verbally, explain that now we are playing the same game silently. Each student should get out a piece of paper and write their name in the top right-hand corner. They are to write their own version of Walter, borrowing ideas from you and their group's oral version. When the signal is given, they place their paper in their right hand, pass to the right, and accept with their left hand. Then they add their name to the top of the paper, read what is handed to them, and add to it. Sometimes give the students three or four minutes, other times give them just enough time to read what has been written and add a few words; mix it up.

After each piece of paper has been around the group at least once, ask them to put this group work in a pile in the center of the group. Explain that since they have all added to the stories, they all own it; it is public domain. Ask if they learned anything while reading each other's contributions. This is not copying; it is called "cooperative learning."

Now give them the rest of the period to work independently on their own version of "Walter the Water Molecule." Ask them to get out a clean sheet of paper and begin to write. Their goal is to get once around the cycle. They can go around in one sentence, "Walter went into a cloud and fell down as rain, which was soaked into a plant that evaporated Walter back into a cloud." But is that a very interesting story? What makes a good story? Detail, detail, detail. What makes for good science? Detail, detail, detail. They can get two As for one assignment by simply adding detail. They can get an A in language arts for a good story and an A in science if they use their science vocabulary and teach their peers something about the water cycle.

Collect their papers at the end of the period.

Assessment: Each paper can be graded for language arts and science. They should at the very least use the four words: evaporation, condensation, precipitation, and collection.

Follow-up Activities: This story is a great introduction to a series of hands-on water activities, including but not limited to a stream table, erosion control, playground water run-off maps, weather, cloud formations, internal anatomy and blood flow charts, drinking water issues, bottled water versus tap, water quality analysis, and benthic macro-invertebrate indicator species. Many of these lessons are in my book *Learning from the Land*.

Encourage your students to develop their own follow-up lessons using an inquiry approach. After they have heard and told several versions of the story, ask them what questions their stories raised. They can make an individual list of three big concept questions, and then you can discuss the questions as a class. Students can then formulate a hypothesis, design an investigation, and answer their own questions in student-centered inquiry.

Comments: Everyone loves Walter. When I was a keynote speaker at an international wetlands conservation conference, I had a room full of more than three hundred foreign and domestic scientists and policymakers make the connections between their local wetlands and the wetlands of the dignitaries sitting next to them in this same exercise. Every year, I work several Project W.E.T. or Make-A-Splash events where thousands of school kids get to hear and then make up their own versions of the story. Again, allow me to emphasize two points: This story is infinitely adaptable to your local watershed, so make it your own by naming places your students feel connected with; also, science is a verb, and there are many possible hands-on science activities that can come out of this story. Did you notice that even in this brief retelling I ask students to go home and *do* science by collecting balls of hail?

"BIRD IS THE WORD": USING POETRY AND STORYTELLING TO TEACH FIELD ECOLOGY

The Whooping Crane's Migration

At first light, a crane lifts its long legs, stretches its wings, whoop, whoop, whoop, singing up the sun!

Whooping **C**rane's dance! Their **R**ed head and long tail feathers give them the appearance of **A** fancy dancer to rival the Lakota. **N**earer and nearer his mate, clacking beaks together, soon they are **E**ntangled in the dance of love. These cranes will bond for life.

Look, now, can you see the male and female are working together to build a nest of cattails, sedges, bulrushes, and other aquatic plants? The mound of vegetation slowly takes shape here in a swampy estuary where their young are free from harm. The mother lays her eggs and both parents take turns warming them, protecting them. The mother bird plucks a few feathers from her breast. In this way, she can line the nest with the insulation of her feathers, and her bare skin touches the eggs so more of her warmth incubates them.

Four weeks pass.

Do you see the eggs begin to stir? They wriggle. A small crack appears. The egg tooth emerges first; this special bump on the beak of the baby bird helps it to crack the egg. Their feathers are wet with albumen. Two chicks emerge from their eggs. The mother keeps them warm, hidden beneath her wings.

The father brings snacks—small fish, tadpoles, and insects—all partially digested by his stomach acids. He regurgitates the food into their hungry beaks. These first few weeks are the most precarious. A red fox has been seen hunting the shoreline of the swamp. Hawks by day, owls by night prowl the sky. The parents are ever diligent watching over their young.

The long-legged babies slowly lose their newborn fluff. Dirty beige flight feathers begin to grow. Three more weeks pass before they begin dancing and flapping, stretching their wing muscles in preparation for flight. The parents lead them on a parade through the cattails and along the edges of the swamp. They are looking for anything that moves!

See the parents gobble up small snakes, large crawfish, fish, mice, frogs, and toads, almost anything they can catch. For the first few weeks, the parents then turn and share their food with these two awkward chicks, but as they grow taller and more agile, the teenage whooping cranes begin snatching up beetles and grasshoppers, slugs, and snails. Watching their parents, they learn what is good to eat and, more important, how to catch it.

Now nearly as tall as their parents, the young cranes begin whooping, leaping, dancing, and stretching for the clouds. They watch their parents fly and yearn to join them in the sky. Because of their weight, long legs, and wings, the crane must get a running start. They begin to flap as they run, and a strong gust coming across the field lifts them into the air. Can you feel the joy they must feel as they take their first flight?

This first flight leads to many more. Though more graceful than a pterodactyl, they share the same ancient affinity for the clouds. The family of whooping cranes flies farther and farther in their search for food. They scour the surrounding prairies, wheat fields, and forest edges, always on the lookout for a coyote or pack of wolves.

Where has the summer gone?

The once far-flung families begin to gather at Necedah National Wildlife Refuge, a large wetland in the heart of the glacial till of Wisconsin. Nearly three dozen endangered birds, where once there were none, are preparing for their historic flight of 1,225 miles to a wetland in south-central Florida.

Most of these birds learned the route from a small, ultralight aircraft and team of ornithologists who wisely thought to expand the range of the nearly extinct species. In the 1960s and 1970s, there was only one flock that nested in northern Canada and spent the winter on the Gulf Coast of Texas. One hurricane could wipe out an entire species. These ornithologists—people who study birds—thought that if they could establish a second flock in their former range, it would be insurance against a calamity. Their plan worked.

We are now witnessing the first successful flight of young whooping cranes that are learning the route from their parents, not a plane!

The day has come; a cold, freezing fog hovers above the ground. The older birds, who have made the trip on their own several times, know—they know—that *this* is the day. This cold wind coming down from Canada will make their journey easier.

It is dawn; do you see the young cranes leaping and whooping it up? They seem to know instinctively that it is time. Several whooping cranes take three or four long, strong strides, flapping their wings, striving towards the sky! They flap vociferously. They catch the wind and begin to lift. In the next several moments, all of the cranes are in the air. Slowly they circle looking for that thermal, a place where the earth reflects heat and the rising warm air lifts the cranes higher and higher.

The cranes form a large V, with some of the older cranes who best know the way leading the flock. In a V, the lead bird cuts through the wind like an arrowhead, making it easier for the birds coming behind. When he gets tired, he falls to the back to rest and lets another bird lead. From great heights, the flock can glide rather effortlessly all day. In this way they can cover one or two hundred miles every day they fly.

They fly over Rockford and Peoria, Illinois. Just south of Peoria along the Illinois River in a farmer's field, they find a small pond that is not yet frozen. The flock decides to rest and refuel, taking a couple of days to regain some strength. Word spreads throughout the community; they get their pictures on the front page of the local papers. Birdwatchers come to ogle them. As long as the people stay far enough away and use their binoculars to get a closer look, the birds are not bothered by the attention. As long as they do not have to take off and fly away scared at an odd hour, wasting precious fuel, having humans near, but not too near, actually keeps the coyotes and other predators at bay.

After a few days of devouring fish and crawdads, the cranes take flight once more to southern Illinois, on to Tennessee, through Georgia, and eventually they arrive at their winter home in the swamps of Florida.

The winter is mild, unlike last winter when several cranes perished in the cold. This subtropical climate is perfect for the young cranes. They whoop and dance, practicing for the springtime to come. But all is not well.

Late in the winter, late at night while the cranes are sleeping, a bobcat stealthily stalks the flock. She creeps closer and closer. On padded feet she silently, patiently, crawls the last fifty feet. With a burst of speed she lunges, leaps, and grabs a sleeping young crane by the neck! The parents squawk! They attack the bobcat, flapping and pecking, but it is too late. The bobcat shakes her head, snaps the neck of the crane, and runs off, carrying the crane away.

Yes, it is sad to watch the death of a creature so rare and so beautiful, but the bobcat has young growing inside her, and the death of a crane means that several kittens will be born soon, plump and healthy.

Most of the cranes survive the winter with their . . .

> long legs for stalking in the shallow swamp,
>
> a long neck and wings for long distance aerodynamic flight, and
>
> a long beak for snatching up frogs and fish, snakes, and mice.
>
> *Whoooop! Whoop! Whoooop!* Song of the whooping crane!
>
> They dance when the earth rises,
>
> when the snow melt floods the rising creek.
>
> they dance when the pasque flower pushes up through the springing earth.
>
> They dance when the sun rises,
>
> when the flocks of birds rise from the trees,
>
> rising from the everglades to the great North woods.
>
> In the tall prairie grasses,
>
> head bobbing like cattails in a spring storm.
>
> Wings extended, long legs strutting.
>
> They dance!

As springtime returns to the far North woods, these ancient birds return to their former homelands, return from the brink of extinction, to once again whoop it up on the prairies. Can you look into the future? Do you see the great-grandchildren of these cranes, now in large flocks, making this same migration, season after season? If you can dream it, maybe, we can work together to make it come true.

"Bird Is the Word": Using Poetry and Storytelling to Teach Field Ecology

Grade Levels: 3–12

Time Estimate: Four hours

Objectives:

- Students will improve their observation skills.

- They will learn to write more fluently.

- They will learn to think like a poet/scientist: observe, collect and analyze data, ask difficult questions, and look for answers.

- Students will use metaphor and analogy to explain complex science concepts.

- Students will learn observation through drawing, poetry, and creative writing.

- Students will demonstrate their ability to write solid expository essays.

National Standards:

- NCTE 4—Students adjust their use of spoken, written, and visual language to communicate effectively with a variety of audiences and for different purposes.

- NCTE 5—Students employ a wide range of strategies as they write and use different writing process elements appropriately to communicate with different audiences for a variety of purposes.

- NCTE 6—Students apply knowledge of language structure, language conventions, media techniques, figurative language, and genre to create, critique, and discuss print and non-print texts.

- NCTE 7—Students conduct research on issues and interests by generating ideas and questions, and by posing problems. They gather, evaluate, and synthesize data from a variety of sources to communicate their discoveries in ways that suit their purpose and audience.

- NAS 1—Science as Inquiry: Abilities necessary to do scientific inquiry; Understandings about scientific inquiry

- NAS 3—Life Science: Structure and function in living systems; Reproduction and heredity; Regulation and behavior; Populations and ecosystems; Diversity and adaptations of organisms

Materials:

- Pen and Paper

- Large unlined art paper and colored pencils, crayons or markers

- Optional: Stuffed, mounted birds from a local museum or nature center

Background Information: This lesson is built on the idea that deepening students' ability to observe will help them write more fluently. If field ecology is like short-story form, then the skills of a poet are very similar to the skills of a scientist. This is a scientific vocabulary, but poets are observant; they collect and analyze data, ask difficult questions and look for answers. Conversely, you could use a poet's vocabulary to describe science: Scientists use metaphor and analogy to explain complex concepts; they are interested in the deeper implications, the hows, whys, and what-ifs. This series of lessons will help students learn observation through drawing, poetry and creative writing. Students will then use storytelling to write solid expository essays.

Instructional Procedures

In this simple, four-step process, students will draw their favorite bird, write several poems, write a story about a day in the life of their bird, and write an essay about that bird.

Step 1: First, ask students, "What is your favorite bird?" Give them a large sheet of paper and invite them to draw the bird true to life. A couple of exhibit cases or mounted birds from your local science museum or nature center can both inspire and instruct students' scientific accuracy. If you have established bird feeders outside your classroom with a variety of foods and birds, students can sit at the window and draw from life.

Encourage students to add a nest, eggs, and a picture of the bird's young. Highlight the differences between male and female birds of this species. Consider this sketch a rough draft. Provide photographs and other paintings of their favorite birds. On a large sheet of paper, ask students to draw a life-size image of the bird in its natural habitat. Examples of John James Audubon's artwork can serve as a model.

Step 2: Through Socratic questioning, discuss what makes a poem: alliteration, rhyme, rhythm, repetition, and meter; imagery, emotions, and philosophy; similes, metaphors, analogies, symbolic language, and personification. Allow their comments to lead the conversation but take notes on the board.

Next, ask students a hundred questions about their bird. Ask the questions rapid fire, often repeating the question with a different vocabulary word to encourage thinking. Tell the students they do not need to answer all of the questions but to answer as many as they can. The truth is, there are really only three basic questions:

• What does my favorite bird look like?

• Where does it live?

• What does it do?

Encourage poetic language and short descriptive phrases. Repeat several key questions in different words. Challenge students to brainstorm on paper as many answers to these questions as they can:

What does it look like? How big or little is the bird? Compare it to something. Make a list of all of the bird's parts. Describe all of the parts of the bird and how it uses these parts, comparing them to tools. How does it use its beak, its tail, its wings? How does it move? Use all of your senses. What are the colors you see? What are the textures you would feel? What are the sounds you might hear? What smells or feelings might you imagine? What are the different colors of the male and female in this species?

Where does it live? Ask students to think in terms of descriptive words. Where does it build its nest? How does it build its nest? What does it build its nest out of? What habitat or ecosystem does it live in? What plants and animals are its neighbors? What is the weather like? What part of the world does it live in? Where does it feed? Where does it get water? Where does it hide? Where does it sleep? If it migrates, what does it see along the way? How does this bird see its world?

What does it do? Ask students to use a lot of verbs. How does it feed? How does it migrate? How does it attract a mate? How does it tend to its nest? How does it raise its young? What are its enemies? How does it survive? What does it do in each season? What is it good at doing? What is its role in the ecosystem? If it could talk, what might it say? Actually it does talk, although not in English; use its language in your poem and then add an English translation. How does it feel about the things going on around it? If you could get inside its head or heart, what does it love, worry about, want more than anything? What can you learn from this bird? How can its wisdom help us to be better animals?

For the questions they cannot answer, students can either: look them up in a book, surf the Web, or better yet, go outside and observe to learn directly from their favorite bird.

Their answers to these questions with a little bit of editing can be turned into an instant poem. If they simply rearrange the answers to the questions, add water, and stir, they have poetry. Their answer sheet with very little rewriting can be turned into several poems.

Ask students to reread what they have written; maybe insert a phrase to make it more poetic or to better answer a question with which they felt rushed. As they read, they should underline their favorite lines, at least five, maybe more. With very little editing they can copy these lines onto a clean sheet of paper, maybe juggle the order, add a descriptive phrase, and— *shazam!* —they have a free-verse poem!

At this point teachers may want to read the "Whooping Crane" poems at the end of this lesson.

Next, ask them to choose their three favorite lines and make a haiku. Remember that haiku are about one intense moment, using present-tense language, and they always have a tension between two yin-yang images or ideas.

For a third poem from the same list of facts, students can write the name of their bird in big bold letters going down the side of their paper to make an acrostic poem. Using the answers to their questions, they can look for words that begin with the letters in the name of their bird. Remember that acrostic poems are not just a list of descriptive words; they can also use short phrases to describe the setting or tell a story.

If they describe each part of the bird and compare it to something wonderful or beautiful, this list is a type of poetry called a brazo. A brazo is an Italian form of love poems. A classic brazo might go like this: Your eyes are like two deep pools, your lips like two red roses, etc.

Students can write a rhyming poem, add a chorus, and it is a song; stretch it into an event, and the rhyming poem becomes a ballad. (Please visit www.foxtalesint.com for more information about poetic forms.) From this same list of facts students can write several forms of poetry all about their favorite bird—all within one hour.

Step 3: Next, students can use their poem as an outline for a story about their favorite bird. Discuss the ingredients for a good story: characters, setting and plot. The bird is the main character. The habitat is the setting. And the bird's behavior is the plot. Encourage them to go back and look at the initial three questions:

	LANGUAGE ARTS	SCIENCE
What does my favorite bird look like?	Character	Animal
Where does it live?	Setting	Habitat
What does it do?	Plot	Behavior

They have already answered these questions, so they already have an outline for their story and solid information for science.

At this point, read or tell the story of "The Whooping Crane's Migration." Briefly discuss how the poems were actually embedded into the story. The descriptive language and metaphors help make the details of the story more vivid.

Students can take each line or stanza from their poem and make them into scenes or paragraphs. Remind them that a good story also has an engaging beginning, an exciting middle, and a satisfying end.

Ask, "Where does your story begin?" Maybe they could start by describing what their bird looks like and where it lives. "What happens first? Then what happens? Then what happens? What is the exciting middle? How does the story end?"

A story also needs a problem and a solution. What problem does this bird face? This could be the exciting middle of the story. How does it survive; how does it solve this problem? This is the satisfying end of the story.

For bonus points, encourage them to explore some broader scientific idea like the food chain or animal adaptation, extinction or migration. What questions do they have about their bird, and how could they research the answers and include the information in their story?

If time allows, invite students to close their eyes and imagine that they are the bird. Imagine they are flying or hunting for food. Imagine that they run into a problem. Ask them to use all of their senses as they imagine. How do they feel about the problem? How does this bird get out of the jam? How do they feel at the end? What did they learn from all of this? After they daydream, they may want to make a quick outline of their story.

Another strategy that is often helpful is to tell the story before it is written. Working with a partner, invite students to take turns telling their stories after their daydream.

Give them time to make a rough draft. Ask them to go back over their story and look for places to add some drama, some action, more excitement, or more detail. At this point you might allow time for them to visit the library or surf the Internet to do some research about the bird. This research could also be assigned as homework: "Tomorrow, bring to class a list of at least ten facts about your bird."

Step 4: Good essays tell a story. A good essay uses poetic language, imagery, and metaphor to explain complicated ideas. The main difference between a story and an essay is the tone. Whereas a story is written to entertain, an essay is written to inform. Actually, a good essay is entertaining and a good story can be informative, which is exactly the point of this exercise.

Draw three overlapping circles on the board, a triple Venn diagram.

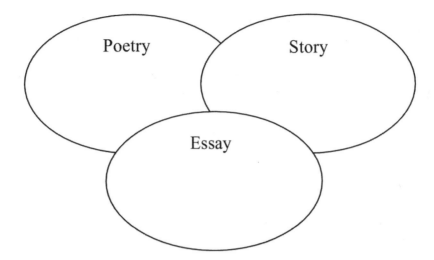

As a class, discuss the differences and similarities between poetry, narrative, and expository writing. The haiku can be the theme of students' essays, the distilled essence. The longer poem is the outline. The story provides a sequence of events. All they have to do is change the tone, rework the opening, and write a closing to create a strong essay about their favorite bird. Using phrases from their poem and whole sentences from their story, ask students to write an essay about their bird.

Using the standard rubric for expository writing, students can write an opening sentence that introduces their main point, give two or three sentences that elaborate on that point, write three paragraphs that go into more detail about the bird, and then write a closing statement that reinforces their thesis.

Ask students to spell out what their essay is about in their first paragraph. Their second paragraph can explain the bird itself. The third paragraph can be about the bird's relationship to its habitat. And the fourth paragraph can be about the bird's behavior, focusing on its role in the ecosystem. Why is this bird important? Their closing paragraph should restate your opening point in new words.

Shazam! Using sentences from their poem and their story, they not only have one of the best essays they have ever written, but it is also probably one of the easiest!

Assessment: Students' answers to the 100 questions can be collected for a simple pass/fail grade if they made a reasonable effort.

Their poetry can be evaluated for style and content with an emphasis on their use of metaphor, simile, personification, and the traits of good poetry that were emphasized in the class discussion.

With both the story and the essay, teachers can offer two grades for one assignment; students can earn an A in language arts for a good story and an A in science for lots of good facts. Extra points can be given for students who find creative ways to embed their poetry.

Follow-up Activities: This same series of lesson plans can be used with mammals, insects, dinosaurs, trees, flowers, fish, rocks, and minerals. I have also used this set of lessons to help students write poetry, stories, and essays about Abraham Lincoln and other historical characters and periods.

Encourage students to collect all four steps into a mini-book: Their picture can be their cover, the poems an introduction or afterword, and their story and essay can include additional illustrations. The class can collect all of the poems into one book, stories into a second, and essays into a third manuscript. Their large pictures can be framed with a construction paper border and the poems mounted in the corner of the frame for an interdisciplinary art exhibit.

With science museum murals in mind, students can work in small groups to create a large mural of their habitat with each student adding their bird to the mural. Wetland birds can work together, forest birds can work together, and prairie birds can work together.

If students are drawing waterfowl, they can enter into the State and National Junior Duck Stamp Competition, with the possibility of winning a trip to Washington, D.C., for the awards banquet. For more information, including a sixty-page booklet of lesson plans and contest rules, please visit duckstamps.fws.gov.

If students have chosen an endangered or threatened bird species or a bird whose habitat is threatened, their expository essay, poem, and story could be the foundation for a persuasive essay. This editorial could be sent to public officials or the press as a guest editorial. Offer extra credit to any student who gets published or receives a response from an elected official.

For older students, a study of the life and work of John James Audubon might prove inspiring. For every one of the 485 birds that Audubon painted, he wrote a short essay about the life and habits of the species based on his own observations. Read aloud excerpts from Audubon's Bird Biographies. Excerpts from "The Passenger Pigeon," "The White Headed Eagle," or "The Black Vulture or Carrion Crow" are recommended. (Please see the next lesson.) In all three essays it is easy to see that the facts were collected firsthand from extensive hours of field observation. You can discuss with your students the principles of field ecology and the scientific method embedded in these essays. Invite your students to choose a bird that lives in their neighborhood, a species that they see often. They can take field notes on its behavior and use this information to write a biography of their favorite bird.

With approximately five to ten minutes for each of the four steps in this lesson plan, it can be easily condensed into a fast-paced set of lessons to be performed in your local natural history museum or outside on the school grounds with a study of plants. Require that all of the students are to focus on one subject: birds, mammals, plants, or dinosaurs. If you have sufficient adult supervision for your museum visit, you could allow students to use this set of lessons for whatever area of the museum they choose, as long as an adult is supervising the small group that chooses that hall of the museum. It works best if they have already walked through the set of lesson plans in class before they go on their field trip.

Saving the best for last, knowing that science is a verb, provide an opportunity for your class to participate in the Great Backyard Bird Count or Feeder Watch, jointly sponsored by the National Audubon Society and Cornell Labs at Cornell University in New York (www.birds.cornell.edu). This amazing Web page provides dozens of lesson plans that allow students to participate in ongoing scientific research.

The following two pages provide three poems and an outline for both a story and an essay.

Whooping Crane

Poetry by Brian "Fox" Ellis

> **C**rane dance
> **R**ed head and long tail feathers
> **A** fancy dancer to rival the Lakota
> **N**earer and nearer his mate, clacking beaks together
> **E**ntangled in the dance of love, crane dance

Long legs for stalking in the shallow swamp

A long neck and wings

for long-distance aerodynamic flight

A long beak for snatching up frogs and fish, snakes and mice

CRANE HAIKU
At first light, a crane
lifts its long legs, wings stretch
singing up the sun

Whoooop! Whoop! Whoooop!

I am the whooping crane!

I dance when the earth rises,

when the snow melt floods the rising creek.

I dance when the pasque flower pushes up through the springing earth.

I dance when the sun rises,

when the flocks of birds rise from the trees,

rising from the everglades to the great North Woods.

I dance in the tall prairie grasses,

my head bobbing like cattails in a spring storm

wings extended, long legs strutting,

I dance!

The Crane's Migration: An Outline for a Story

The story opens with a description of the crane's dance, raising young and teaching the young to fly.

The heart of the story is the long trip south, soaring over America and the perils they encounter along the way. The parent bird teaches the young which way to fly; what to look for in a place to rest; how to keep watch at night, narrowly averting a bobcat attack; and then they fly back to the North.

The story ends with them returning safely to their nesting grounds, where the story begins again.

The Endangered Whooping Crane: An Outline for an Essay

The opening paragraph describes the beauty and importance of the crane and its relationship to its environment.

The heart of the essay is the need to protect wetlands and the need to protect habitat in order to protect the bird. The emphasis is on the idea that migratory birds highlight the need to protect habitat across the country, so they have safe places to rest along the way.

The essay ends with a description of the nesting grounds and hope that the young being born this year will have a home for the future.

"THE RUBY-THROATED HUMMINGBIRD": A LESSON IN RESEARCH AND REWRITING

The Ruby-Throated Hummingbird

by John James Audubon, edited by Brian "Fox" Ellis

Where is the person who, upon seeing this lovely little hummingbird moving on humming winglets through the air, suspended as if by magic in it, flitting from one flower to another, with motions as graceful as they are light and airy, and yielding new delights wherever it is seen—where is the person, I ask of you, who, on observing this glittering fragment of the rainbow, would not pause, admire, and instantly turn his mind with reverence toward the majesty of creation?—There breathes not such a person; so kindly have we all been blessed with that intuitive and noble feeling—admiration!

Its gorgeous throat in beauty and brilliancy baffles all competition. Now it glows with a fiery hue, and again it is changed to the deepest velvety black. Upon closer inspection the smallest feathers of the "ruby throat" are designed with a slight curvature, much like the mirror a surgeon wears on his forehead to concentrate the light. The feathers, rays, barbs and barbules capture the light, reflect and refract it, like a prism, so that the brightest ruby hue flashes at you if you are facing this flicker of light. The upper parts of its delicate body are of resplendent changing green; and it throws itself through the air with a swiftness and vivacity hardly conceivable. At rest, its heart beats more than 250 times per minute, and when it is flitting about, its heart rate leaps to 1,250 beats per minute! To balance this exuberance, to conserve energy, when it is cold or asleep, it can slip into torpor, a state of semi-hibernation, where its temperature drops from 110

degrees to 55 degrees Fahrenheit and its heart rate slows to 55 beats per minute. With 75 to 80 wing beats per second, this gleam of light, moving from one flower to another, is the only bird that can fly backward, one of the few that can hover and does so by moving its wings in a figure-eight pattern. In this manner, it searches the extreme northern portions of our country, following with great precaution the advances of the season, and retreats with equal care at the approach of autumn.

Please participate with me in this migratory math: If the wings beat 75 times per second, and there are 60 seconds in 1 minute, and 60 minutes in 1 hour, and the ruby-throated hummingbird will fly more than 10 hours at night as it crosses the Gulf of Mexico from the tip of the Yucatan Peninsula to the gulf coast, how many wing beats does it take to make this journey? 75 x 60 x 60 x 10 equals 2,700,000 wing beats in one flight across the Gulf of Mexico in its annual spring migration!

No sooner has the warmth of the sun brought the vernal equinox, and millions of plants have stretched their leaves and blossoms, than the little hummingbird is seen advancing on fairy wings, carefully visiting every opening flower-cup. Like a curious florist, he removes from each flower the insects that might cause their beautiful petals to droop and decay. Poised in the air, it is observed peeping cautiously, and with sparkling eye, into their innermost recesses. And the bird, as it leaves the flower, sips so small a portion of its liquid honey that the theft of nectar is looked upon with a grateful feeling by the flower, which is thus kindly relieved from the attacks of her destroyers. The hummingbird has several unique adaptations as an insectivore and nectivore. The tongue attaches to the back of the skull to give it extra length for extension. It is forked, though this is rarely seen, and each fork has tubular channels to aid the bird in the absorption of nectar through capillary action. Can you curl your tongue? Like a dog drinking water, the hummingbird quickly slides its tongue in and out of the flower to draw in the sweet elixir. You can see this in a hummingbird feeder with the ripples created in the surface as the tongue moves rapidly in and out.

In exchange for this sip of nectar the hummingbird gleefully pollinates the flowers. The tubular flowers, honeysuckle and trumpet vine, touch-me-not, and cardinal flowers—each offers its honey sweetness to bribe the hummingbird to carry pollen from one flower to another. Upon careful examination, one will see that each flower positions its pistil and stamen so its pollen will dust a different portion of the hummingbird's head, neck, or throat. The fuchsia will deposit its pollen on the chin while the fire pink dusts the bill, and the jewel weed or touch-me-not places its pollen on the forehead of the little bird. In a busy day of sipping nectar and eating insects the hummingbird's fairy wings will carry it to many species of plants, but the pollen of each species is carefully stored on the head, the cheek, the underside of the bill or the chin, so when it visits the same species of flower late in the day, the pollen is not wasted, the proper dusting of pollen finds the proper pistil.

The prairies, the fields, the orchards and gardens, nay, the deepest shades of the forests, are all visited in their turn, and everywhere the little bird meets with pleasure and with food. Within its territory this glorious gardener knows where each flower is blooming and makes its rounds with the consistency of a soldier on watch, chasing away any rivals. In the same manner in which the fur trappers of our earliest history would check their trap-line every day, the hummingbird knows which flowers are producing nectar and where the tastiest insects are found. Sipping nectar for energy, they depend on insects for protein. The ruby-throated hummingbird has several  means of catching bugs: Like a peregrine falcon it will gather insects on the wing. I have seen it perched on a slender, leafless twig of a dying oak and dart out into a swarm of tiny flies or a cloud of gnats and catch as many as 25 to 30 gnats in a matter of moments. The hummingbird zips out and snap-snip-snap-snip, snaps up half a dozen gnats before flying back to its perch to enjoy what it has caught. Within a quarter hour it has made a dozen forays into the swarm, more efficient than a tyrant flycatcher! This wise little bird has learned to follow the rounds of the sap sucker and where this woodpecker has made holes in the bark of trees the hummingbird will sip the sap and glean the insects trapped in the sap. Like a nuthatch they will scour the bark and underside of leaves for beetles, larva, and eggs. And in a manner similar to some of the woodland warblers and wrens, I have seen the blur of wings whirl up a rush of wind and roll over the dead leaves on the forest floor. The hummingbird will devour insects thusly exposed.

But what would the hummingbird do without the aid of spiders? The hummingbird will poach insects from the spiders' webs. And if no other bugs are to be found, the hummingbird will eat the spider! Though I have not seen this with my own eyes, others have said this is a grave risk, for they have seen hummingbirds

entrapped by the spider's web. And of course, the spiders' web is the glue for making the hummingbird's nest.

If you have seen these winged jewels, then you can imagine the pleasures which I have felt whilst watching the courtship of a single pair of these most favorite little creatures, when engaged in the demonstration of their love to each other—how the male swells his plumage and throat, and, dancing on the wing, whirls around the delicate female; he will fly up and swing down like a pendulum swinging back and forth, then look how quickly he dives towards a flower, and returns with a loaded bill, which he offers to her; how full of ecstasy he seems to be when his caresses are kindly received; how his little wings fan her, and he transfers to her bill the insect and the honey which he has procured with a view to please her; how these attentions are received with apparent satisfaction; how, soon after, the blissful compact is sealed; how, then, the courage and care of the male are redoubled; how he even dares to give chase to the Tyrant Fly-catcher, hurries the Blue-bird and the Martin to their boxes; and how, on sounding pinions, he joyously returns to the side of his lovely mate.

Could you, please, imagine casting a momentary glance on the nest of the hummingbird, and see, as I have seen, the newly hatched pair of young, little larger than bumblebees, naked, blind, and so feeble as scarcely to be able to raise their little bills to receive food from the parents.

The nest of this hummingbird is of the most delicate nature, the external parts being formed of a light grey lichen found on the branches of trees, all so neatly arranged round the whole nest, as to seem part of the branch or stem itself. These little pieces of lichen are glued together with spiders' silken strong webs. The next coating consists of cottony substance, and the innermost of silky fibers obtained from various plants, all extremely delicate and soft. On this comfortable bed the female lays only two eggs, which are pure white and almost oval. Ten days are required for their hatching, and the birds raise two broods in a season. In one week the young are ready to fly, but are fed by the parents for nearly another week. They receive their food directly from the bill of their parents, which disgorge it in the manner of canaries or pigeons. It is my belief that no sooner are the young able to provide for themselves than they associate with other broods, and perform their migration apart from the older birds, as I have observed twenty or thirty young hummingbirds resort to a group of trumpet-flowers, when not a single old male was to be seen.

They do not receive the full brilliancy of their colors until the succeeding spring, although the throat of the male bird is strongly imbued with the ruby tints before they leave us in autumn.

I have seen many of these birds kept in partial confinement, when they were supplied with artificial flowers made for the purpose, in the corollas of which water with dissolved sugar was placed. One does not live on sugar alone; they seldom lived many months. On being examined after death, they were found to be extremely emaciated. Others, on the contrary, which were supplied twice a-day with fresh flowers from the woods or garden, placed in a room with windows merely closed with mosquito gauze-netting, through which minute insects were able to enter, lived twelve months, at the expiration of which time their liberty was granted to them.

In this, my portrait of the ruby-throated hummingbird, I have represented several of these pretty and most interesting birds, in various positions, feeding, caressing each other, or sitting on the slender stalks of the trumpet-flower and preening themselves. The diversity of action and attitude thus exhibited, may, I trust, prove sufficient to present a faithful idea of their appearance and manners. A figure of the nest you will also find has been given; it is generally placed low, on the horizontal branch of a tree, seldom more than twenty feet from the ground. They are far from being particular in this matter, as I have often found a nest attached by one side only to a twig of a rosebush, currant, or the strong stalk of a rank weed, sometimes in the middle of the forest, at other times on the branch of an oak, immediately over the road, and again in the garden close to the walk.

No one is sure how many of these swift moving birds exist as they are so difficult to count. Where there is an abundance of food they are quite common. Where the habits of man have destroyed their habitats they are more rare. But our habits can improve their habitats. Like the demise of so many species of birds, when we destroy their homes, their sources of food and places where they raise their young, their numbers will plummet. Allow me to ask: If I were to burn down your home, destroy your crops and marketplaces, raid your pantry, and weaken you to a state where you could not bear young, how long would your species survive? If we are to make room in our lives for these winged jewels, we must preserve what habitat is left to them. Placing hummingbird feeders in your yard is a great place to begin, but it is only a beginning. Plant the flowers we know they love and encourage a wild corner for them to hide in and raise their young. The diversity of native plants in your yard will increase the diversity of insects, their primary food. Think how sad our lives would be without these glittering fragments of the rainbow. If they bring you joy, like they do me, then let us do what we can to see their numbers increase!

Source material: Audubon's *Ornithological Biography* (1832), *Sibley's Guide to Bird Behavior* (2001), *Garden Birds of North America* by Henry Hill Collins Jr. and Ned R. Boyajian (1965), and my personal observations.

"The Ruby-Throated Hummingbird": A Lesson in Research and Rewriting

Grade Levels: 5–12

Time Estimate: Two to three hours

Objectives:

- Knowing it is easier to teach rewriting strategies when working with someone else's writing, students will demonstrate their skills in deciphering historical text and then rewrite this text with more modern language and updated scientific information.

- Students will compare and contrast Audubon's essay about their favorite bird with more contemporary scientific essays.

- Students will immerse themselves into the life of one bird and in so doing learn general concepts in ornithology that can be applied to other bird species.

National Standards:

- NCTE 5—Students employ a wide range of strategies as they write and use different writing process elements appropriately to communicate with different audiences for a variety of purposes.

- NCTE 6—Students apply knowledge of language structure, language conventions, media techniques, figurative language, and genre to create, critique, and discuss print and non-print texts.

- NCTE 7—Students conduct research on issues and interests by generating ideas and questions, and by posing problems. They gather, evaluate, and synthesize data from a variety of sources to communicate their discoveries in ways that suit their purpose and audience.

- NAS 1—Science as Inquiry: Abilities necessary to do scientific inquiry; Understandings about scientific inquiry.

- NAS 3—Life Science: Structure and function in living systems; Reproduction and heredity; Regulation and behavior; Populations and ecosystems; Diversity and adaptations of organisms

Materials:

- Paper and pencil

- Access to Audubon's *Ornithological Biography*: www.audubon.org/bird/BoA/BOA_index.html

- *The Sibley Guide to Bird Life and Bird Behavior* by David Allen Sibley (2001)

- *Stokes Field Guides to Bird Behavior* by Donald and Lillian Stokes (1996)

Background Information: Most folks know John James Audubon as one of the most important ornithologists in history, as well as a world-renowned wildlife artist. You might be surprised to find that in his day he was also considered one of America's greatest authors. For every bird he painted, 485 species, he wrote three to five pages about their life, habits and habitats. These were later published in seven volumes as *The Ornithological Biographies*. He also published fifty short stories about his travels in the wildest places in North America.

By today's standards his writing is flowery, dated, and filled with romantic euphemisms and run-on sentences that are difficult for today's students to decipher. Yet there is a wealth of information worth sifting through. This sifting process can be a great way to teach students the skills they need to decode nonfiction essays while learning to rewrite overwrought material. If they can read and decode Audubon, then there isn't anything they can't tackle! Although his writing is dated, one aspect of his style was actually ahead of its time—namely, his ability to weave expository writing with a narrative thread. Most modern, award-winning science essays blur this line between narrative and expository writing, making for more compelling reading. Audubon was a master of this style and is therefore a great role model for students to emulate.

This lesson is a great follow-up to "Bird Is the Word" (see page 148). This is also one of the few stories in the book that I would highly encourage you to read rather than learn and tell. Because it lacks the typical plot line of a normal narrative and is packed with scientific detail important to the lesson, reading aloud with the same emotional fluidity and interactive flair of storytelling is the best strategy.

Instructional Procedures

Introduction: Begin by asking students to get out a sheet of paper and a pencil and to take notes on the following narrative essay. Warn them that some of the language is flowery and antiquated, but there is a lot of good information. Their job is to listen for the important facts and write them down.

To introduce the story, you may want to give a brief introduction to John James Audubon. I perform as Audubon and have only used this lesson after a performance, but here is a short introduction you can use.

"How many of you have heard of John James Audubon? The Audubon Society was named for him, an organization dedicated to protecting birds and their habitats. He was born in 1785 and died in 1851. He was the first man to paint a portrait of all of the known birds of North America—485 species—including more than a dozen that he was the first to name. His artwork hangs in some of the finest museums in the world, and he made his living selling hand-colored prints of his *Birds of North America*. Although Audubon was often poor, if you owned a complete collection of his prints today, it would be worth more than $4 million.

"In the early 1820s and 1830s, he traveled in the wildest places in America, from Florida to the Rocky Mountains, Texas to Nova Scotia, to collect birds. He also wrote fifty short stories about his adventures, kept a journal along the way, and for every bird he painted, he wrote a short biography or scientific essay that blended his observations with delightful, although sometimes over-the-top, flowery language. Here is his essay on the ruby-throated hummingbird, which has been edited and updated with new scientific information. As you listen, make notes of the important facts."

Read aloud the story.

Activity: Immediately following the story, discuss the information contained within and the style of writing. What were some of the most important facts? Make a list on the board; encourage students to add to their lists. What are a few passages that you really liked? What are the parts where the writing seemed over the top?

Next, ask students to get out a sheet of paper and pencil and to make a two-minute, quick sketch of their favorite bird, fill the page with a large drawing, and try to convey as much information as they can. Make it clear that this rough sketch will not be graded for art class, but might be part of their science grade, so if they want to label parts or make notes in the margins, that might be helpful to them later.

Ask them to turn to a partner and take turns using their sketch as a teaching tool; share with your partner all that you know about your bird, answering the following questions:

What does this bird look like, including differences between male and female?

Where does it live (forest, prairie) and what kind of nest does it make?

What does it do (how does it eat, fly, swim, build a nest)? Think in terms of verbs.

With this information in hand, tell students that you are not asking them to write a new essay on their favorite bird; rather, you are inviting them to rewrite John James Audubon's essay on their favorite bird. Rewriting and editing are very important skills, and sometimes they are easier to learn when working with someone else's writing.

Give students time in the computer lab to find and print a copy of Audubon's essay about their bird, or assign this research as homework if your students have access to the Internet and a printer (www.audubon.org/bird/BoA/BOA_index.html). Ask students to read the essay and use a highlighter to highlight the important facts in each paragraph. Ask them to write a short phrase or one-sentence synopsis of each paragraph. Set this aside to return to later.

Provide students with copies of *Sibley's Guide to Bird Behavior* and *Stokes Field Guides*. Also provide access to www.birds.cornell.edu/AllAboutBirds/. Ask them to read at least one other modern ornithological essay about their bird, so they can look for new information to add to their Audubon essay. They should take notes on a separate sheet of paper and begin to think about where they might add these facts to Audubon's essay.

Especially with older students, a brief review or introduction to footnotes, quoting your source material, and the laws regarding plagiarism would be most appropriate at this point.

Here is where the fun begins! Instruct students to reread their essay on Audubon with the goal of cherry picking the best parts to make a short, sweet, slightly condensed edition of the essay. Their goal is to play with Audubon's language, to try to maintain elements of his style of writing, but to update the essay with more modern language and modern science. They should aim for 1,000 to 2,000 words, which means a few essays might need expansion, but most can be cut in half. A few of the longer essays can even lose two-thirds of the drivel.

If they are working on paper, students can read Audubon's essay again. Instruct them to underline their favorite parts, parts they want to keep, and draw a line through the boring, confusing, or unnecessary parts—parts they want to cut out or rewrite. They can also number the facts on their research notes and simply write the number of which fact they want to put in the right places. These notes can be rewritten into a new version of Audubon's essay.

If working on a computer, students can cut and paste the entire essay into a new document. As they read through it, they can cut the boring or confusing parts and reorganize the parts they want to keep. Encourage students to simplify some of the long, convoluted sentences. One can often cut a run-on sentence in half by adding a period and a capital letter in the middle. With a few of Audubon's longer run-ons, I can cut them into three or four complete sentences. Students can type in the new facts trying to emulate some of Audubon's style of writing while using a more modern vocabulary. Students can also add some of the information they already know about the bird and true stories about their encounters with this species trying to write in Audubon's style.

If you feel your students need more detailed instruction, review paragraphs one, two, and three of my edited version of the hummingbird essay, versus the first three paragraphs of Audubon's original. Walk students through, sentence by sentence, and look at the edits I made. Emphasize the places where I added scientific information and simplified the text. Paragraph one I simply shortened. The second paragraph was nearer the end of the essay. I moved it and added most of the science about how they get their ruby throats. Paragraph three I wrote adapting an idea from *Garden Birds of North America* by Henry Hill Collins Jr. and Ned R. Boyajian (1965).

Or, as the teacher you can choose your favorite bird essay by Audubon and ask your students to help you. As a class you can work together to rewrite a paragraph or two, providing students with another example of this process.

Allow students plenty of time to rewrite Audubon's essay.

Assessment: The final essay can receive up to three grades: one on mechanics, grammar, and punctuation; one grade on the accuracy and depth of scientific information; and a third grade on the style and fluidity in the writing. With the first two grades, it is easy to count the facts or subtract the mistakes. With the grade on style, we are actually asking students both to maintain the voice of Audubon in the sentences they add and to update the language, simplify the grammar, and improve the fluency of the piece, so admittedly this is a more subjective grade.

Follow-up Activities: These essays can be collected into a classroom book or shared with the class orally. You can also work with the art teacher to create large watercolor sketches of the birds to illustrate the essays.

In the spirit of Audubon, encourage your students to conduct field research about their bird, to go outside and observe it. Cornell Labs (www.birds.cornell.edu) has several great field ecology lesson plans online, so your students can participate in ongoing research about the birds of their region.

Comments: I shared this lesson plan with a seventh-grade teacher to get his feedback, and he recommended the Cornell Labs Web site as another resource for students to gather information about their favorite bird. This page has lots of cool facts that can enrich student essays with the latest scientific information. www.birds.cornell.edu/AllAboutBirds/BirdGuide/.

"MON-DAW-MIN": AN OJIBWA STORY ABOUT THE COMING OF CORN WITH A WILDFLOWER OR WILD EDIBLE WALK

Many long winters ago, the people of this land were hunters and gatherers. There were times of great feasting and times of great hunger.

During the summer they would follow the herds of bison, gather the berries and nuts from the fields and forests, dig the roots and tubers, learning from the land where and when to gather their foods.

But during the winter when the snow was deep and the ground was frozen, there was little to eat and it was difficult to hunt. During these lean times the people would grow hungry. Sometimes they would starve before the spring returned to the earth.

Among the people there was a young man named Wunza. He was old enough that he would soon go alone into the wilderness to fast and pray, to seek a vision, to ask those age-old questions that we still wrestle with today. Who am I? Why am I here? What are my gifts and talents? What can I do to make the world a better place? In this time he knew he should pay close attention to his dreams and to the plants and animals that might come to visit. Each of them may hold an answer to his prayers.

As spring was changing to summer, Wunza was changing from a boy to a man. His village would have held a feast for him but there was little food to be had. One warm spring morning as the sun rose over the eastern hills, Wunza went out alone into the wilderness.

What caught his eye as he walked along were all of the shades of green, light and dark green, reddish green and yellow green, green with hints of blue and purple. He saw the plants were in various stages of growth. Some of the early blooming woodland flowers were already fading and making seed, yet some of the prairie grasses were just beginning to sprout. The wild strawberries were flowering and would soon be bearing fruit.

He saw the gophers nibbling grasses and he noticed which leaves they passed over. The squirrels were eating maple seeds now, but he knew they would eat acorns, walnuts, and hickory nuts each in their season. He saw holes in the old trees where woodpeckers had stored last year's acorns. Everywhere he looked he saw food! He was so hungry.

His one wish, his one desire, was to find a way to feed the people. He wondered if there was a way to learn from the animals how to survive the long winters. Somehow he knew the plants could help.

He carried his wish in his heart as he looked for a secret spot to sit for seven days and seven nights. When he found the place along the edge of the prairie, along the edge of the forest, he made a circle of stones. He spread his buffalo robe on the ground and settled down to pray, to seek a vision. To ask and answer those great questions.

Think about it. Who are you? Why are you here? What are your gifts and talents? What can you do to make the world a better place? These are the questions Wunza asked himself over and over.

The first four days were the hardest. He was so hungry he had trouble sleeping. On the fourth night he fell into a fitful sleep with strange dreams. In his dreams a young man came from the sky world to visit him. He was dressed in robes that were light green and flowing like many wide blades of grass. He had silky, golden hair. This was strange, because Native people have hair that is midnight black.

The young man fairly shouted with enthusiasm, "Wunza, I am Mon-daw-min! Creator has heard your prayers and sent me to help you. Get up and wrestle me! If you win, I will teach you the secret life of plants! I will help you to feed the people! Get up! Get up!"

Wunza was weak with hunger, but he loved to wrestle. No sooner had he stood on his two feet before Mon-daw-min pounced on him. The two boys rolled in the dirt. They tussled. They grunted. They loved the sport of it! Finally, Mon-daw-min picked up Wunza and threw him to the ground.

"Oh, Wunza, you seem to have fallen. Get up, get up!" said Mon-daw-min. "You can do better than that. Maybe tomorrow, when I return, you can win and your wish will come true."

And with that lightning flashed, thunder crashed, and Mon-daw-min disappeared.

When Wunza awoke in the morning, he rubbed his eyes and remembered his dream. He could not wait until the next night and another chance to wrestle Mon-daw-min.

That night, no sooner was he asleep, than a broad shouldered man appeared. He was taller and his robes were darker green. His hair was silky but more brown than gold.

"Wunza! Do not look surprised. It is I, Mon-daw-min. Are you ready to wrestle? Get up, boy, and show me your strength!"

Wunza stood up. Weak from hunger, he was not at all sure he could win. He lost last night to a younger man. How could he win against this strong man? Wunza leaped at Mon-daw-min. Mon-daw-min stepped aside and scooped the boy up as he passed. He tried to throw the boy to the ground, but Wunza landed on his feet. Mon-daw-min pounced. The two fell to the ground. They rolled in the dirt. They tussled. They groaned. They both laughed as they strained and grunted! Finally, Mon-daw-min rolled over Wunza and pinned him to the ground.

"Oh, Wunza, you have fallen again. Get up, boy, get up!" said Mon-daw-min. "I admire your daring will, but I think you can do better than that. Maybe tomorrow, when I return for the last time, you might win and your wish will come true."

And with that lightning flashed, thunder crashed, and Mon-daw-min disappeared.

When Wunza awoke in the morning, he rubbed his eyes and remembered this dream, too, but was it a dream? He could not wait until the next night and another chance to wrestle Mon-daw-min.

That night, Wunza sat by his small fire, watching the stars twirl in the sky above him. For the first time he noticed how all the stars seem to circle the one star, just as his people dance around the Council fire. For the first time he began to feel his place amongst the stars, and with that thought he fell asleep. No sooner was he asleep than an old man appeared. He was bent with age. He wore weathered brown robes. His clothes rustled as he moved. His hair was falling out. He was missing a few teeth. His voice was horse when he said, "Wunza! Do not look surprised. It is I, Mon-daw-min. Are you ready to wrestle? Get up, boy, and show me your strength. Maybe tonight you can win and I will teach you my secret!"

Wunza was reluctant. His parents had taught him to respect his elders; he did not want to hurt the old man. But he was taught to respect his elders; the old man told him to stand up. As he stood, still unsure, the old man leapt onto Wunza. They both fell down. They rolled in the dirt. Struggling together they both stood, grunting and pushing against one another. As Wunza planted both feet firmly on the ground and wrapped his arms around the old man he felt a strange strength come into him. His toes and feet tingled, as the power seemed to rise from the earth into his legs, his torso, his arms and head. His whole body rippled with this power. He lifted the old man and threw him to the ground.

"Wunza (cough, cough), I knew you had it in you. You have won! Now I will tell you what to do to feed the people so they will never be hungry again. Listen closely. In the morning when you awake you will find my withered body. Do not shed a tear for me. I will return if you do as I tell you. Dig a shallow grave and bury me. Tend this plot of land carefully removing all stones and weeds. In the dry season bring me water. When I sprout, place fresh soil around my roots and continue to pull the weeds. When I am grown your wish will come true. But Wunza, you must not forget to save some seed to plant for the next season."

And with that lightning flashed, thunder crashed, and Mon-daw-min disappeared.

In the morning when he awoke, it was just as the old man said. Lying beside him was the withered, broken body of the old man. Wunza did as he was told and carefully prepared the soil. He buried Mon-daw-min in a shallow grave and watered the earth with his tears. He tended the plants throughout the summer. Soon the young Mon-daw-min appeared with light green robes, and silky yellow hair. Later in the summer the strong young man with darker green robes, darker hair, and broad shoulders appeared. In the early autumn, the young man grew old and wilted.

And in this way Wunza learned the secret of maize, what you call corn. He shared this story with the people. When he harvested the corn, he had enough to feed the entire village. He saved some seed as he was instructed and soon taught the whole village the gift of corn. He taught them to grow their food. They were never hungry again. From that day until this one, Mon-daw-min has provided for the people.

Let me ask: Do you like popcorn, hominy, nachos, and corn-fed beef? Then say thank you to Mon-daw-min. To this day he still feeds the people.

"Mon-Daw-Min"—An Ojibwa Story about the Coming of Corn with a Wildflower or Wild Edible Walk

Grade Levels: 3–12

Time Estimate: 1.5 hours

Objectives:

- Students will demonstrate an ability to use a key.

- They will identify one flower and model the skills they need to identify most any plant.

- They will learn to use the parts of a plant to do this.

National Standards:

- NCTE 4—Students adjust their use of spoken, written, and visual language to communicate effectively with a variety of audiences and for different purposes.

- NCTE 6—Students apply knowledge of language structure, language conventions, media techniques, figurative language, and genre to create, critique, and discuss print and non-print texts.

- NCTE 7—Students conduct research on issues and interests by generating ideas and questions, and by posing problems. They gather, evaluate, and synthesize data from a variety of sources to communicate their discoveries in ways that suit their purpose and audience.

- NAS 1—Science as Inquiry: Abilities necessary to do scientific inquiry; Understandings about scientific inquiry

- NAS 3—Life Science: Structure and function in living systems; Reproduction and heredity; Regulation and behavior; Populations and ecosystems; Diversity and adaptations of organisms

Materials:

- Sketch pad or clipboard and paper for each student

- Several copies of Lawrence Newcomb's *Field Guide to Wildflowers* (Little, Brown and Co., 1977)

- A box or two of 64 colors of crayon or several sets of colored pencils

- Several different field guides to wild edibles; I recommend *Peterson's Field Guide to Wild Edibles* (1977), any one of several books by Bradford Angier or Euell Gibbons, and Jean Craighead George's (1995) *Dandelion Salad*

Background Information: If you have never used a key to identify a plant, it is important that you familiarize yourself with Newcomb's (1997) *Field Guide to Wildflowers*. This is also a lesson where it is important to have access to a field of wildflowers or a prairie or garden where a variety of flowers are blooming. The teacher does not have to know every flower. It is actually more instructive if one can say, "I don't know, but let us find out together," and use the key.

Classification and identification skills are vital to good science. This hands-on experience will allow students a chance to use a key to identify almost any flower they find.

The overall arc of this lesson is an adaptation of "The Flow Hike," first proposed by Joseph Cornell (1998) in his groundbreaking book on environmental education, *Sharing Nature with Children* (Dawn Publications). The basic concept for a flow hike is to begin with awareness, move into hands-on activities, and then end with a contemplative introspective activity to allow students to process what they have learned. Cornell's book gives a much more in-depth outline of the process as well as exciting activities for building nature awareness in children.

Instructional Procedures

Introduction: Before telling the story, begin with a discussion of our food, what folks like to eat, favorite recipes, and their ingredients, all with an emphasis on plants. What plants do we eat? Somewhere in this discussion, I love to quote Studs Turkel, "We are all just a lucky pile of mud." Think about it: We are what we eat, and what we eat grows in the earth, so it only follows that we are lucky piles of mud. Most mud just lies there, but we are lucky, we can tell stories and go for a hike in the woods and learn about wild foods!"*

Take the class outdoors and sit under a shady tree and then introduce the story.

The following story is from the Ojibwa or Chippewa people who live in the northern Great Lakes region. Some folks might say it is just a myth, but I believe that myths speak of higher truths, and if you listen carefully to this story, you can learn much about how plants grow and our food supply. When we are done with the story, we will talk more about these things, but I want you to ask yourself, "What can I learn from this story. What can I learn from Mon-daw-min?"

Tell the story of Mon-daw-min.

Activity: After the story ask: What did Wunza learn? What was his gift to the people? What can we learn about plants and farming from this story? Did you know that Native Americans first domesticated most of our food plants? Many come from Central and South America, but when the Europeans first came to North America, they "discovered" these foods and imported them back to Europe. Eventually the world began to grow corn, tomatoes, potatoes, blueberries, pumpkins, turkey, and several species of beans, squash, and hot peppers.

Hike out to your favorite prairie, garden, forest, or forest edge where a wide variety of flowers are blooming. As you hike, challenge students to notice colors. Ask them to look for all of the colors of the rainbow. Or give each student a few colors of crayon and ask them to find plants that match these colors.

About halfway through the hike, stop the group and ask them to notice what stage of development the plants are in at this moment. As they walk along, like Mon-daw-min, they can learn from the plants. Are these young sprouts, strong young adults in flower, or old men and women wilting and bearing seed or fruit for the next generation?

When the class arrives at the prairie or wildflower garden, organize students into small groups of four. Ask each group to look for as many different shapes of leaves that they can find. Discourage them from picking; encourage them to use their sketchpad to simply draw the basic shape of the leaf. Give them about five minutes for this activity. Challenge them to work together and discuss the shapes as they go. This not a contest, but encourage students to find as many shapes as they can, paying attention to the details of vein structure, pointed or round edges, smooth or jagged edges, and the like. Call them back together and ask them to share their findings. At this point introduce key leaf shapes: lobed, toothed, smooth, and divided into leaflets versus entire leaves.

In this discussion, allow them to lead with their examples and use their descriptive vocabulary to introduce the scientific terminology from the field guide. Encourage them to write the key words next to an example of this leaf type.

Now ask students to quickly revisit five of their plants and look at how leaves are attached to the stem. Give them just two minutes before calling them back to discuss their findings. Introduce the key concepts of leaves attached singly, alternating up the stem; paired opposites; whirled; or basal. Again, use their examples and their descriptive vocabulary to introduce the scientific terminology from Newcomb's wildflower guide.

Now pass out crayons or colored pencils with sketchpads and ask students to pick a favorite flower and make a careful sketch, working individually. They should fill the page with their sketch, not make a tiny picture in the corner. Challenge them to pay attention to detail, the shapes and number of petals, the way petals are arranged (are they regular or irregular?), the colors, and how the flower is attached to the rest of the plant. For older students, have them include and label the parts of the plant (leaf, root, stem) and parts of the flower (pistil, stamen, petal, sepal). They should include this in their drawings, making notes in the margins around their pictures to clarify. After five minutes, ask each student to stand and describe his or her picture or flower for a partner.

After they have had some hands-on experience with plant parts and the vocabulary of the key, introduce Newcomb's *Field Guide to Wildflowers* and "The Five Key Questions."

Use one of the student's plants as an example. Ask students, "Is the flower regular or irregular in shape, or are the flower parts indistinguishable? How many petals? (Count the number of petals out loud.) Is it an herb, shrub, or vine? If a wildflower, does it have leaves? Are they all at the base, arranged singly on the stem alternating, or are they opposite in pairs or in whorls? Are the leaves entire, or are they toothed or lobed or divided?"

After answering the questions, model the use of the key, and identify the flower. Discuss one flower as a group, then pass out copies of the book and walk the class through the process together with another student's flower. They can follow along in the books that they share with their partners.

Ask them to try to identify their flowers. First they should answer the five questions on the back of their sketch. The questions lead to a number, for example 457. Students should write down the number and the page number the key sends them to. The number will lead them to the corresponding page so they can discern the name of their flower. Admittedly, this can be a little confusing at first, but working with a partner, they can discuss what they think and follow it until they get it right. If their initial step-by-step following of the key leads them astray, challenge them to double check their answers to the five questions. After they have got it right, then they can help their partner. With a little practice, students do figure this out, and then they want to try another flower, and another, until soon they begin to feel like experts.

Next, lead a discussion about western taxonomy and native awareness: "In not so ancient times, it was important to know what plants grew around you and how to identify them, or you would starve, like the people in the story. One could also learn about wild edibles from a grandma or grandpa; German or Cherokee, all cultures had to know what they could eat and what was poisonous.* Newcomb's *Field Guide to Wildflowers* is a western scientific approach that is linear: step A, then B, then C, and so on. It works very well, but it isn't the only way to know a plant. For native peoples throughout the world, it was through stories and personal experience that people learned how to identify plants, which plants were edible,* which were medicine, and which were poisonous."

Discuss these questions: "How many of you could go into your backyard and identify five plants? Do you know which ones are edible* and which are poisonous? How do you know? How did the first people learn which plants could be eaten? How did they teach their children?"

Next, invite students to sit quietly with their plant and learn directly from the plant. Challenge them to use both their scientific mind to ask questions and look for answers but also to use their creative mind to imagine a conversation, create a poem or song, or imagine watching the plant's entire life, past and future, from seed to flower to seed again.

Give students a choice: Using their illustration, scientific knowledge, and any poetic ideas they learned from the plant, they can write a fable, a myth, poem, or modern folktale about the origin and uses of this plant.

Give them a moment to share their creativity with a partner.

Once back in class, ask students to rewrite and edit their story or poem before sharing it with the class.

Assessment: More important than if they got it right, right away, evaluate their answers to the five questions as compared with their sketch. Their poem or story can be graded as a piece of creative writing with bonus points for botanical information.

Follow-up Activities: Their picture and creative writing can be paired for a bulletin-board display. With help from parents, either a large sign that includes the students' information about the plants in this garden or individual signs for each of the plant species can be made. "Bird Is the Word" on page 148 can be adapted to include poems, stories, and essays about plants and is a great follow-up to this lesson.

Comments: *At several points in this activity, I give disclaimers about wild edibles. I often say, "*Do not eat wild edibles* unless you are with an expert. There are many things out there that are very poisonous. If you eat the wrong plant, your mother might be upset. Seriously, even on this hike, you do not put anything in your mouth unless you show it to me first. We will learn how to identify plants, which is the first step toward being an expert, and if you listen carefully, I will teach you how to tell two plants apart. *But please do not go out on your own and start eating stuff! You might die!*" Only if you feel confident in your ability to identify plants and have a working knowledge of edible plants should you introduce the idea of wild edibles and then allow students a chance to eat a few plants. If the idea makes you *at all nervous,* do not even think about it.

I have led this set of activities more often in an environmental education setting. Almost every summer for the past several years, I have had at least a few kids get hooked on the idea of plant identification and then beg their parents to buy Newcomb's *Field Guide to Wildflowers*. Parents have called to ask about the book and then started to identify plants as a regular hobby!

ROCKET TO THE MOON/POSTCARDS FROM MARS: PUTTING THE SCIENCE BACK IN SCIENCE FICTION

The Story: This is one of only two lesson plans in the book that I do not begin with a story. The story grows organically out of their research into astronomy, questions they ask and find answers to. When I have invented a story on the spot and used it as a model, they tend to replicate my story, so it is best to let them imagine from scratch. You will also note that this is really two lesson plans that work well independently, but also work better in sequence.

Grade Levels: 2–7

Time Estimate: Two hours

Objectives:

- Students will demonstrate fluid narrative writing with an integration of solid scientific knowledge.

- Students will learn research skills with an emphasis on researching on a need-to-know basis.

- Intrinsically motivated, students will teach themselves and their peers about their favorite part of the solar system.

National Standards:

- NCTE 1—Students read a wide range of print and non-print texts to build an understanding of texts, of themselves, and of the world; to acquire new information; and for personal fulfillment. Among these texts are fiction and nonfiction, classic and contemporary works.

- NCTE 3—Students apply a wide range of strategies to comprehend, interpret, evaluate, and appreciate texts.

- NCTE 4—Students adjust their use of spoken, written, and visual language to communicate effectively with a variety of audiences and for different purposes.

- NCTE 5—Students employ a wide range of strategies as they write and use different writing process elements appropriately to communicate with different audiences for a variety of purposes.

- NCTE 7—Students conduct research on issues and interests by generating ideas and questions, and by posing problems. They gather, evaluate, and synthesize data from a variety of sources to communicate their discoveries in ways that suit their purpose and audience.

- NCTE 8—Students use a variety of technological and information resources to gather and synthesize information and to create and communicate knowledge.

- NAS 2—Physical Science: Properties and changes of properties in matter; Motions and forces; Transfer of energy

- NAS 4—Earth and Space Science: Structure of the earth system; Earth's history; Earth in the solar system

- NAS 5—Science and Technology: Abilities of technological design; Understanding about science and technology

- NCTM 6—Problem Solving

- NCTM 10—Representational Models

Materials:

- Paper and pencil

- Books about the solar system, planets and space travel

- Access to the Internet is optional

- An 8½ x 11–inch piece of cardstock for each student works best, but unlined paper also works well

- A set of markers, crayons or colored pencils

Background Information: Traditional science fiction had an emphasis on the science. Isaac Asimov was not only a great writer, he also exhibited the traits of a great scientist—namely, he asked difficult questions and then hypothesized potential answers. He followed ideas to their logical extreme, exploring the "what ifs" and "whys" of human existence and technology.

Students love solid science fiction because of the way it blends facts with imagination, science with creativity. Science can be dramatic. Discuss research with a working scientist and there is often great passion for their work, a sense of adventure and discovery. Science fiction allows students to stretch their imaginations in a way that can also affirm the logical mind of science-process skills. It encourages them to ask questions and look for answers. It motivates research by giving purpose to their pursuits.

Instructional Procedures: Postcards from Mars

Introduction: This is a great lesson plan for introducing the planets and giving students a fun way to focus their research and writing. It can be used to teach research skills, introduce science fiction, strengthen writing skills, and introduce students to the planets of our solar system. This lesson plan can also be used as a follow-up lesson when studying the solar system, a way of sneaking in an evaluation of their knowledge base while having fun doing it.

Activity: Ask your students to imagine that their classroom is a spaceship and that they can travel to any planet they like. They could visit one of their moons or rings. What kind of adventure would they have? What would they see along the way? How would they get there, and how long would it take? Explain that today they are writing science fiction. Traditional science fiction is a mix of fact and fiction, good science and a great imagination.

Ask each student to get out a sheet of paper and pencil to first:

Write the name of the planet they are planning to visit at the top of their page.

Brainstorm what they know about this planet. Make a list of facts.

Make a list of questions. What do they want or need to know about their planet to make a trip there?

Allow them about 10 or 15 minutes to look for answers. Provide a stack of books from the library, access to their science textbooks, or access to the Internet.

Now with facts in hand, tell students they are going to write a postcard home from their favorite planet. On one side they are to draw a picture of their planet with points given for accurate details: Does it have rings, moons, clouds, or bands of color? Explain that as they draw, they can think about shaping their adventure into a story. How can they use the facts to propel the story? Allow students about five minutes to draw and ten or fifteen minutes to write their postcard. They can write to their mother, father, grandma, or dog. Warn students that they will receive extra points for each fact they use well.

Teachers may want to draw a sample postcard form on the board so that students understand where text goes and where to save space for the address and stamp.

When they are finished and graded, teachers can mail them to the addresses provided by students as a pleasant surprise for parents and grandparents who still love to get snail mail.

Instructional Procedure: Rockets Beyond the Moon!

Introduction: Begin with a brief discussion of science and fiction. Ask students to define, compare, and contrast these terms. State the goals of this lesson: to write an exciting adventure that is in part made up—but possible—it could be true—at least it could be true in the future. The more true facts they have about their planet, the more points they can earn.

I always offer two for the price of one! Students can earn two As for one story. They can earn an A in language arts for writing an adventure, filled with drama, well-drawn characters, a clear setting, and exciting action. They can also earn an A in science for spicing the story with lots of cool facts about their planet, the solar system, and things they might see along the away.

Activity: Pass out the worksheet "Rockets Beyond the Moon!" Walk students through the questions to help them outline their story. At the top of their page, ask them to put their name and date, and then write the name of the planet they would like to visit. If this room were a spaceship, where would they like to travel?

If they have already written their postcards, you can skim through the next three paragraphs. Ask them to get out their original list of facts, questions, and answers.

Ask them to brainstorm a list of facts on paper. What do they already know about this planet? How far do you have to travel? Is it closer or farther away from the sun? Is it larger or smaller than the earth? Does it have moons? How many?

Ask them to brainstorm a list of questions. What do they want to know? What questions can they not answer that might be important to their survival? What facts might help them pack or prepare?

At this point, especially if you are near the beginning of the unit, allow students 10 minutes to research their planet. I like to challenge them: How many facts can you find in 10 minutes? Try to find one fact a minute, 10 facts in 10 minutes.

Shifting gears, ask them to make a short list of who would go with them. Including themselves, write a brief description of the job skills, knowledge, or expertise required of each person. Why would they bring this person along? How do they ensure the success of the mission? Give them just two or three minutes to jot this down.

Ask students, "What would you pack? What is essential for survival? What does your spaceship look like? What are the major features?" Allow two or three minutes for students to write and draw.

Knowing a story has a beginning, middle, and end, as well as a problem and solution, ask students to use the back of the sheet to make an outline of their story. The main question is: If you went on this adventure to this part of the solar system with these people and tools, what would happen along the way? And then what happens? And then what happens? Allow students about five minutes to make an outline of their story.

Next, ask students to close their eyes and daydream an adventure; imagine packing, preparing, and taking off. What do they see, hear, and feel as they fly through space? What happens along the way and when they get there? What do they learn about the solar system that you can only learn from being there? What problems do they face, what goes wrong, and how do they fix it? How do they finally, finally make it home alive?

When they open their eyes, ask them to turn to a partner and take turns telling their story. As their partner listens, they should note any questions that come up and ask them when their partner is done.

Allow students plenty of time to turn their notes into a story. Remind them that good science facts make better science fiction! Their rough drafts could be collected at the end of the period, or finishing the rough draft could be homework. The following day, use storytelling as a rewriting strategy (see page 69) and assist students in making a final draft.

Assessment: The worksheet can be collected and graded on both the quality and quantity of facts. The story can be evaluated for grammar, spelling, stylistic elements, and the way planetary facts help to propel the story.

Follow-up Activities: These stories can be collected into a book of science fiction, posted on the Web, or performed for their peers.

This same set of lesson plans can be used to write ecological survival stories if you simply adapt a few of the questions. Instead of a planet, what habitat do they wander into, how do they get there, who goes with them, what plants and animals help them survive, and then how do they get out of the jam?

Comments: This lesson sprang out of one of those serendipitous teachable moments when I was presenting an artist-in-residence program at a school, and the moment before I stood up to teach, the classroom teacher asked if I could help her students get a little more excited about planets. I love postcards, and they seemed like a fun way to motivate research and convey the facts that students learned. The story is actually an adaptation of a wilderness survival lesson plan, so the follow-up activity actually came first. If you and your students are also big fans of Jean Craighead George and Gary Paulsen, you can easily adapt the worksheet to emphasize the ecological survival, realistic fiction that is a perennial hit with students.

Rocket Beyond the Moon!

Name: _____ Date: _____

Where would you go in the solar system and why?

_____

What do you know about this planet or moon? List at least three facts:

_____

_____

_____

Questions? Spend some time looking for answers!

_____

_____

_____

Who would you take with you and why? What are the job skills you need?

NAME   JOB SKILLS

_____   _____

_____   _____

_____   _____

What would you take with you?   Draw and describe your space ship.

_____

_____

_____

_____

_____

_____

On the back of this sheet, make an outline of your story:

1.   Begin with the beginning: preparing/packing/training.

2.   Leaving/traveling.

3.   What problems do you encounter on the way or when you arrive?

4.   How do you solve the problems?

5.   How do you bring them home alive?

 From *Content Area Reading, Writing, and Storytelling: A Dynamic Tool for Improving Reading and Writing Across the Curriculum through Oral Language Development* by Brian "Fox" Ellis. Westport, CT: Teacher Ideas Press. Copyright © 2008.

CHAPTER 5

STORYTELLING, MATH, AND PROBLEM SOLVING

MATH STORIES: TELLING AND WRITING

It has become a cultural cliché: "If a train is leaving Washington at 75 miles an hour and another train is leaving . . . blah, blah, blah." We hear it in sit-coms and romantic comedies, and it rarely gets a laugh because it is such an oft-told tale. Yet this is what most folks think of when they think of math stories—stiff, tired clichés.

But the truth is, math is directly or indirectly a part of every story. As has been said a dozen times throughout this book, every story needs a problem and a solution. Every story provides an inherent opportunity to teach math and problem solving. Sadly, most authors do not see the math hidden in their own stories. It has been my life mission to get out the yellow highlighter and draw attention to the math in every tale.

As you will see in the first story, the problem-solving and computational skills were there all along; all that the story needed was that yellow highlighter.

I am trained as a science teacher. Counting, classification, measurement, and statistical analysis are the foundation of good science skills. In most of the science stories I write and tell, I often lead the audience by the hand into the problem and then pause the story to give them a chance to do the computational skills. It could be as simple as counting the petals of a flower in "Mon-daw-min" or as complex as computing the number of wing beats for a hummingbird to migrate across the Gulf of Mexico (see Chapter 4 for these activities).

The basic idea is a simple one—an old idea turned on its head: Instead of writing and telling math stories, look for the math in every tale.

"THE END OF THE WORLD": EVERYDAY MATH IN EVERY STORY

The End of the World

I need your help with this story. Actually there are two ways you can help. First, think about wild animals that live in India where this story originates. Keep this to yourself for now; I will call on you when we need this information, but think about your favorite wild animals from India.

Also, whenever I say, "The ground is breaking up!" I want you to say, "It's the end of the world!" Say it like you mean it! Let's practice: "The ground is breaking up!" [Point to the audience.] "It's the end of the world!" Now don't forget, it comes up about 10 times!

Once upon a time, a long time ago, there was a little rabbit. Little rabbit was hopping along. Little rabbit was feeling kind of hungry. This little rabbit looked up and saw a mango tree. Oh no, all of the mango were green. None of them were ripe. You cannot eat a mango if it is not ripe. Then he thought, "If I sit here underneath the mango tree and I watch for them, one of them will fall."

And that is what he did. He lay back looking up at the green mango, hoping they would get ripe. And as he was laying there he began thinking. He was resting and thinking and thinking and resting, and what do you think he was thinking about?

He thought, "What will the world be like when I grow up? What will the world be like when I grow old? What will the world be like when I die?"

WHAM! Just as he thought that thought, he heard a great big CRASH!

The little rabbit jumped up and he took off running. He screamed, "The ground is breaking up (all together): it's the end of the world!"

The little rabbit took off running as fast as he could. As he was running along, he met another rabbit, and the other rabbit said, "Whoa, slow down, why are you running?"

And the first rabbit said, "The ground is breaking up; it's the end of the world!"

Then there were two rabbits running as fast as they could. They met a third rabbit, and the third rabbit said, "Slow down, where are you going?" And the first two rabbits said, "The ground is breaking up; it's the end of the world!" Now there were 3 rabbits and 4 rabbits and 5 rabbits and 10 rabbits and 100 rabbits and soon there were 1,000 rabbits all running across the savanna.

They ran past a bear. The bear was sleeping. He heard all of that noise. The bear jumped up and he saw 1,000 rabbits. He said, "Where's the fire; where are you going?' And they said, "The ground is breaking up; it's the end of the world!"

"Oh, no!" said the bear, "I'm getting out of here too." The bear took off running. He met another bear and the other bear said, "Hey buddy bear, where are you going?" The rabbits and the bear said, "The ground is breaking up; it's the end of the world!"

Soon there were 2 bears and 3 bears and 4 bears and 5 bears and 10 bears and 100 bears and 1,000 bears and 1,000 rabbits all running across the savanna.

Next, they met a . . . [*At each of these encounters, pause and let the audience choose, as long as it is an animal from India and not a lion. If someone says lion, say "that is a great idea, but let's save that one," and call on someone else.*] . . . a snake, a long king cobra. Now some people say that a snake slithers with his belly on the earth, so he can feel the vibrations of the earth. Could you imagine the vibrations of 1,000 rabbits and 1,000 bears?

The cobra poked his head up out of the tall grass and said, "Whoo-o-oa s-s-s." When he saw all of these creatures he said, "What's-s-s going on here-s-s?" They said, "The ground is breaking up; it's the end of the world!"

"Oh no-s-s, I'm getting out of here, too-s-s." Soon, they met another snake and 3 snakes and 4 snakes and 5 snakes and soon there were 10 snakes and 100 snakes and 1,000 snakes, and 1,000 bears, and 1,000 rabbits, and next, they met a... [*let the audience choose*] . . . a peacock.

Now peacocks live in tribal groups, and they usually put one peacock up in a tree as a sentry—a guard—to watch out for their enemy. The peacock up in the tree said "Brrrrk, brrrrkk" when he saw all of those animals. He said, "Help, help, something is wrong here, wrong here, why are you running, why are you running?"

All of the animals said, "The ground is breaking up; it's the end of the world!"

"Baak, I'm getting out of here, baak, I'm getting out of here." Soon, there were a 1,000 peacocks, 1,000 snakes, 1,000 bears, and 1,000 rabbits.

They met a herd of elephants. The leader of the elephants said, "What is going on around here?"

All of the animals said, "The ground is breaking up; it's the end of the world!"

Soon there were 1,000 elephants, 1,000 bears, 1,000 snakes, 1,000 peacocks, 1,000 rabbits, and they met the warthog and the gazelle and the deer and the Bengal tiger and the monkey. Soon there were 10,000 animals and all of them were running.

Now sleeping on a rock at the edge of a cliff there was a lion. The lion heard all of that noise, and he saw all of that dust, *and* he saw where they were running. He knew what was going to happen. But then he thought, "I can't let that happen, but what can I do?" One lion against 10,000 animals? Think about it, what would you do?

[*At this point, I sometimes pause and ask the audience members to turn to a partner and brainstorm possibilities. Put yourself in the lion's paws; if you saw 10,000 animals running toward a cliff, what would you do? I give them a minute to discuss with a partner, call on a few of them, and then tell them what the lion did.*]

The lion saw those animals running toward that cliff; he had to try something. He didn't know if it'd work, but he jumped down off of the rock, and he ran right out in front of them. Then as they were running toward him, he blocked the way and he *roared* as loud as he could roar. [*All together, I will count to three and then you roar one time. One, two, three, ROAR!*] The animals heard that roar and they stopped. The rabbits stopped, and the bears stopped, and the snakes and the elephants and the monkeys and the warthogs stopped, until all 10,000 of them stopped.

From *Content Area Reading, Writing, and Storytelling: A Dynamic Tool for Improving Reading and Writing Across the Curriculum through Oral Language Development* by Brian "Fox" Ellis. Westport, CT: Teacher Ideas Press. Copyright © 2008.

The lion said, "What is going on here? Why are you running? Do you not see what could have happened if you would have kept running? What's going on here?"

They all said, "The ground is breaking up; it's the end of the world!"

"Whoa, whoa, How do you know the ground is breaking up? How do you know it's the end of the world? Feel the ground right now; feel the earth, it's solid. Who told you the ground was breaking up?"

The gazelle said, "It wasn't me, it was the deer." And the deer said, "Wasn't me, it was the monkey." And the monkey said, "It wasn't me, it was the warthog." Warthog said, "Wasn't me, it was the elephant." Elephant said, "Wasn't me, it was the peacock." "Baak, wasn't me, baak, wasn't me, it was the snake." "Ssswasn't me, it wasss the bear." "Wasn't me, it was the rabbit."

And 1,000 rabbits all looked at each other and one of them said, "It wasn't me it was him," "her," "her," "him," "him," "her" "her" "him" "her" "him" "her." Soon 9,999 animals were all looking at the little rabbit who said, "It was me. I did it. I heard this sound; it sounded like the ground was breaking up. It's the end of the world."

"No it's not," said the lion, "Where did you hear that sound? Show me where you heard the ground breaking up."

"No, I'm not going to show you, I'm not going back there."

"Show me," said the lion.

"No, I don't wanna."

The lion picked up the little rabbit and put him on his back and said, "I'll take you there." The rabbit guided him until they crossed the savanna. Off in the distance they saw that big mango tree.

The rabbit said, "It was over there by that mango tree."

"Which one?"

"I'm not getting any closer."

"Yes, you are." And the lion took him over to that spot. They saw in the grass where the rabbit had been laying down because the grass was stilled smashed. Right next to that spot there was a . . . a mango. The juice was still dripping from the fallen fruit.

The lion said, "Look, this is what you are afraid of, a mango? Ummm, that is nothing to be afraid of." Then the lion turned to the animals and said, "When you are afraid, simply face your fears and you will see that often there is nothing to fear. And do not always listen to what others say; sometimes you must think for yourself."

And so they have from that day until this one.

"The End of the World": Everyday Math in Every Story

Grade Levels: K–12

Time Estimate: 60 minutes

Objectives:

- Students will participate in simple counting, addition, multiplication, and place value exercises.

- They will also begin to look for the everyday math in every story.

- Using a folktale of their choosing, they will create simple math problems.

National Standards:

- NCTE 1—Students read a wide range of print and non-print texts to build an understanding of texts, of themselves, and of the world; to acquire new information; and for personal fulfillment. Among these texts are fiction and nonfiction, classic and contemporary works.

- NCTE 2—Students read a wide range of literature from many periods in many genres to build an understanding of the many dimensions (e.g., philosophical, ethical, aesthetic) of human experience.

- NCTE 3—Students apply a wide range of strategies to comprehend, interpret, evaluate, and appreciate texts.

- NCTE 4—Students adjust their use of spoken, written, and visual language to communicate effectively with a variety of audiences and for different purposes.

- NCTM 1—Number and Operations

- NCTM 8—Mathematical Communication

- NCTM 9—Connections Between Mathematical Ideas

Materials:

- Paper and pencil

- Access to the library and collections of folktales

Background Information: As I was wrapping up the rough draft of this book, I had a conversation with my daughter Laurel about this chapter. I asked her what were her favorite stories that involved math? She startled me when she mentioned this story, because I had not thought of it as a math story. Once she mentioned it, lights flashed, thunder clapped, and the obvious truth rang out: This story is the perfect embodiment of my goal with this chapter. Math is a part of every story, and math need not be the focus of the story to be a math story. Thank you, Laurel.

Without much conscious thought, I had habitually done with this story the same thing I am asking students to do with their favorite story, get out the yellow highlighter and make obvious the math that is hidden in every story.

Even before it was published, I was a big fan of the idea behind *The Math Curse* by Jon Scieszka (1995). I remember when I was a third-grade teacher I had a similar conversation with my students. Math is everywhere!

Math is also a part of every story. What makes a story? Problems and solutions make a story. What is math? Math is a way to solve problems. If you look and listen carefully, you can find simple math problems in every story.

In this Indian folktale, the obvious math includes the addition and multiplication of animals, from 1 rabbit to 10,000 animals. The idea of 10,000 things is important in Eastern thought, as it symbolizes the complexity of the universe. I invite the audience to chant along: soon there were 10 monkeys, 100 monkeys, 1,000 monkeys, and in this way I emphasize place value.

I also engage the audience members by allowing them to name the next animal. After I start with rabbits and bears, they choose the next few animals, and we make the sound of that animal. The students love to roar, hiss, crow, and so forth. It does make it tricky for the teller to remember the order of animals as you go along if you let them choose, but the audience will help you remember. I always end with lion.

Instructional Procedures

Introduction: Begin this lesson with a discussion of ways in which math is a part of everyday life. Ask students to look around the room and see how math helps to hold things up, move things about, and make sense of their world. Call on a few students to share ways in which they have used math to solve a real life problem.

Introduce the idea that math is a part of every story by discussing a favorite classroom story they have all heard. As a class discuss the math within the story. Write a few math facts and problems on the board as the class shares ideas.

For example, in the first story in this book, "The Stonecutter" (see page 25), you can figure out how many stones he cut in a day and estimate how many stones he would need to cut to literally move a mountain. You can create a series of math problems around the wealthy merchant: How much does silk cost? How much money does he make from each kimono he sells? How much does he pay his servant? How many kimonos must he sell to pay his servant? With the wind or storm, you can compute the wind speed to rip up a tree or create a chart for the wind speed of F1, F2, F3, F4, and F5 tornados.

Ask them to listen carefully to the following story, making note of the math.

Tell the story!

Activity: After the story is told, discuss specific examples of the math concepts: First we count the number of rabbits and eventually we are doing simple addition, adding the number of rabbits, bears, monkeys, and so on. This is a great example of the idea that eventually addition becomes cumbersome and multiplication is speedier.

One of the concepts I emphasize in my telling and in this written script is place value. Ten peacocks become 100 peacocks, become 1,000 peacocks and eventually there are 10,000 animals. The animals multiply in multiples of 10!

As this discussion progresses, make notes on the board, ask them to speak the language of math, and to help you to write math problems and formulas, e.g., 1,000 rabbits + 1,000 bears =

2,000 animals. If each animal has four feet, then 2,000 x 4 = 8,000 feet. Once they get the idea, invite them to turn to a partner and help each other invent two math problems from the story.

As an assignment, ask students to choose one of their favorite folktales and to write several math problems. As a challenge, tell them the more problems they can create, the more points they can get. Invite them to make it easy for themselves; choose a story they know well, like the *Three Little Pigs*. At the same time, they should choose one they don't think anyone else will choose. At this point, teachers may wish to take students to the library and focus on 398.2, folktales from around the world. Or give them access to folktale archives online or provide a stack of folktale collections and picture books based on folklore. Allow ten to fifteen minutes for students to find and review a story, looking for the math hidden within.

Ask them to make a story map with five pictures like the story maps at the beginning of each story in this book, or to write a brief five-sentence synopsis of the story. And then ask them to fill the page with math problems, including the answers. Give your students approximately ten to fifteen minutes to work on this rough draft. For homework they are to create a simple worksheet with an outline or story map at the top, and their problems neatly transcribed without answers. Make it clear that these will be worksheets prepared and copied for the rest of the class.

Over the next several days, start or end each math class with a story. Allow students to perform their stories for the class, and after each student tells his or her story, pass out a math worksheet, based on the students' assignments.

Assessment: The original worksheet can be collected for a math grade. Each student can collect his or her worksheets from the class and grade them, putting points at the top that are then tallied by the teacher. The students' performances can be graded using the rubric at the end of Chapter 1.

Follow-up Activities: This kind of activity can be used as a simple but effective way of tying math into the rest of the curriculum. On an irregular basis—but not every lesson, to keep it fresh and unexpected—ask students to prepare a math worksheet from the stories they are reading, writing, or telling in science, social studies, or literature. For example, warn students in advance to include some math in their stories that evolve from the lesson plans, "Bird Is the Word," "Postcards to Mars," "Oral History Interview," or "Recipe for a Story." When students perform for the class, ask listeners to also look for the math problems and make note on the back of the rubric sheet as they evaluate the tellers.

Comments: Again, I must thank my daughter for making the obvious visible. When students are forced to write boring math stories, math is less meaningful because there is no emphasis on the plot or the story. When asked to write exciting stories and slip in some math, it becomes a game and they begin to see the math in everyday life.

"DIVIDING THE GOOSE": FRACTIONS AND THE QUAKERLY QUERY

Dividing the Goose

A long time ago in a small Russian village, there lived a poor farmer who struggled to feed his family. One year there was a terrible drought. His crops did poorly. As winter raged on, and on, and on, it appeared that his family was going to starve.

But this was a clever man who said to his wife, "Help me to roast the goose. We shall serve it to the baron so at least his family shall feast."

Now at first the wife was going to protest, "We can hardly feed our own children, why should we give our last goose to the Baron, whose children grow fat while we starve?" But she bit her tongue. She knew she had a clever husband; that was why she married him. She knew he was up to something. So she helped him to pluck and roast the last goose.

They put it on their best platter. They adorned the platter with carved beets and carrots. It was a meal befitting a king! The poor farmer draped the goose with a clean towel and a warm blanket and headed to the baron's palace.

The baron was at first surprised by the poor farmer's generous offer to provide a feast for his family. But he knew him to be a clever man and warmly welcomed him into the banqueting chamber.

With a deep bow the farmer placed the roasted goose on the table. When he straightened up, he noticed the goose was dwarfed by the amazing array of roasted deer and pig, huge pots of boiled potatoes swimming in butter, vast trays of fresh vegetables, puddings and pies, cakes and breads. It took all of his self-restraint to keep from drooling, the farmer was so hungry.

The baron stroked his beard. He looked at the goose. He looked at the farmer. He looked at his wife, his two sons, and his two daughters. A grin crept across his face. The baron said, "Please will you have supper with us? But alas, I see we have a problem with your goose. Before you sit to dine, you must divide the goose so my entire family is happy. If you can do this, then you not only can eat dinner with us, but you can take the leftovers home to feed your family."

This was the kind of thing the farmer was hoping for when he brought the goose to the baron's dinner.

From *Content Area Reading, Writing, and Storytelling: A Dynamic Tool for Improving Reading and Writing Across the Curriculum through Oral Language Development* by Brian "Fox" Ellis. Westport, CT: Teacher Ideas Press. Copyright © 2008.

[At this point pause and say to the audience, "Put yourself in the farmer's shoes. What would you do? How would you divide the goose? Imagine a goose to be like a large chicken or a small turkey. If you were listening carefully, you know how many people were eating dinner. How would you divide the goose? Think about it. Now turn to a partner and discuss the possibilities!" Give the students just one minute to talk it over, and then have them write a numerical problem and mathematical computation to express their solution.]

Well, this is what the farmer did. He took a carving knife and he cut off the legs, handing the drumsticks to each of the sons saying, "Soon you will be running this kingdom as wise rulers, and these legs will help you to run it well." The boys chuckled and began devouring the delicious drumsticks.

He cut off the wings and handed one to each daughter saying, "Soon you will spread your wings and take flight, and these wings will help you to soar!" The girls demurely smiled and daintily nibbled on the goose. The baron wiped a clandestine tear from his cheeks with the thought of his daughters growing up and taking flight; "more like swans than geese," he thought.

The farmer sliced off the rump and handed it to the baron's wife. She was at first a little embarrassed until he said, "You sit here on your throne, and we know who rules the ruler (with a wink), and this shall help to cushion your seat."

At this everyone laughed aloud, with the baroness laughing the loudest.

The farmer cut off the bony neck and handed it to the baron. Falling to one knee, he said "You are the true ruler of the roost, the leader of your people, and the head of the family, so it is only fitting that you have the neck."

Finally the clever farmer said, "And since I am your guest and a poor and hungry farmer, I will take the rest of this goose home to feed my family." Of course everyone noticed that most of the goose was still on the platter.

The entire court burst into applause. Everyone was thoroughly entertained by the clever farmer. The farmer feasted with the baron's family and left that night with a cart full of food, enough to feed his family through the rest of the winter. The chef even slipped in a large bag of potatoes and a few extra heads of cabbage.

Now, if you think this is the end of my story, you would be mistaken!

Another farmer heard what had happened and decided to go two better. He asked his wife to roast three geese so he could take them to the baron. Oh, she complained bitterly, "How shall we feed our children? I was planning to make feather pillows and a down comforter. Please do not kill our last three geese."

"You can still make your pillows, silly woman; we are not going to eat the feathers!" With that the second farmer slaughtered three geese, roasted them, and took them to the baron's castle.

Though there were more geese, the baron was less impressed. No bowing or kind words were offered by the oaf. But the baron proffered the same deal, "Before you sit to dine, you must divide the geese so my entire family is happy. If you can do this, then you not only can eat dinner with us, but you can take the leftovers home to feed your family."

The second farmer was at a loss, three geese and seven people for dinner. Though he may not have known what a prime number was, he was having a hard time dividing them. Quietly, the baron sent a rider and a horse for the first farmer.

[Again, ask students to turn to their piece of paper and try to solve the problem, showing their work!]

From *Content Area Reading, Writing, and Storytelling: A Dynamic Tool for Improving Reading and Writing Across the Curriculum through Oral Language Development* by Brian "Fox" Ellis. Westport, CT: Teacher Ideas Press. Copyright © 2008.

Well, the clever farmer knew exactly what to do. He said, "This is easy! Six people and three geese, I will divide each goose in half: half a goose for the baron, half for his wife, and half for each of the four children. As for my friend and I, we are poor peasants. We should not be so presumptuous to think that we can eat at the baron's table whenever we wish. We shall return home to eat with our families." And with a bow he turned to leave.

But the truth is . . . he rarely left the baron's side again. From that day forward, the clever farmer and his family resided in the castle. The baron counted on him to be his most trustworthy advisor in all things mathematical. The baron knew, as the farmer had so clearly shown him, that real problem solving is so much more than simple addition, subtraction, multiplication, or division—for it also takes a bit of wit!

From *Content Area Reading, Writing, and Storytelling: A Dynamic Tool for Improving Reading and Writing Across the Curriculum through Oral Language Development* by Brian "Fox" Ellis. Westport, CT: Teacher Ideas Press. Copyright © 2008.

"Dividing the Goose": Fractions and the Quakerly Query

Grade Levels: 3–12

Time Estimate: One hour

Objectives:

- Students will demonstrate listening skills in discerning the important facts in a math story.

- Students will use creative problem solving and division in dividing the goose.

- Students will learn to highlight the math in a problem-solving story.

National Standards:

- NCTE 4—Students adjust their use of spoken, written, and visual language to communicate effectively with a variety of audiences and for different purposes.

- NCTE 5—Students employ a wide range of strategies as they write and use different writing process elements appropriately to communicate with different audiences for a variety of purposes.

- NCTE 11—Students participate as knowledgeable, reflective, creative, and critical members of a variety of literacy communities.

- NCTM 1—Number and Operations

- NCTM 6—Problem Solving

- NCTM 7—Reasoning and Proof

- NCTM 8—Mathematical Communication

- NCTM 9—Connections between Mathematical Ideas

Materials:

- Paper and pencil

Background Information: I call this a Quakerly Query, because it was at a Quaker college when I was first introduced to this two-fold idea: Stories can be models for creative problem solving, and sometimes the solution isn't obvious—it raises further questions and requires contemplation. The Quakerly Query by tradition is a question not easy to answer. The truth is that *all* cultures and faiths have this tradition of using stories to teach wisdom and problem solving. It is a core value in the Jewish faith embodied in the Midrash, the stories that help common folks understand the deeper meaning of the Torah. From the fables of Aesop to the parables of Jesus, these types of stories are a deep pool of wisdom at the heart of all cultures.

Another source for these types of stories are the highly recommended books *While Standing on One Foot* (1993) and *The Cow of No Color* (1998), both by Nina Jaffe and Steve Zeitlin and published by Henry Holt. Although the first book is poignantly Jewish and the second focuses on tales of justice, they both include these kinds of creative problem-solving stories. These authors also pause the story with italicized text to invite the listeners to debate possible outcomes. The math is not always evident nor always present, but often it can be highlighted when the teacher tells the tale. In the bibliography are other stories in which the math is more evident.

This idea of telling half a story and then pausing, letting the audience discuss the facts and solve the problem, can be used for many kinds of stories in most subject areas. Using true stories from great scientists you can introduce both the science content and science-process skills. In language arts you can help students refine concepts such as foreshadowing and irony by allowing them to finish a story that you start. It is also a potent way to introduce morality and social justice with a story that asks, "What would you do in this situation?"

This Russian folktale is a wonderful opportunity to teach creative problem solving. The story demonstrates that it takes more than computation skills to effectively use math to get oneself out of a jam. There is also a higher level of division involving fractional answers and an unusual sense of fairness.

Instructional Procedures

Introduction: With very little fanfare, introduce the idea that the following story has an unusual math problem and requires creative thinking to solve it. Ask students to get out a piece of paper and pencil and listen for the math facts that might help them to solve the problem.

Activity: Tell the story, pausing twice to allow students a chance to do the problem solving.

The first problem can be discussed with a partner, but students must write down their solution, showing their work, the facts they found to be important, and how they arrived at their solution.

The second problem should be solved independently. Students should write out a math problem, but narrative text is also encouraged, allowing students a more creative solution. When they are done with their guess, finish the story.

When the story is over, discuss the details of both of their solutions and the two solutions created by the clever farmer. Few students will come to the same conclusion, but their creativity should be rewarded, highlighting both the computational skills involved and the problem-solving strategies.

Assessment: These papers can be collected for a math grade with bonus points for creativity. Even if they came up with a different solution, if their math works, they should get graded accordingly. If their math does not work, they can still get points for showing their work and extra points for any narrative explanation.

Follow-up Activities: Another way to run this lesson plan involves students in actually writing a narrative ending to the story after the second farmer's problem is introduced and the baron sends for the first clever farmer; ask students to get out a clean piece of paper and write the ending of the story before you read or tell the traditional ending.

Or students can be asked to rewrite the entire story using the same characters, setting and plotline and the same sequence of events, but they can insert their math and their solutions to the problem of dividing the goose.

This clever farmer—and his clever wife, if the girls want a female character—can become the star of a series of stories. Ask students to use the same character and setting to create a new story. Now that the clever family has become advisors to the baron, how can they use math to solve a new problem that might come up for the royal family? First, introduce the day, the new characters, and the new problem. Use creative problem solving, a twist the audience may not see coming, and make sure that the basic math skills are obvious. Encourage students to use the math that has recently been covered in class, be it fractions, multiplication, or geometry. These stories can be performed for the class and collected into a book. Students can add new stories to the book whenever the clever farmer and his wife solve new problems.

Comments: Students love this story! More important, they love this process. The idea that they can be like detectives and use what they have just learned in math class to figure out a puzzle will make math fun and meaningful. And though I have heard lots of clever answers, no one has given the same answer as the clever farmer.

"A FATHER'S GIFT OF CAMELS": A STORYBOARD AND PRIME NUMBERS

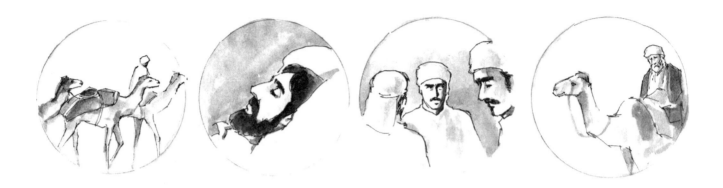

In the ancient lands now known as Saudi Arabia, there lived a wealthy merchant. He had a large herd of camels. He traveled the Silk Road through the highlands of the Middle and Far East. He crossed the deserts of Africa. He went wherever his business took him. He bought and sold silk, salt and exotic spices, jade, rubies, and pearls, gorgeous hand-woven carpets, olive oil and dried figs. He did quite well for himself, and his family prospered.

When his time came to leave this world, he left his herd of camels to his three sons. His hope was that his sons would follow in his footsteps, travel the world, and build a successful business just as he had.

After the funeral, once the tears were dried, the three sons got together to read the father's will and divide the family's wealth.

The old man had 17 camels. To his oldest son he gave one-half of his herd. To the second son he gave one-third of his camels. To his youngest son he gave one-ninth of the herd. The three boys were puzzled by this. Their father had taught them the value of math; he often said, "To be a successful merchant you must know how to add and subtract, multiply and divide, quickly, in your mind."

But the boys saw no solution. What is half of 17? What is one-third of a prime number? Do we slaughter a camel? What would you do?

[*At this point, ask the students to get out their pencil and paper and play with the facts. If anyone can figure out the solution, offer a prize, even if it is just a round of applause or standing ovation from their peers.*]

As the boys were discussing their dilemma, on the verge of an argument, an old man happened upon the scene. He heard the harsh words and steered his camel toward the noise. He asked if he could be of some assistance. The oldest son explained, "Our beloved father recently passed away and he left his camels to us, his three sons. I, the oldest son, will get one-half of the 17 camels."

The second son chimed in and said, "I will receive one-third of the 17 camels."

"But I only get one-ninth," said the youngest son, "What is one-ninth of seventeen?"

From Content Area Reading, Writing, and Storytelling: A Dynamic Tool for Improving Reading and Writing Across the Curriculum through Oral Language Development by Brian "Fox" Ellis. Westport, CT: Teacher Ideas Press. Copyright © 2008.

The old man got down off his camel. He said, "I see a solution. Let me give you my camel, this will make it all easier."

"No, no, no," all three boys responded.

"That is very generous of you, but we cannot accept." The oldest son tried to politely decline the offer, but the old man would not give up.

"But I insist. Here, take my camel. Now you have 18 camels."

The oldest son grinned, saying, "Ah yes, half of eighteen is nine, I will take nine camels, half of this herd."

The second son said, "I see! One-third of eighteen is six. I will take six camels, one-third of the herd."

The youngest son, smiled, "One-ninth of eighteen is two. I get two camels, a boy and a girl, and one day I will have as many camels as my father had!"

After each son took his camels, they noticed there was one left. The old man got back on his camel and quietly rode away.

From *Content Area Reading, Writing, and Storytelling: A Dynamic Tool for Improving Reading and Writing Across the Curriculum through Oral Language Development* by Brian "Fox" Ellis. Westport, CT: Teacher Ideas Press. Copyright © 2008.

"A Father's Gift of Camels": A Storyboard and Prime Numbers

Grade Levels: 3–12

Time Estimate: 25 minutes

Objectives:

- Students will practice division skills.

- Students will model creative problem solving.

- Students will use a storyboard to help map out a math problem.

National Standards:

- NCTE 11—Students participate as knowledgeable, reflective, creative, and critical members of a variety of literacy communities.

- NCTE 12—Students use spoken, written, and visual language to accomplish their own purposes (e.g., for learning, enjoyment, persuasion, and the exchange of information).

- NCTM 1—Number and Operations

- NCTM 2—Algebra

- NCTM 6—Problem Solving

- NCSS 7—Production, Distribution, and Consumption

Materials:

- Paper and pencil

Background Information: I first heard this story told by Jean Liggett, my first storytelling mentor. By day she was a quiet librarian who also ran the peer-tutoring program where I worked a minimum-wage job to help pay for college. Frequently, she would disappear to tour the world regaling audiences with wild stories of her world travels. Everywhere she went, she collected tiny toys, souvenirs that became symbolic memory keepers to help her remember a story. She kept them in a large basket and often let a child pick a toy, and that is how she would choose the next story to tell. In the basket was a small wooden camel.

"One small camel can solve a mighty big problem," is how she would start the story.

Although I use very few props when I tell stories, this is a story where you are heartily encouraged to cut out 18 camels or draw 17 camels on the board before you begin and add 1 camel when the time is right. Tape or a magnet on the back of the camel will help it stick.

Instructional Procedures

Introduction: Warn students that they will be asked to solve the problem in the middle of the story and that they should listen for clues that will help them. Insist that they have paper and pencil ready before you begin the story, so they can do the math.

Activity: As you tell the story, place 17 camels on the board.

After you set up the problem, pause in the middle of the story and ask students to first work out a possible solution on paper: Write out the important math facts, create an equation using numbers to write the problem, and try to solve it to the best of their ability. Warn them that this is not easy, and you do not expect anyone to get it right the first time. Allow two or three minutes of independent work.

Then invite them to turn to a partner and discuss their solution. Do not erase anything, but give them a few minutes to see if they can work out a new, better solution with their partner. After a few minutes, open the discussion to include the entire class.

If any students get the same answer as the old man, please encourage them to stand up and take a bow—give them a round of applause or standing ovation! When the class begs for the right answer, tell the rest of the story.

When the story is over, ask this simple question: What are the math concepts involved in this story? Take notes on the board. Using a Socratic questioning approach, help students who understand to explain it to those who may be a little foggy about the concepts. The conversation should cover fractions, common denominators, the idea of prime numbers, and borrowing to help solve a problem.

Give each student a copy of the black-line master and allow a few minutes for them to cut out 18 camels. While they are cutting out camels, make a storyboard or story map on the board, asking students to help you remember what happens next—and then what happens, and then what happens—until they have the outline. Ask them to take turns rehearsing the story with a partner.

For homework, challenge students to go home and tell the story to everyone who will listen. The more signatures they collect, the more points they get. Students can write their own note:

I heard _____ tell the story of "A Father's Gift of Camels."

Signed _____

Signed _____

Signed _____

Assessment: Collect students' rough notes from listening to the story and award points based on how well they listened, the math facts they heard and noted, and the design of their math problem. Award extra points if they took notes on the conversation with their partner and the classroom conversation, and give bonus points if they got it right! Students can also earn credit for the number of signatures on their homework assignment.

Follow-up Activities: This story can become a model for students to create their own complex math problem story. Instead of camels, they can rewrite the story using an imaginary argument with a friend over dividing up a bag of candy or they can set the story in the Wild West and have cowboys dividing horses. Using the five Ws and an H on pages 42–43, students can take this old story and make it new.

Comments: I love this story. I love stumping the audience, and I love the "Aha!" moment when they figure out what the old man is doing just before I get there. But I will also admit that the fractions can be confusing, and on more than one occasion, I have misstated the fraction, using one-third, one-sixth, and one-ninth, or was it one-half . . . . Review the fractions each time just before you tell the story.

CHAPTER 6

CREATING THEMATIC UNITS

STORIES AS THE WARP AND WEAVE FOR INTEGRATING THE CURRICULUM

If I were the curriculum coordinator for a large urban school district, I would encourage every teacher to make storytelling the core of the curriculum. Stories are an exciting way to introduce ideas, immerse students in the various content areas, and tie the curriculum together in ways that make sense for students. Storytelling is also a powerful tool for students to show what they have learned. As outlined in the preface, storytelling is the perfect "warp and weave" for integrating the curriculum. The goal of each of the preceding chapters was to demonstrate how to use storytelling in each individual content area. If the preface and introduction are the heart and soul of this book, then the following chapter is the DNA, the code that gives the instructional manual for making it all work together.

In this chapter, I share with you one way to use one story to create an interdisciplinary unit that neatly ties together African culture, literature, geography, ecology, math, economics, dance, and art—all strands woven out of a single story. More important, there is a frame, a format for extracting similar interdisciplinary units out of every story in this book. There is indeed a *math* lesson in every *science* story that can be viewed through a *cultural* or *historical* lens, all wrapped with *poetry* and *literature*.

If you teach in a junior high or high school with departmental teams, please allow me to gently twist your arm. Get up and walk down the hall to your colleague's room with this book in hand. Share the lesson plan of the "Talking Yam," telling them you are going to make their life easier by providing a lesson plan for them, one that each of them will do a piece of and therefore reinforce what the others are doing, making everyone's job a little easier and their students' education more meaningful! Continue the conversation: Using the format for creating your own interdisciplinary units, open a monthly dialogue on ways you can use storytelling to weave the curriculum together all year 'round.

A careful glance at the table of contents reveals that there are also threads throughout the book that can be used to tie together the various stories and create dozens of interdisciplinary units. Here are three examples:

1.   "Bird Is the Word," page 148, is a great introduction to . . .

2.   rewriting "Audubon," page 159, which could lead into a . . .

3.   The activity beginning on page 152, about students' favorite bird.

These lessons together can interweave scientific illustrations, poetry, narrative, and expository writing with a cultural folktale, maps of bird migrations, field ecology, and a study of ornithology. A similar set of lessons could weave fables with ecological studies of mammals or plants or insects or rocks, instead of birds.

Another lesson on personal and family history:

1.   "Buzzard Baked Beans" and a "Personal Narrative," page 63, introduces . . .

2.   "Prairie Fire" and an "Oral History" project, page 89.

And if you weave in a genealogical timeline, a family tree, and a family portrait, this narrative makes a personal connection to history, the math of a timeline, the genetics of inheritance, and the art of portraiture or fine art photography and computer graphics.

Follow the strands and weave together a dozen interdisciplinary lessons.

In this chapter, I have also invited two of my friends and colleagues to contribute stories and interdisciplinary lesson plans. Phyllis Hostemeyer is not only a dynamic and hilarious storyteller, but also one of the most sought-after school consultants who motivates and inspires teachers to step up to best practices in language arts and literacy instruction. Dr. Kevin Cordi shares a portion of his newly minted Ph.D. thesis based on dozens of years of teaching storytelling fulltime in a California high school. His lesson is an innovative adaptation of process drama to blend storytelling with authentic student-led inquiry. Because I also believe that everyone tells stories in their unique way and it is good to see several models, Kevin and Phyllis present different models for designing lesson plans. Use these models to create your own.

But first, it is my turn.

"THE TALKING YAM": A THEMATIC UNIT ON WEST AFRICA AND CULTURAL BIO-GEOGRAPHY

Theme: Cultural Bio-Geography: How cultures reflect their ecosystems through their folklore.

Grade Levels: 5–12

Time Estimate: 5–7 class periods

The stories people tell about themselves are the best way to get an insider's view of a culture and its relationship to the environment. Imagine a triangle of social studies, science, and language arts. Folktales are the key to understanding the reciprocal relationships between these content areas.

Goals: The primary goal of this unit is to help students see how cultures are influenced by their ecosystem. Folktales give us an in-depth look at a culture as its members see themselves. Students will also get a deeper look at their own culture of origin as reflected by the other cultures.

National Standards:

- NCTE 1—Students read a wide range of print and non-print texts to build an understanding of texts, of themselves, and of the world; to acquire new information; and for personal fulfillment. Among these texts are fiction and nonfiction, classic and contemporary works.

- NCTE 2—Students read a wide range of literature from many periods in many genres to build an understanding of the many dimensions (e.g., philosophical, ethical, aesthetic) of human experience.

- NCTE 3—Students apply a wide range of strategies to comprehend, interpret, evaluate, and appreciate texts.

- NCTE 4—Students adjust their use of spoken, written, and visual language to communicate effectively with a variety of audiences and for different purposes.

- NCTE 5—Students employ a wide range of strategies as they write and use different writing process elements appropriately to communicate with different audiences for a variety of purposes.

- NCTE 6—Students apply knowledge of language structure, language conventions, media techniques, figurative language, and genre to create, critique, and discuss print and nonprint texts.

- NCTE 7—Students conduct research on issues and interests by generating ideas and questions, and by posing problems. They gather, evaluate, and synthesize data from a variety of sources to communicate their discoveries in ways that suit their purpose and audience.

- NCSS 1—Culture

- NCSS 3—People, Places, and Environments

- NCSS 6—Power, Authority and Governance

- NCSS 7—Production, Distribution, and Consumption

- NCSS 9—Global Connections

- NCTM 1—Number and Operations

- NCTM 6—Problem Solving

- NCTM 8 Mathematical Communication

- NCTM 9—Connections Between Mathematical Ideas

- NAS 3—Life Science: Structure and function in living systems; Reproduction and heredity; Regulation and behavior; Populations and ecosystems; Diversity and adaptations of organisms.

- NAS 4—Earth Science: Structure of the earth system; Earth's history

"The Talking Yam" (also known as "Talk, Talk")

[*Suggestions for telling: This is a fun story to play with character voices and accents. There are also lots of opportunities for wild gestures, pulling up the vine, plucking a branch, laying it down, running in place, having a net on your head, taking a bath, and including the regal authority of the oba. Invite the audience to say everything that is in parentheses and italics.*]

Before I begin this story, I would like to ask: Have any of you ever talked to someone, maybe an adult, who just ignored you? How did that make you feel? I find it interesting that every culture tells stories about a time when the animals could talk and the people still listened. This is a story from West Africa about that time when the people first forgot how to listen and the creatures were not very happy about it!

Now I need your help with this story. It repeats itself, *a lot*. If you hear me say something that I have already said, please say it with me the second time and the third time, and by the fourth and fifth time, you can say it on your own. If you join in, you will learn this story.

Early one morning, a farmer went out to harvest some yams, some sweet potatoes. He grabbed one of the vines to pull, when the yam said, "Get your hands off of me!" W-H-A-A! (Can you say that? *"Get your hands off of me!"*) He jumped back, and his dog teased him. His dog said, "You better listen to your yam!" (*"You better listen to your yam!"*) He wasn't taking this from a dog! So the farmer plucked a branch off the tree and the tree said, "Put that branch down!" (*"Put that branch down!"*) He put the branch down, and the branch said, "Put me down gently." (*"Put me down gently."*) He was about to put the branch on a rock when the rock said, "Get that thing off of me!" (*"Get that thing off of me!"*)

The farmer ran away, thinking he was losing his mind. He went running, running, running down the road when he met a fisherman with a net coiled on top of his head, heading to the river to catch some fish, because that is what a fisherman does. The fisherman said, "Whoa, why are you running on such a hot African morning?"

(This time say the plant and animal parts along with me.) The farmer said, "I know you are not going to believe me. I hardly believe it myself, but this morning when I went out to pull up a yam, my yam said, 'Get your hands off of me!' Then my dog made fun of me, my dog said, 'You better listen to your yam!' I wasn't taking this from a dog! So I grabbed a branch off the tree and the tree said, 'Put that branch down!' I went to put the branch down and the branch said, 'Put me down gently.' I put the branch on a rock when the rock said,

'Get that thing off of me!' That's when I knew I was losing my mind. That's when I took off running and that's when I met you."

The fisherman shook his head. He did not believe a word of it, until his net said, "You better believe him, he's telling the truth." (*"You better believe him, he's telling the truth."*) W-H-A-A! The two of them took off running, running, running down the road until they met a weaver with a bolt of cloth under his arm, heading to the marketplace to sell, barter or trade.

A weaver is a man or woman who weaves thread into cloth. Look now at your shirt; look closely and you might see the threads knit or woven together. Have you ever seen kente cloth from West Africa with its beautiful red, black, green, and gold patterns? The weaver said, "Whoa, why are you running on such a hot African morning?"

The farmer said, "I know you are not going to believe me, but this morning when I went out to pull up a yam, my yam said, 'Get your hands off of me!' Then my dog said, 'You better listen to your yam!' I grabbed a branch off the tree and the tree said, 'Put that branch down.' I went to put the branch down and the branch said, 'Put me down gently.' I put the branch on a rock when the rock said, 'Get that thing off of me!' That's when I knew I was losing my mind. The fisherman said he did not believe me until his net said, 'You better believe him, he's telling the truth.' That's when we took off running and that is when we met you."

The weaver said, "Whether you are telling the truth or not, it's too hot a day to be running." But then his cloth said, "You'd run too if it happened to you." (*"You'd run too if it happened to you."*) W-H-A-A! The three of them took off running, running, running down the road.

Next they met a man bathing in the river. He was under water, so you could not see anything, if you know what I mean. And though you might laugh, how many of you have ever been swimming in a pond, stream, or river?

The man in the river said, "Whoa, why are you running on such a hot African morning?"

(I'll set you up, but this time, see if you can say the plant and animal parts on your own.) The farmer said, "I know you are not going to believe me, but this morning when I went out to pull up a yam, my yam said, 'Take your hands off of me!' Then my dog made fun of me, my dog said, 'You better listen to your yam!' I wasn't taking this from a dog! So I grabbed a branch off the tree and the tree said, 'Put that branch down.' I went to put the branch down and the branch said, 'Put me down gently.' I put the branch on a rock when the rock said, 'Get that thing off of me!' That's when I knew I was losing my mind. That's when I took off running, and that's when I met the fisherman."

"The fisherman did not believe me until his net said, 'You better believe him; he's telling the truth.' Then we met the weaver. The weaver said, 'It's too hot a day to be running.' His cloth said, 'You'd run too if it happened to you.' And that's when we met you."

The man in the river said, "Your friend is right; whether you are telling the truth or not, it is too hot a day to be running. Why don't you peel off those hot, dusty, dirty clothes and take a cool refreshing bath in the river?"

Just then the river said, "I don't want them fools in me!" (*"I don't want them fools in me!"*) W-H-A-A!!! They took off running, running, running down the road.

They were promptly arrested—arrested for disturbing the peace. They were taken before the Oba; can you say oba? The oba is the ruler of his people. Here in America, you would call him the mayor; in Germany, he would be the bergermeister; but in West Africa he is the oba.

The oba sat on his large wooden throne. Can you imagine a throne carved with leopards, snakes, and birds? He looked the folks over carefully. He turned to the farmer and said, "You, sir, you seem to be the root of the problem. What is going on here?"

[*At this point the story is funnier if you have a well-trained audience and they say the plant and animal parts without you. When their turn comes up, point at them and let them jump in.*]

The farmer said (in a pleading voice), "Oh kind and wonderful oba, Oh wise and wonderful oba, I know you are not going to believe me. *Nobody* believes me! But this morning when I went out to pull up a yam, my yam said, 'Take your hands off of me!' Then, then, my d-d-dog made fun of me, my dog said, 'You better listen to your yam!' I was not taking this from a dog! So I grabbed a branch off the tree and the tree said, 'Put that branch down.' That was a big tree, yes sir, so I did as I was told. I went to put the branch down and the branch said, 'Put me down gently.' I put the branch on a rock and the rock said, 'Get that thing off of me!' That's when I knew I was losing my mind. That's when I took off running and that's when I met the fisherman. I-I-I will let him t-t-tell the rest of the story."

The fisherman said, "I heard the same tale you just heard, and I did not believe him until my net said, 'You better believe him, he's telling the truth.' That's when we took off running, we met the weaver, and I will let him tell the rest of the story."

The weaver said, "I, too, heard this tale. I told them it's too hot a day to be running. But then my cloth said, 'You'd run too if it happened to you.' We took off running, and that's when we met the man in the river. I'll let him tell the rest of this story."

The man from the river said, "I wasn't causing any problem. I was just taking a bath. I saw these men come running down the road. I invited them to take a bath in the cool refreshing water, when the river said, 'I don't want them fools in me!'"

The farmer picked up the end of the story. He said, "Oh wise and wonderful oba, I swear to you it is true, the whole truth and nothing but the truth, Oh, kind and compassionate oba."

Well it was true, at least the part about the oba being wise and wonderful. He said, "Get up, man. You are making a fool of yourself. I will make a deal with you. You know how I love yams, sweet potato pie, and sweet potato pudding. But when I sent my chef to the marketplace, there were no yams to be had. I will set you free if you will go and harvest some yams and bring them here before lunch!"

The farmer said, "Thank you I will go and get um . . . there must be some yams somewhere who are not talking." And he ran off.

The oba turned to the fisherman and made the same deal. "You know how I love fish, fried fish, smoked fish, broiled fish, but when I sent my chef to the marketplace, there were no fish to buy. Go! Catch some fish and bring them here before supper time, and I will set you free."

The fisherman said, "I remember where my-my . . . I will get a new net." And the fisherman ran off.

The oba turned to the weaver and said, "Think about this. You know how the children love to wear beautiful new clothing to school. If there is no cloth in the marketplace, how will their parents make new clothes? What will the children wear to school? Do you want them to come to school dressed like the fourth man?" The weaver ran away.

The oba looked the fourth man up and down and said, "Get some clothes on!"

The fourth man ran away leaving the oba by himself. He sat back on his throne scratching his head. He said to no one in particular, "What a crazy village. What crazy people. What a crazy story."

When all of the sudden his throne said, "Well, if you ask me, I think it was a pretty funny story!"

Sources: I first heard this story told by Mapopa Mtonga, a storyteller from Zimbabwe whom I hosted as an artist in residence at the school where I taught in North Carolina. He spent a week teaching storytelling, dance, and drumming. The story is also readily available in several books, such as *The Cow Tail Switch* (H. Courlander, Boston: Houghton Mifflin, 1991); *Talk, Talk* (D. M. N. Chocolate, Mahwah, NJ: Troll Associates, 1993); *Favorite Folk Tales from Around the World* (J. Yolen, New York: Random House, 1986).

From *Content Area Reading, Writing, and Storytelling: A Dynamic Tool for Improving Reading and Writing Across the Curriculum through Oral Language Development* by Brian "Fox" Ellis. Westport, CT: Teacher Ideas Press. Copyright © 2008.

Lesson Plans

Introduction: Before telling the story, you can discuss whether plants and animals talk, how people feel when they are not heard, and the use and respect of natural materials. Inherent in this story is the belief that nonhumans can communicate. There was a time when all people believed this, and some of us still do. You may want to discuss how their pets let them know what they want. For example, how do you know if your dog wants to be let out, wants his belly rubbed, or something to eat? What does your pet do when it feels like it is not being heard? What do you do when you are ignored? How do you feel when you are taken advantage of by someone in power? Do you use natural resources without being respectful? How can we show our respect to natural materials? Some of these questions you may want to discuss after the story.

Before telling the story, pass out copies of the "Multicultural Questionnaire" (see p. 208). As a class or in small groups, ask students to discuss these questions in terms of their culture. You may have to do a little pre-teaching or review of some of the concepts in the questionnaire. Challenge them to listen to the story carefully, and most of these questions will be answered by the story.

Language Arts

Listening and Speaking Skills: Through the call-and-response and repetition of the key lines, students learn to be active rather than passive listeners, knowing when to chime in and when to be quiet. They learn sequential order and cause and effect through the anticipation of who or what will speak next. This story also presents an opportunity to experiment with emotional timbre by exploring different emotional reactions to the farmer's story. With a little coaching, students could discuss culturally sensitive dialects in the retelling of this tale.

Reading Skills: This story can be easily found in multiple versions and in multiple texts (see Resources). Students can read two or three versions of the story and compare and contrast the differences between them.

Writing Skills: Use this story as a model to help students write their own. Invite students to imagine an "average" morning routine for themselves and their family. Ask them to make a sequential list of what they do as a part of their morning routine. In this scenario, who or what would talk to them? What would they say? Who would they tell and how would their friends or family respond? Who or what would talk to each of your family members or friends? Who is the authority figure? Who would put a stop to this nonsense, and what would talk to them in the end? They may want to use a multi-tiered flow chart—a graphic organizer—to map out their story (see diagram 210).

Social Studies Concepts: Cross-cultural comparison. After the story is over, review the Multicultural Questionnaire. Ask students to work by themselves to answer as many questions as they can about West African culture based on the story. Ask students to move into small groups and discuss their answers. Next, ask them to create a Venn diagram to compare and contrast their culture with the culture depicted in this story. What do they have in common with West African people, and how are they different? Discuss these comparisons as a class, emphasizing the similarities between cultures and our basic human needs. What makes us human? Discuss our differences in light of environmental influences and how people adapt to different ecosystems.

The science and math lessons are directly related to these social studies concepts, and social studies are an integral part of these next two lessons.

Science Concept: Ecological influences on culture.

Materials:

- Four maps of Africa: cultural, ecological, elevation, and rainfall

As a class, discuss the ecosystem where you live and how it influences your lifestyle. As urban humans, we tend to think we control our environment; it doesn't control us. Obviously we are fooling ourselves. How do our clothing styles change when the weather changes? How does the food we eat change seasonally? We import a lot of our food, but has anyone eaten any gazelle or breadfruit lately? Clearly, the environment has a major effect—a multitude of effects—on our daily life. Over time the environment shapes the culture of the people living there.

Find four good color-coded maps of Africa: topography or elevation, rainfall, plant life or biomes, and tribal groups (not a political map). Study and discuss each map one at a time. First look at the elevation map. Discuss how the terrain, landforms, mountains, and elevation affect the available water, food, rainfall, and plant life. Ask students to predict where the deserts and rainforests might be. Next, look at the map that shows rainfall. Compare these two maps and discuss if their predictions were accurate. Discuss concrete examples of the ways elevation and landform influence rainfall. Explain the rain-shadow effect on the backside of mountains. Mid-continent regions, removed from the oceans, tend to be drier, like Africa's savannas and America's prairies. Using these two maps together, ask students to predict what types of plants and animals live in each region of the continent. Again, where are the rainforests and where are the deserts? Next, look at the map of ecological regions and discuss their predictions. How does rainfall and terrain affect what types of plants live where? How does the plant life influence the animals? Make a brief list of the plants and animals in each ecosystem. Which ones have adapted to several environments? How have humans adapted to the various ecosystems?

Saving the map of cultural groups as a grand finale, show them the fourth map. When I first saw this correlation, it left me speechless. It expanded my awareness of the many ways the environment influences our daily lives, our culture, our religion, our history, fashion, our foods . . . every facet of our lives. (Doesn't this make it all the more essential that we protect the environment?) Rainfall affects culture, which in turn affects our language. The Inuit of the far north have many words for snow. We have one. Discuss ways that the environment influences daily life and how daily life over time shapes a culture. Go back to the Multicultural Questionnaire and reevaluate question 6.

These maps also raise important questions about the political maps and how European colonists carved up the country, disrespecting the natural and cultural boundaries—bad decisions that still haunt Africa politically and that are one of the roots of ongoing strife, civil war, and recent genocide.

As a follow-up lesson, ask students to work in small groups to study other cultures in Africa, or other continents, and to evaluate how the culture is influenced by their environment. You could use a jigsaw model of cooperation. Each group of four students chooses one culture to study. Within this group each student chooses a topic, such as food and fashion; shelter and jobs; music, dance, and art; or ritual and religions. Students can then do a little independent research into their culture's specific topic. Four small groups can then come together to share notes: the food group meets in one corner; the shelter group meets in another corner; the ritual-religion group in a third corner; and the music, dance, and art group in the other corner of the room.

The cooperative groups then come together and each student teaches their peers about their specialty. Each cooperative group can build a mini-museum exhibit that includes dioramas, displays, and informational placards. The exhibit will be a combination of anthropology and environmental studies with an emphasis on how cultures reflect their ecosystem and on how the available natural materials influence the culture.

Each cooperative group can also research a traditional folktale from its chosen culture and perform it as a skit. Reviewing the Multicultural Questionnaire, the class as a whole can discuss this cultural group in light of their culture and the West African culture depicted in "The Talking Yam."

This same kind of lesson plan can be used with traditional American Indian cultural groups and the ecosystems of North America. In both instances it is important to highlight that these are studies of traditional cultures, historic and current. You may wish to discuss how cultures change through time, how these cultures have been influenced by modern cultures, and how these cultures have contributed to modern culture.

Math Concept: Addition, economics, the value of labor, and profit margins.

Materials:

- Beads

- String

- Heavy-duty paper plates

- Pencil and paper

Within the story of "The Talking Yam," are three references to a marketplace where the weaver will barter or trade his goods, where the farmer could sell his yams, and where the oba sent his chef to buy fish for dinner. This marketplace economy provides an opportunity for a study of economics, labor, art, and math.

Ask students if they have ever been to a flea market, garage sale, church craft fair, or another type of informal marketplace. Discuss how things are "valued" at such a market and how prices vary depending on supply and demand, the materials used, and the labor that goes into it. For example, a quilt that used free materials—old scrapes—as a raw material is still very expensive because of the intensive labor and artistic value added by its creator.

Use this discussion as a springboard for an art project in which the students compute the costs of their materials and labor versus the sale price and profit margin.

At any local craft supply store, you can acquire a wide variety of inexpensive beads. Plastic, glass, clay, wood, shell, bone, horn, semiprecious stones, and seeds are all easily found. Arrange the beads in trays or bowls and label each bowl, including the cost per bead, material, and country of origin. Before you display the beads or let students take any, show them a few basic necklace designs. Invite them to bring some small change to purchase beads. Yes, make it clear that students will purchase beads at wholesale costs, because part of the lesson is about value, profit versus costs.

There are many one-penny beads or beads you can get three for a penny. A student with 10 cents or 15 cents can make a beautiful necklace. There are some beads that are 5 cents, 10 cents, 25 cents, 50 cents, 75 cents, $1.00, $25.00, $100.00, or more. Collectable beads, antiques, and ancient tribal beads are widely available for those who can afford them. Emphasize that it is not how much you spend on beads but the design, use of color, and creativity put into the final product.

When I first presented this lesson to my seventh-grade class, some of the students who could afford only a small handful of beads were more careful about their choices and designs. Later when the class traded and bartered, these students acquired more expensive beads on poorly strung necklaces, which they cut, restrung, and traded for a profit!

When you begin selling beads, emphasize that you are working on an honor system—that students are responsible for their own integrity *and* accuracy in buying beads. Each student takes a paper plate and sheet of paper. As they choose beads to add to their cup, they write down the quantity, type, color, material and costs. Two examples:

5 red glass beads from the Czech Republic at 1 cent each	$0.05
4 white bone tubes from Hong Kong at 15 cents each	$0.60
Total	**$0.65**

20 black glass beads from Czech Republic at 1cent each	$0.20
4 red glass beads from Czech Republic at 1 cent each	$0.04
4 green glass beads from Czech Republic at 1cent each	$0.04
4 yellow glass beads from Czech Republic at 1 cent each	$0.04
Total	**$0.32**

After they choose their beads and tally their sheets, they pay for them. Then they can make their necklaces. With younger children, you may need to walk them through the processes of cutting string to the right length—too long is better than too short; arranging a pattern and stringing the beads; tying knots to space beads; and tying a final knot so it fits over their heads, unless they also purchase clasps.

The final thing students need to do to earn their grade—remember, this *is* a math/economics class—they need to develop a sheet that includes their bead costs, an estimate of the value of their labor, and an appreciation of profit and the retail price.

Costs of beads	$0.32
Labor cost (1/2 hour at $10 per hour)	$5.00
Profit Margin	$4.68
Retail Price	$10.00

This could lead to a fruitful discussion of profit margins, the value of labor, labor management, and minimum wage. Also, now that students have performed some craft work and have an idea of the labor that goes into handmade goods, you can estimate the labor in other goods and discuss sweatshop production versus fine-quality crafts.

Physical Education, Dance, and Music: Invite an African dancer to your school to teach a harvest dance.

Other Lessons: As you can see, this lesson requires some rather complex analysis, comparison and contrast, application of the concepts to the study of a new culture, and internalization of cultural bio-geography. The most important lesson is the yin and yang of helping students to value their culture in comparison to other cultures, while developing tolerance for cultural differences.

Assessment: The stories students write will receive two language arts grades: one for creativity and style and a second grade for spelling, grammar, and punctuation. The Venn diagram will be collected for a social studies grade with points being given for answering all twelve questions on the Multicultural Questionnaire, answering questions twice, both for their culture and the one depicted in the story. Their science projects will receive two grades; one for the research they do on their specific topic and a team grade for the diorama they co-create. The math grade will be based on the costs/profit sheet they generate, along with a brief essay on the value of labor and reasonable profit.

Storytelling and Multicultural Understanding

Within every story there is a wealth of information about the culture that told the tale. If you would like to study another culture and its beliefs, ***cultural anthropology,*** one of the best ways to gain an understanding of their way of life and their values is through their stories. Through their folktales and mythology, you can see a group of people as they see themselves. A careful reading of the tale will answer a variety of questions about their political system, religious beliefs, economics and market systems, their relationship to the environment, the family and social structures, as well as the material culture and what types of food, shelter, and clothing they used. Ways in which we are different and alike can also be seen. Not every story will answer every question, but as you read your story, keep the following questions in mind:

1.   What type of foods do they eat?

2.   What kind of home or shelter do they have?

3.   What kind of clothing do they wear?

4.   Are they farmers, hunters and gatherers, or merchants and craftsmen?

5.   In what kind of environment do they live?

6.   How does the environment influence the answers to questions 1–4?

7.   What type of political system do they have (e.g., monarchy, oligarchy, democracy, or republic)?

 From *Content Area Reading, Writing, and Storytelling: A Dynamic Tool for Improving Reading and Writing Across the Curriculum through Oral Language Development* by Brian "Fox" Ellis. Westport, CT: Teacher Ideas Press. Copyright © 2008.

8. Is there a general equality, or are there vast differences in wealth and power?

9. What is valued (e.g., money, wealth, and power; or wisdom, love, and family relationships)?

10. What are their religious beliefs? Do they believe in spirits, one God, or many gods?

11. What kind of family structure do they have? Does the mother or father have more power? Is it a large family? Do grandparents and other relatives all live together in one household? Is there more than one wife?

12. What kind of taboos do they have? What is forbidden?

You may want to answer these same questions about your culture to make the following chart. List three ways your culture is like the culture in this story, and three ways each are different.

A. SIMILAR	B. DIFFERENT
1.	1.
2.	2.
3.	3.

After you have read your story, answer as many of these questions as you can on another sheet of paper. Support your answers with evidence from the story. For example, in "Jack and the Bean Stalk," we know they are farmers because they have a cow. They drink milk and eat beans. We also know that some people are poor like Jack and his mom, and some are rich like the Giant. Jack was raised by a single mother. They believe in magic, the beans. In some versions of the story, they talk about the king, so we know their political system was a monarchy. Isn't it amazing how much we can learn from a single story?

A Flow Chart for Creating Your Own Version of "The Talking Yam"

What do you see first
thing in the morning?

1

If it could talk,
what would it say?

What do you see next?

2

What would it say?

What do you see next?

3

What would it say?

What would you see next?

4

What would it say?

Next?

5

What would it say?

Who would you meet first?

6

Cycle back

How would they respond?
What talks to them?

Who would you meet next?

7

Cycle

How would they respond?
What talks to them?

Next?

8

Cycle

How would they respond?
What talks?

Next?

9

Cycle

How would they respond?
What talks?

What authority figure would you encounter?

10

How would he/she respond?
And how does the story end?

Format for Creating Your Own Story-Based Interdisciplinary Lessons

STORY: _____

THEME: _____ GRADE LEVEL: _____

GOALS: _____

_____

_____

NATIONAL STANDARDS:

English: _____ Social Studies: _____

Math: _____ Science: _____

OTHER: _____

STORY SYNOPSIS:

_____

_____

INTRODUCTION TO THE UNIT:

_____

_____

LANGUAGE ARTS LESSON PLANS

Listening Skills: _____

_____

Speaking Skills: _____

_____

Reading Skills: _____

_____

Writing Skills: _____

_____

SOCIAL STUDIES CONCEPT: _____

_____

Lesson Plan: _____

_____

_____

_____

_____

SCIENCE CONCEPT: _____

Hands-on Lesson Plan: _____

_____

_____

MATH OR PROBLEM-SOLVING CONCEPT: _____

Lesson Plan: _____

_____

_____

_____

_____

PHYSICAL EDUCATION OR OPPORTUNITY FOR MOVEMENT: _____

_____

_____

MUSIC, VISUAL, OR PERFORMING ARTS: _____

_____

_____

OTHER LESSONS IN COOPERATION, HIGHER-LEVEL THINKING, OR LIFE SKILLS:

_____

_____

EVALUATION: _____

_____

_____

SOURCES: _____

_____

_____

"THE DUNG BEETLE AND THE EAGLE": STORY AND LESSONS BY PHYLLIS HOSTMEYER

A young hare was eating grass and enjoying the early morning sun. As he nibbled the tender shoots, he suddenly noticed an eagle gliding in the sky above him. The young hare froze, hoping that the eagle, with its keen vision, would not notice him. The hare did not want to become breakfast for the eagle. But the eagle spotted the hare and spread her mighty wings. The hare, the fastest of all rabbits, darted up the hill in an attempt to reach his burrow before the eagle could capture him. The raptor dove down in hot pursuit.

Soon the hare spotted a beetle rolling a ball of dung across the field. He took refuge with the beetle and begged, "Please help me; save me from the eagle." The brave little beetle stood up to the eagle and yelled, "Please spare this hare and let him proceed to his burrow. In your eyes I am small and insignificant, but in the name of Zeus, I implore you, do not hurt this hare."

With a flick of her wing, the eagle brushed the beetle aside, grabbed the hare, tore him to pieces, and devoured him. Infuriated by the eagle's brusque behavior, the beetle sought revenge. He secretly flew after the eagle in order to find her nest. The next day, when the eagle flew from the nest, the beetle made his move. He crept into the nest and used his powerful legs to roll the eagle's eggs out of the nest, smashing them onto the rocks below.

When the eagle returned, she was filled with grief and fury and searched in vain for the creature that had destroyed her eggs.

Next season, the eagle moved the nest higher up the cliff. But this did not stop the beetle. He climbed to the summit of the cliff and waited for the eagle to leave. Once again, he entered the nest and rolled each egg out of the nest, smashing them onto the rocks below. The eagle grieved for her little ones.

The next season the eagle searched for a new place to lay her eggs. Not finding any place safe on earth, the eagle flew to Mount Olympus and implored Zeus for help. The eagle pleaded, "For the past two years some creature has visited my nest while I was gone and crashed my eggs onto the rocks below. I think someone is trying to make the eagle extinct. Please, please help me, Zeus."

Concerned for the future of the eagle, Zeus agreed to protect the eggs. The eagle built a nest in the lap of Zeus and left the eggs there, confident that they would be safe. But even this did not stop the vengeful beetle.

The beetle worked in his dung pile to create the largest ball of dung that he could carry. He then flew to Mount Olympus with the ball of dung and dropped it directly into Zeus' lap. Shocked by the large ball of dung, Zeus jumped to his feet, and with that the eagle's eggs once again crashed to the rocks below.

From *Content Area Reading, Writing, and Storytelling: A Dynamic Tool for Improving Reading and Writing Across the Curriculum through Oral Language Development* by Brian "Fox" Ellis. Westport, CT: Teacher Ideas Press. Copyright © 2008.

Zeus now ordered the eagle and the dung beetle to come to a meeting. And when Zeus makes an order, creatures listen! Zeus asked the beetle, "Why are you destroying the eagle's eggs? Are you trying to erase all eagles from the face of the earth?"

The beetle told the story of the hare, saying, "The poor hare begged me to protect him. Knowing that I was too small to stop the eagle, I begged her in the name of Zeus to let the hare run free. Instead, she brushed me aside and devoured the hare."

Zeus thought for a moment, and then he spoke. "Eagle, what you did was wrong, and I understand why the beetle is angry. But, Beetle, the revenge you have taken on the eagle far exceeds the crime. If you continue with this behavior, the eagle will soon be extinct. You must stop this behavior."

The beetle screamed, "Never! I will not stop until the eagle is wiped from the face of the earth."

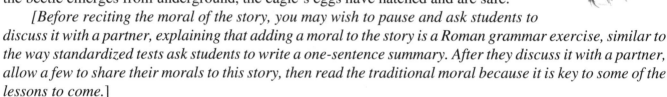

Not wanting to see either creature destroyed, Zeus devised a plan. And that is why today, the mighty eagles lay their eggs between January and March while the tiny beetle is still living underground. By the time the beetle emerges from underground, the eagle's eggs have hatched and are safe.

[Before reciting the moral of the story, you may wish to pause and ask students to discuss it with a partner, explaining that adding a moral to the story is a Roman grammar exercise, similar to the way standardized tests ask students to write a one-sentence summary. After they discuss it with a partner, allow a few to share their morals to this story, then read the traditional moral because it is key to some of the lessons to come.]

Moral: Revenge sows seeds of hate and often reaps a bitter fruit.

Language Arts

National Standards: Nl-eng.k-12.2 understanding the human experience.

Students read a wide range of literature from many periods in many genres to build an understanding of the many dimensions (e.g., philosophical, ethical, aesthetic) of human experience.

This is an excellent story for discussion through the use of Taffy Raphael's QAR (Question-Answer Relationship). A variety of questions for each category of QAR follows.

On My Own Questions: What is revenge? Why do some people seek revenge?

The following words have similar denotations. Discuss the connotations of each the following words: *revenge, retribution, payback,* or *settling scores.* What are the shades of difference in each of these words? What images come to mind for each word? In what context would you use these words?

Right There: What was the hare doing before being chased by the eagle?

Whose name did the beetle use while imploring the eagle for mercy on the hare?

Who pushed the eggs from the nests?

Where did Zeus live?

Think and Search: Where did the eagle build each of the nests?

Explain the steps the beetle took to destroy the eagle's eggs.

Compare the beetle in this fable to the beetle in Arnold Lobel's fable *King Lion and the Beetle* (Scholastic, 1980).

Author and Me: Was the beetle justified in seeking revenge against the eagle?

What would have been a better way for the beetle to show his displeasure with the eagle?

What irrational thinking lies beneath seeking revenge?

Concept Ladder: Have students work in small groups to fill in sections of the "Concept Ladder" on revenge. At this point, students are simply filling in the ladder as an "On My Own" activity. They are using their background knowledge and experiences to fill in what they know and understand at this point. It is not necessary to complete the steps of the ladder in any specific order. Students are not expected to complete the ladder at this point.

Using the partially completed ladders, begin a class discussion on their views about revenge. This will provide a strong foundation to begin comprehension of the fable. After reading and discussing "The Dung Beetle and the Eagle," let students return to their concept ladders. They might decide to erase or change some of their original ideas. They should definitely be ready to add ideas to the ladder. The goal is to develop a deep understanding of the concept and to be able to apply the ideas to their own lives.

Synonyms:

How can it be prevented?

How does it hurt people?

Non-examples:

Examples:

Associated Feelings:

Causes:

Definition:

Allen, Janet. *Words, Words, Words: Teaching Vocabulary in Grades 4–12.* Stenhouse Publishers. 1999.

Social Studies

Materials:

- Jewelry catalog

- Pictures of jewels

- Pieces of jewelry

Remember the scarab bracelets that were so popular in the early 1970s? If you still have one, now is the time to bring it out. The scarab or dung beetle was often cut from stone and placed on the chest of the deceased in ancient Egypt. A scarab of black resin with an inscription from the *Book of the Dead* was suspended from King Tut's neck. He was also wearing a scarab bracelet. For more information access www.touregypt.net/featurestories/tutsmummy.htm. To see a picture of one of the scarab jewels entombed with King Tut, visit http://dsc.discovery.com/anthology/unsolvedhistory/kingtut/tomb/slide_08.html.

Primary Grades

On My Own: What are some types of jewelry that people wear?
Why do we wear jewelry?

Right There: Show some different pieces of jewelry and ask if students know what each piece is called: necklace, pin, brooch, bracelet, and so forth.

Think and Search: Allow students to look at the jewelry and pictures of jewelry.
What is this jewelry made from?

Author and Me: Can you think of some unusual things that people use to make jewelry? Possible answers include gold-plated leaves, leather, teeth, claws, glass, wood, feathers, nails, and the like.

Explain that the scarab was often carved into stones and glass to serve as a special piece of jewelry in ancient Egypt. Students will probably find it amusing or amazing that the image of an animal that lives in a dung heap would be turned into an elegant piece of jewelry.

Why do you think someone would want to wear a scarab as a piece of jewelry?

Can you think of other jewelry we wear that means something special to the person who wears it?

For a concise history of scarab jewelry in ancient Egypt and pictures of scarab jewelry, visit the Web site www.shopategypt.com/egyptian_scarab.htm.

Grades 3, 4, and 5

Materials:

- http://plasma.nationalgeographic.com/mapmachine/

- www.si.edu/Encyclopedia_SI/nmnh/mummies.htm

National Standards:

- Standard 10: The Characteristics, Distribution, and Complexity of Earth's Cultural Mosaics

• Standard 17: How to Apply Geography to Interpret the Past

On My Own Questions: How do our burial customs show our honor and respect for the dead?
What are some ways that we show honor for our dead?
How do we honor national heroes?
How do we honor family members who have died?
Why is it important to honor them?
Suggested article on mummies: www.si.edu/Encyclopedia_SI/nmnh/mummies.htm.

Right There Questions: What conditions exist in Egypt that caused some bodies to be mummified by accident?
When did the Egyptians begin to mummify bodies intentionally?
How long did the mummification process take?

Think and Search Questions: Explain the mummification process.
What valuable information can we gain from studying ancient mummies?

Author and Me Questions: http://plasma.nationalgeographic.com/mapmachine/
Use the National Geographic Web site to gather climate information on Egypt. What is the relationship between Egypt's climate and mummification?
Would any regions of the United States be able to maintain mummies effectively? Why or why not?
Is it possible that burial customs in our region could be changed because of changes in the environment?
Select areas of the world and use the National Geographic map to determine their average precipitation and average temperature. Which of these areas might effectively practice mummification?

Location	Average Precipitation	Average Temperature	
Egypt			

Science—Primary

Materials:

• Pictures of the basic elements of a food web and a ball of string.

National Standards: Content Standard C. As a result of activities in Grades K–4, all students should develop an understanding of

- the characteristics of organisms,

- life cycles of organisms, and

- organisms and environments.

Objectives:

- Define the food web.

- Explain how organisms within a system are interdependent.

- Analyze how events and choice can impact a food web.

- Prepare 3 by 5 cards so that the following parts of a food web are represented. Each student will be given one of the food web cards and they will form a large circle. Cards: Sun; Plants; Insects/Spiders; Reptiles or Amphibians; Raptors; Other Birds; Herbivorous Mammals; Carnivorous Mammals; Decomposers—Dung Beetle. Make sure to have enough cards for your class.

Give the ball of string to the student who represents the sun. The student will roll the string to someone in the circle and explain the relationship. For example, the sun gives energy to one of the plants (e.g., an oak tree). The plant now holds onto a piece of the string and rolls the ball to another person in the circle. The oak tree might roll the ball to a mouse that eats the acorns. The mouse now rolls the ball to a hawk that eats the mouse.

Try completing various webs. What would happen if all of the plants were removed from the web? What would happen if the decomposers were removed from the food web? Have students discuss various natural events. How might a tornado affect the food chain in our region? How might a drought affect the food chain? How might a very mild winter affect the food chain? How might logging affect the food chain? What other activities by humans could affect the food chain?

Science—Middle to Upper Elementary

Materials:

- Article (from Web site: http://managingwholes.com/dung-beetles.htm) to supplement science textbook and the "Anticipation Guide" provided below.

Instructional Procedure: Students complete the anticipation guide before reading the article. They read the statements individually and decide if they agree or disagree with the statement. They can now discuss their choices in small groups and make changes based on those discussions. Students then read the article. They return to the anticipation guide and mark whether they agree or disagree with the statement.

Pre-Reading	Statement	Post-Reading
Agree Disagree	Healthy soil is a crucial component to maintain diversity of plants and animals.	Agree Disagree
Agree Disagree	Insecticides are designed to destroy parasites and will not hurt insects that are beneficial to the environment.	Agree Disagree
Agree Disagree	Dung beetles can bury a ton of wet manure per acre every day.	Agree Disagree
Agree Disagree	Dung beetles can help to negate the harmful effects brought on by drought.	Agree Disagree
Agree Disagree	Since dung beetles and earthworms are both decomposers, they cannot thrive in the same ecosystem.	Agree Disagree

Post-reading discussion questions: Beetles accelerate the degradation of dung and return it to the soil. How can this benefit cattle ranchers?

- Pasturelands return to grazing areas more rapidly.

- Nitrogen is returned to the soil rather than being lost to the atmosphere.

- Parasites do not have time to breed and hatch in the dung.

Can you think of other advantages that farmers and ranchers might realize through the decreased use of insecticides?

Art

National Standards: NA-VA.K-4.1 Understanding and applying media, techniques, and processes

- Students know the differences between materials, techniques, and processes.

- Students describe how different materials, techniques, and processes cause different responses.

- Students use different media, techniques, and processes to communicate ideas, experiences, and stories.

- Students use art materials and tools in a safe and responsible manner.

Materials:

- Pictures of various beetles

- Colored paper

- String

- Glue

- Nontoxic school paints

Begin with a review of what children have learned about beetles.

Right There Questions: What is the name of this insect?

How many legs do all insects have?

How many body parts do all insects have?

Can anyone tell me the names of each body part and point to them on the picture?

Think and Search Questions: How do we know that a spider is not an insect?

How is the spider different than the beetle?

Instructional Procedure:

- Look closely at the pictures of the beetles. Discuss symmetry. Have children point out the symmetry in the beetle's body.

- Fold construction paper in half and show children how to draw and cut on one side, so that the final parts of the bug will reflect symmetry.

- Using heavy construction paper, each child will make the three body parts for the beetle.

- Provide sponges, paint, and small brushes so that children can paint a design on the body of the beetle. Designs should repeat and reflect designs that could be found in nature.

- Glue the body parts down to a large sheet of construction paper.

- To create legs and antennae, students can use pipe cleaners, or they can drag pieces of string through glue. Add these parts to the beetle.

- Once the beetles have dried, children can use pencils or metallic pens to add details such as eyes and veins on the inner wings.

- Have the children name their beetle and write a few sentences about it.

   Helpful Web Sites

- **www.bbc.co.uk/nature/wildfacts/factfiles/498.shtml**

This site has clear pictures of dung beetles and a concise list of facts.

- **www.dawnsbrain.com/?page_id=98**

Dawn's Brain has a research paper that was written for an entomology class.

This is my version of Aesop's fable, "The Eagle and the Dung Beetle." For other versions of this fable, consult Margaret Read MacDonald's *Three Minute Tales: Stores from Around the World to Tell or Read When Time Is Short* (August House, 2004); the Web site www.mythfolklore.net/aesopica/oxford/153.htm; and Taffy E. Raphael, Kathy Highfield, and Kathryn H. Au's *QAR Now: A Powerful and Practical Framework That Develops Comprehension and Higher-Level Thinking in All Students (Theory and Practice)* (Scholastic, 2006).

STORY AS INQUIRY: *PROCESS DRAMA AND ENSEMBLE STORY LEARNING BY KEVIN CORDI*

Picture a classroom where the students think and act as engineers on the *Titanic*. One student is concerned about what type of wood was used to build the shell, another student wonders about the impact of the iceberg, and all the others are wondering just how to explain why it sank on that terrible night. In a few days, they will have to explain it to the press. There is a nervous tension surrounding the meeting, but everyone has an investment in being able to tell the right story.

This is the story we created in Cleveland, Ohio, using the teaching method of process drama outlined in this work. You, too, will be able to help your students to imagine being in a different time or place, while also being present in the moment.

I have always used story in my teaching and eventually created a position at a California high school, becoming the first full-time storytelling teacher in the country. For fourteen years, story was my curriculum. I taught beginning and advanced storytelling, as well as English and other cross-discipline courses using storytelling. I also advocated "students-as-tellers" in a collective form, creating an award-winning, traveling youth storytelling group called Voices of Illusion. The students in this group performed statewide and nationwide for 11 years.

It was not until 1998, however, when I was studying with Dr. Brian Edmiston, author of *Imagining to Learn,* for my Ph.D. at the Ohio State University that I was introduced to a dynamic new method to engage learners through story. What would happen if a story's direction could be negotiated between student and teacher? How could storytelling in the classroom transform learning? How is this kind of storytelling different from a traditional storytelling experience? How could a storyteller or teacher use stories to encourage learning while intentionally involving *all* students in the process? Likewise, what would happen when students co-created stories for learning? Further, how could ensemble learning be achieved?

These questions piqued my curiosity. Through my own studies, I discovered a method of learning using story that aims to do the following:

- Employ narrative or story to help students further develop meaning in a collective fashion

- Develop stories using an inquiry-based understanding, which can redefine traditional storytelling

- Demonstrate a proven and effective method not only to use the standards but also to develop them through story

- Most important, design a way that teacher and students can question *together,* rooted in what they find, develop, and produce through inquiry

This unit will help to answer the following questions:

- How can we use story not only to introduce a theme but also to design and develop it?

- How can students reach beyond simply telling a story to actually experience it?

Classroom Drama

These questions can be framed in the teaching pedagogy known as process drama (Heathcote, 1995; O'Neill, 1995; Edmiston & Wilhelm, 1998); and ensemble story learning (Cordi, 2007). Process drama has many names—*educational drama* (Heathcote, 1995; O'Neill 1995); *story drama* (Booth, 2006); and *dramatic inquiry* (Edmiston, 2006). Although process drama employs standard acting conventions, the outcomes are quite different and do not result in performance as an end goal. It is not theatrical drama. Morgan and Saxton (1987), in their book *Teaching Drama*, distinguish between theater and drama, advising us, "In theater everything is contrived so that the audience gets the kicks. In the classroom, the participant gets the kicks" (p. ?). In process drama, drama is used as a tool to help students engage by learning new material or exploring topics the class wishes to pursue further. It includes storytelling to help students construct meaning. Rarely is this type of drama performed for an audience other than the fellow student actors; instead, the class, along with the teacher, uses dramatic conventions to further understanding. Students do more than inquire; they experience, engage, and evaluate the story. With the example woven throughout the following text, classroom students "built" the *Titanic* and evaluated how well it was constructed under their direction.

Understanding Process Drama

Although parameters employed in process drama are built on the idea of "students as experts" and "teacher-in-role," what is emphasized by those using the method can be different. For example, scholar David Booth (2006) highlights the role of story in his story drama work, whereas Edmiston (2006) highlights the inquiry involved when using drama, believing story does not happen without inquiry: "Dramatic inquiry allows people collectively to move inside and across time-spaces at the same time to remain outside in everyday life as they experience, represent, and evaluate whatever they regard or agree is significant" (Edmiston, 2006, p. 9).

I define this type of process drama as "ensemble story learning" because students work together to understand the stories that are inherent in the drama. These stories can take many forms, such as writing, drawing, telling, and role-playing. As an ensemble classroom, students share their story using these many dramatic conventions. Unlike traditional storytelling, many stories are explored concurrently in some dramatic way by all participants. As a class, teacher and students share stories; however, the stories can be diverse and contrasting, like an ensemble.

Three main dramatic parameters in process drama include:

1. *Teacher-in-role.* The teacher is "in role" alongside students. For example, when the class is studying the Civil War, a teacher might become a solider for a time, then transform into a Civil War nurse. The teacher mediates his or her role so that it helps to improve student inquiry.

2. *Mantle of the expert* (MOE). As a teaching pedagogy, MOE positions students as "want-to-be-experts" in the field they are studying (Heathcote, 1995). Students studying cave mining do not study it as if they are students who want to know more about cave mining; instead, they assume the role of "want-to-be-miners."

   When children take on a "mantle" of expertise, they adopt the viewpoint of an older, experienced adult who already has expertise and who is working to acquire more expertise because of a particular project. Edmiston suggests that children who are using MOE "frame" their relationships with other people and the topic when they act as experts and not students (Edmiston, 2006).

3. *Client (enterprise).* In process drama, students work for an imaginary client or enterprise. For example, students studying the stages of a butterfly may be "hired" or commissioned to create a program with a museum curator.

Before the Ensemble Story—Prework

In October 2007, I worked with classroom teacher Jonathan Fairman and his students at the Cleveland School for the Arts in Ohio to build an inquiry-based story unit on the *Titanic*. First, students were asked what they already knew about the *Titanic* and what they wished to learn. After an initial assessment, we realized that most students' touch point for the *Titanic* was the 1997 blockbuster film. One student shared, "I know that Jack met Rose and fell in love on the *Titanic*, but what I would like to know is how cold that water was when they almost drowned."

We needed to spark an interest beyond the film interpretation to build ensemble story learning and wanted to capture student experience beyond the film through story engagement. As we incorporated story and inquiry, students worried less about Jack or Rose and instead became engineers on the *Titanic*. Students asked questions and provided information to *build* the story. One such exchange illustrates how the process can unfold.

Student (in the role of engineer): "My name in Sherry Evans (a pseudonym) from Kentucky. We were just talking about how the iceberg was formed. We looked at where the *Titanic* was sailing, and we were wondering about the iceberg and how it affected the boat."

This student's story launched our inquiry about icebergs, leading another student to question the boat's construction.

Second Student (in role of boat constructor): "My specialty was construction of the boat. Ma'am, when we were going out to buy the wood, I received a telegram from Mr. Smith, and he said we don't have enough money for the wood. I went out and bought the wood and noticed that this wood was a little more flimsy than the wood we were supposed to buy. The iceberg actually cut the wood, and this might have been because we could not get the other wood."

Special Note: Before entering the class, I researched the making of the *Titanic* and discovered that the ships were made of steel—not wood. Although the students were creating story, it was more important for them to voice authority and expertise on the subject, rather than stop the interaction for correction. However, as the mediating teacher, I encouraged students to research the plausibility of constructing a ship out of wood. Although it would have been easy to tell the students that the ship was made out of steel, students instead were able to discover the truth on their own. Students uncovered that some resources had reported that rivets were cheaply made and could have contributed to the *Titanic*'s sinking. As a group, we were able to build inquiry, which later led to further research and fact checking.

Students were engaged in learning, no longer relying on the movie's faded storylines. They began telling the story they wanted to learn—why the ship they helped to build had sunk. When students are engaged in socially constructed learning, learning is amplified, especially when engaged in play (Vygotsky, 1978). Sharing stories and drama are forms of play. "Play is a rehearsal for life" (Paley, 1992). By creating meaningful play, students can create meaning for their lives and the lives of others (Paley, 1992; Hall, 2007; Edmiston, 2007).

Building Inquiry with Standards

Teachers are typically trained and expected to build curriculum based on state mandates. Story can offer a creative way both to teach standards and to design curriculum rooted in student interest and curiosity. Teachers often wonder why students are not invested. Standards by themselves do not include students' voices and can sometimes isolate them from learning. However, if standards teaching is rooted in student curiosity, students not only will invest in story but also will become active in creating the learning as well.

True learning comes when curriculum is built from inquiry (Harste, 2001). Education as inquiry provides an opportunity for learners to explore topics of personal and social interest collaboratively, using the perspectives offered by others as well as various knowledge domains (Harste, 2001). Clearly, curriculum can be built when students ask questions based on the questions they develop. Inquiry drives a student's search for meaning. Although the Cleveland students did not have a firm grasp on the issues surrounding the *Titanic*, they did have a strong curiosity, which was the anchor point to fuel their interest.

Ensemble story learning is congruent with the National Teachers of English (NCTE) standards. These include:

- NCTE 1: Students read a wide range of print and nonprint texts to build an understanding of texts, of themselves, and of the cultures of the United States and the world.

- NCTE 3: Students apply a wide range of strategies to comprehend, interpret, evaluate, and appreciate texts.

- NCTE 4: Students adjust their use of spoken, written, and visual language (e.g., conventions, style, vocabulary) to communicate effectively with a variety of audiences and for different purposes.

- NCTE 7: Students conduct research on issues and interests by generating ideas and questions and by posing problems. They gather, evaluate, and synthesize data from a variety of sources.

To build inquiry, a first step involves activating prior knowledge within students. With our students in Cleveland, we told them to "look to someone next to you and say what you know about the *Titanic*. Then, turn to someone and say what you would like to know about the *Titanic* that you don't already know."

This probing further ignited their curiosity. Students began asking questions such as, "Is it true that poor people were in the 'ghetto of the boat' and were not allowed to come up when the water flooded the ship?" As students generate storylines, encourage them and help them to explore collectively the stories, as in the *Titanic* example. From these interests, the inquiry can build. In fact, the muddier the water or the more varied the positions, the more curious students can become about the inquiry.

To encourage narratives, we covered the classroom floor with pictures, articles, and other material concerning the *Titanic*. This information came both from well-known sources like the *Titanic* museum, but also from the movie script. I deliberately tried to "muddy" the waters or find information with multiple perspectives and positions that could be questioned as fact or fiction. We displayed a map of the ship levels, various texts and prints of the *Titanic*'s course, and numerous stacks of sticky notes to spark interest and connection. For further interaction with the texts around the room, we asked students to review and determine what they wanted to explore in greater detail. They were to post this information to share with the group. Unlike traditional storytelling in which stories have a clear beginning, middle, and end, we wanted to explore many stories from all angles given the information we had, because as Edmiston (2006) points out, "the best stories often begin in the middle." These "student posts" became ideal launching points. As a class we then began to question:

- How long did it take for the *Titanic* to sink?

- How much time did they have to prepare before the ship sunk?

- It says here that there were only five survivors left living. The youngest would be ninety-nine years old; what happened to him?

- I read that it took $7 million to build the *Titanic*; was that considered a lot at the time?

In traditional storytelling, tellers search for the best way to invite students into the story. For example, with the *Titanic,* we could begin as the ship is being built, after it has taken off, or even at some point in the future. With process drama, however, many nonlinear possibilities can be explored at the same time, including the past, present, or even a possible future trip for the ship.

Dramatizing the Story

As the conversations unfolded, it was clear the class wanted to know why the ship sank, so we began to use drama to explore the story. Students and teachers were invited to position themselves within the story as experts with firsthand knowledge of why the ship sank. To create this atmosphere, we employed dramatic teaching, with "teacher-in-role" and "mantle of the expert" (Heathcote, 1995).

Keeping this in mind, we asked the students, "Who might want to know about why the ship sank?" Students gave us responses: historians, film producers, and engineers. I asked, "Would you like to be engineers in this story?" They agreed. The story began.

The Story of the Drama

As the teacher, I assumed the role of an engineer with the following interaction:

Teacher-in-role: "All right this meeting starts at 2:15 P.M.; can you check your clocks please? We are going to be here for a long time. Did we bring enough drinks? Who was responsible for the drinks?"

Student: I was.

Teacher: We are going to be here for awhile because we have something to figure out. We built this ship. We are getting a lot of flack from the press. We have many people who want to know why it sank. I am not blaming anyone here, because I helped build it; we have engineers, we have steelworkers; you did the research. Can you tell us some possible reasons why this ship went down?

Student: I can.

Teacher:	Can you stand and be addressed (with clipboard)? Your name please?
Student:	My name is Cashmeer.
Teacher:	Where are you from?
Student:	I am from Ireland.
Teacher:	What is your specialty?
Student:	I was a chef on the boat. What people don't know is that when we received the food, we had a rookie on the job, and we left the window open, and I think that might be why it sank.

A note concerning roles: The roles in process drama, or what I refer to as "ensemble story learning," are not assigned. Instead, students invest in what role they want to bring to the drama. In this example, students were steelworkers, carpenters, and iceberg specialists. Each role created by the students added to the story being shared.

Accepting all responses: Teachers can borrow from improvisation. In improvisation troupes such as Second City, each idea that is given is accepted. For example, to build story, students' additions are never negated. This is called, "yes, and." For example, instead of saying, "No, you are wrong, the ship sank from the iceberg," we might say, "Yes! The window may have contributed to the sinking, but we also know that an iceberg was hit." This way, students are not dismissed but encouraged to press on with their interests and curiosity. This is how the teacher serves to mediate, so that the story continues and all students are involved in the process, and you can swerve away from a less fruitful path toward the truth.

Research from Inquiry

After the story drama, we continued the inquiry, asking students to research "in role" for a follow-up meeting with the press. As iceberg specialists and engineers, students examined photos to uncover cracks in the hull, explored the Internet to discover what others had said about the building of the ship, and listened to courtroom testimony. They examined passenger lists and scrutinized the expertise of the crew. Students *had become* the engineers. Their collaborative inquiry drove the research. They discovered which facts were accurate or inaccurate and reported them to the press. For example, their earlier belief in wooden construction led them to learn about steel construction and the types of steel used. They determined that the type of steel and rivets used had contributed to the durability of the ship.

Map to Learning

If the story is aligned with the curriculum, ensemble story learning can help guide the way. Together the mediating teacher and students decide how to proceed with the story. The students help create a map to help the teacher know where to use drama or story. As expected, this type of ensemble story learning takes a great deal of trust, time, and practice and is best conducted over a few weeks, as opposed to one class period. Some of the techniques used in the *Titanic* example included the following:

- The teacher had students interview "in-role" others who had a hand in building the ship.

- Students researched the Internet to find additional diagrams.

- The class listened to trial proceedings available online.

- The class watched documentary films to see what other engineers reported.

As an ensemble, the class worked toward the same goal of uncovering and experiencing the story of the *Titanic*. However, the findings can be diverse, and it is this difference that is used to help extend the learning. Drama and curiosity serve as the arena in which students can present various perspectives, explore new information, and discover from watching, reading, or finding new texts. They can even dramatize and see what transpires from the process.

Ensemble story learning is not scripted but is designed by the group decisions and ideas. The key word is "map." A map only suggests routes; people can explore many directions to arrive at the same point, but a map shows you the possible routes to take. With any given map, there are many alternative routes to explore when seeking a destination. Students add layers of new or unknown information to build their map of inquiry. As the teacher lets go, the stories and ideas will flow. As expected, ensemble story learning must unfold over time. It is best to experiment slowly until comfort levels increase. Start with smaller projects, and as students and teacher grow comfortable with their roles, explore larger issues.

Using Ensemble Story Learning with Other Curriculum and Grade Levels

Ensemble story learning can be used successfully with all grade levels and abilities. Recently, I incorporated ensemble story learning in a British classroom with students aged five to eight years. For two days, students became part of a mountain-climbing rescue team. With children's drawings and wooden structures, the children built rescue helicopters and hospitals with everyday classroom objects. For example, a calculator, with a little imagination, can calculate the weather and record what to include for the rescue mission. They also tried to anticipate danger and train medical teams. Students used many paths to create the rescue drama. For example, they used math for calculations and referenced the previous history of the climbers and the staff when making decisions. Students continued to use drama to venture five years into the future to visit those who had been hurt. Clearly, the students took to this immediately. This was meaningful play at work.

Ensemble story learning works well with students with special needs as well. In a recent classroom visit, four kindergarten students who were blind led an adventure mission to Mars. Under the direction of the students, the room transformed into a space station, the planet Mars, and even a press room. The students chose to dramatize a Mars scenario where the blind students led the adults around because we had lost our sight from the dust on Mars. In their story world of Mars, they were the ones who helped us see. They used their Brailler and other devices to communicate with the Martians, and together we negotiated with the United Nations to permit both a Russian and a Chinese astronaut to join the ship. Several teachers commented that they had never seen this type of energy and work commitment from their students.

Likewise, I worked with a group of third graders who became "fairy tale helpers," electing to help Jack's sick grandmother with the coin stolen from the giant, Jim. They debated whether to use the money to help her sickness or to give it back to the giant. These choices were difficult. Some opted to share their story with the giant and ask for help, whereas others hid the coins. Ensemble story learning launched a group discussion in which students could examine multiple perspectives. From this discussion, we were able to use drama to show the choices from the story dramas the students designed.

Recommendations—Conclusion—Something to Wrap Up

Whether teaching a unit on the Civil War, understanding the dangers of bullying, or exploring the intricacies of the atom, students architect the story creation through mediated story work. For ensemble story building to work best, please note the following:

- There is no set script; the students design the work.

- Students are encouraged to build and question the story.

- Teachers mediate student choices.

- The teacher, either in-role or not, chooses which stories to use to help extend the learning with the class. This is not to say students cannot help extend the learning, but that the teacher needs to decide how it can be used to promote inquiry.

- Teachers can employ improvisational techniques including—"Yes and . . ."—to accept all choices, being careful when saying no to ideas presented.

- When developing process drama, work toward the student who is paying the least attention. Then you will have everyone's attention. Try to make this your goal.

- Finally, remember this experience should be rewarding for all students. It is not as important to tell the right story, but instead to share new ways stories can be told, questioned, evaluated, and discussed.

A Note about Performance of Ensemble Story Learning

Although the intent of this work is not meant for performance (the process is the goal), it can be used to build performance work. Drawing on such work as O'Neil and Lambert's (1982) book *Drama Structures,* one can see how this inquiry work can be drawn together to form a dramatic story presentation. However, this is up to you. The value of the learning can be from the "doing" of the work, but with some attention to theatre conventions, story work can form the basis of a fine production. All that is needed is a class willing to go beyond the inquiry and place it in the form of a tellable story.

Resources

Booth, D. (2005). *Story drama: Creating stories through role playing, improvising, and reading aloud.* Markham, Canada: Pembroke.

Edmiston, B., & Wilhelm, J. (1998). *Imagining to learn: Inquiry, ethics, and integration through drama.* Portsmouth, NJ: Heinemann.

Harste, J. (2001). What education as inquiry is and isn't. Retrieved May 1, 2008, from www.mantleoftheexpert.com.

Morgan, N., & Saxton, J. (1987). *Teaching drama: A mind of many wonders*. London: Hutchinson.

Norfolk, S., Stenson, J., & Williams, D. (2006). *The storytelling classroom: Applications across the curriculum*. Westport, CT: Libraries Unlimited.

O'Neill, C. (1995). *Drama worlds*. Portsmouth, NH: Heinemann.

O'Neill, C., & Lambert, A. (1982). *Drama structures: A practical handbook for teachers*. Cheltenham, England: Heinemann.

Paley, V. G. (1986). "On listening to what children say." *Harvard Educational Review, 56*(2), 122–131.

Rokos, K., & Christie, J. (2007). *Play and literacy in early childhood: Research from multiple perspectives*. New York: Lawrence Erlbaum Associates.

Sima, J., & Cordi, K. (2003). *Raising voices: Creating youth storytelling groups and troupes*. Westport, CT, Libraries Unlimited.

Vygotsky, L. S. (1978). *Mind in society: The development of higher psychological processes*. Cambridge, MA: Harvard University Press.

Kevin Cordi is a nationally known storytelling and story teacher who has taught and told in thirty-five states, as well as in England, Japan, and Scotland. He holds a master's degree in storytelling and education and is a Ph.D. candidate at the Ohio State University, studying the importance of ensemble story learning and dramatic inquiry. He is the co-author of *Raising Voices: Creating Youth Storytelling Groups and Troupes* and the founder of Y. E. S. (Youth, Educators, and Storytellers) for the National Storytelling Network. His story work has been commissioned by the John F. Kennedy Center for the Performing Arts, *Highlights for Children*, and *Newsweek*. Kevin may be reached at **www.kevincordi.com** or e-mail at *kcteller@ sbcglobal.net*. He would like to thank his editor-in-life for working on this—his wife, Barbara Allen-Cordi.

CHAPTER 7

BUILDING A COMMUNITY OF LEARNERS

WE ALL TELL STORIES—PRINCIPALS AND PARENTS, CUSTODIANS AND SECRETARIES, POLITICIANS AND POLICE OFFICERS

One of my favorite memories of an artist-in-residence program is of a principal in North Carolina who stepped way outside her comfort zone as a formal, somewhat authoritarian administrator to take the microphone during an assembly and tell a funny story about her grandmother. Having spent two weeks in the building, I saw how she was always warm with the students, knew their names, and said hello in the hall, but students seemed a little intimidated by her authority. The students were delighted by her story. Some kind of metamorphosis took place when she performed; the students' jaws dropped, like, "Who is this woman we have never seen before?"

Everyone loves it when their teacher stands up in the auditorium and tells a folktale with wild gestures and outrageous sound effects. The janitors and lunch ladies all have a tale to tell.

Storytelling themes can bring the school community together and allow folks to get to know another side of the people they work with every day. Not every lunch lady has to be pushed into something she doesn't want to do, but with the right encouragement, at least a few representatives of the diverse school culture can be recruited to be a part of a school-wide storytelling festival. Maybe the school nurse has a fondness for fairy tales, or the D.A.R.E. officer, as part of his training in character education, learned one of Aesop's fables. As you plan your storytelling unit, put the word out that you are looking for storytellers; gently twist a few hesitant arms, and you might be surprised at who volunteers!

Many school communities have a read-aloud program where guest readers come and share their favorite children's picture book. This year recruit the mayor, city council members, or local news anchors to come and *tell* their favorite folktale. With a mini-workshop on storytelling or an oral history project to prep them, visiting grandparents can be encouraged to share stories from their childhood.

Most important, parents—who should always be encouraged to be active members of the school community—parents can be recruited to visit and share stories from their culture of origin, immigrant tales, personal narratives about the neighborhood's history, or simple songs and finger play. The following lesson plan is one that I have presented at family literacy nights more than 100 times in the past two dozen years. Admittedly, it is my favorite program because it empowers parents in their role as a child's first teacher. Even functionally illiterate parents can build literacy skills with their children through oral-language development. Further, parents who may not have had a positive school experience can have a fun night at school, increasing the likelihood they will return on friendlier terms in the future.

PRESENTING A FAMILY STORYTELLING EVENING

The goal of the evening is to encourage families to celebrate literacy and family heritage through the telling of family stories.

The plan: I always start with a brief welcome that includes a sincere thank you and praise to the parents who came because action speaks louder than words, and their presence says loud and clear that they value their children and their children's education. I also give a brief (two-minute) lecture on the importance of reading aloud and telling family stories for giving their children the tools they need to succeed in school, noting that children who succeed in school tend grow into people who succeed in life. The emphasis is that family stories give us a bigger sense of who we *are*. Then I outline the evening, warning them that they will get a chance to tell a few stories later.

Then I tell a family story. I cannot emphasize enough how important it is to tell a story to model the process, inspire ideas, and give everyone that good feeling that a heartwarming, funny family story can create. I often begin with "Prairie Fire!"

Next, we play a few basic storytelling games to warm them up to the idea that they already know how to tell stories. I lead the games asking them to turn to their family members to play, working in small groups to make sure that everyone gets a turn. If I have just completed an artist-in-residence program, the students know these games and enjoy teaching them to their family as I facilitate. The games include:

- "Counting to Five with Feeling"

- "Counting to Five, Changing Your Voice to Become Different Characters"

- "Imitating Animals, the Phone, the Wind, and Practicing Sound Effects"

- "The Magic Something"

- "An Imaginary Journey into a Favorite Picture Book"

- To put it all together, we all learn "Once There Was an Old Witch"

All of these games can be found in Chapter 1, "How to Learn and Tell a Tale."

Throughout this process, I keep emphasizing the idea that they already know how to tell stories by asking questions such as, "How many of you raise your voice when you are excited? How many of you impersonate the nagging voice of your parent/child when talking to your spouse/sibling? Parents, have you mastered 'the look'? Raise your hand if you talk with your hands moving."

At this point, I either tell another very short family story, or I invite a few students to come up and tell a traditional folktale. If you include several students in the program and make sure everyone knows in advance, then you are sure to have an audience of friends, siblings, parents, and distant relatives.

Next, I tease the parents; now it is their turn. The way it works is this: Ask the students to be the listeners and the parents to be the speakers. Ask the students to repeat after you when you read the prompt. This way the parent hears the prompt twice and has more time to formulate a response. Ask the parents to respond to the prompt with whatever comes to mind. They should simply begin speaking, telling their children any tidbit of information or story that comes to mind. Give them only one or two minutes to respond, then ask for silence or ring a bell or clap twice—somehow signal time is up. The idea here is simply to open the floodgates of vivid memory. Read three or four prompts in this manner. (Note that this is an adaptation of the "Oral History Interview" on page 95.)

Following is a set of prompts, but feel free to write your own. Make sure they are general enough to elicit a response from everyone, yet specific enough to create vivid images. Knowing your families and their common experiences, create prompts that will elicit a variety of responses.

Tell me about your grandma, grandpa, or some other older person you have known.

Tell me about a family vacation—where you went and what you did.

Tell me about your first day of school or some early school memory.

Tell me about your favorite childhood game, how to play it, and the last time you played.

Tell me about _____ (fill in the blank).

Next, I tell a brief family story that is my response to one of the prompts. This models a more complete story. I always end the evening with the part the students love best: I give the parents homework! I tell them that they need to sit down with the family elder and conduct this kind of interview to collect family stories, *before it is too late!* The students are to make sure that their parents do their homework. At the end of the session you could even go so far as to put out a sign-up sheet to get parents to commit to coming to school to tell a story to your class.

I then thank them for coming and encourage them to keep the stories alive. Following is one of the handouts I give them to encourage more stories.

Turning Family Photos into Family Stories

They say a picture is worth a thousand words and it is true. Old family photos are a great way to unlock the floodgates to long-forgotten family stories. Sit down with your grandmother and a photo album, and she will fill your ear with tales both tall and true.

A few well-worded questions will help you to get beyond a simple description of the pictures. Ask questions such as, "What was he or she well known for doing? How did you and grandpa meet? Where are some of the places you went in that car? What did you do for fun when you lived there? Whatever happened to that old dog?" Look at each picture carefully and come up with questions that will invite your elders to go into detail.

Recently, I was talking to my Aunt Irene about this picture. She told me that my great Uncle Johnny was born and raised in Wayne County, Tennessee, near the home of Davy Crockett. His mother was Cherokee; her name was Hannah Jane Reed. He was related to the Clantons who faced Doc Holiday and Wyatt Earp in the famous shoot-out at OK Corral, but as usual, Hollywood got the story all wrong.

When people remember Johnny Clanton, they say that he was a great hunter. I have mixed feelings about hunting, especially fox hunting, but my Aunt Irene assured me that they never killed the fox. It was a game of wits. In the evening, the men would gather with their hounds. They would build a big fire and sit around listening to the hounds chase the fox. If something happened and the hounds did not come back, a man could leave his coat by the fire, and when he came back the next morning, his dog would be sitting by his coat waiting for him. They say a good fox hound was worth something. Maybe that is why my uncle chose to have his hound dog in the picture with him. And do you see who is sitting on his lap?

Look through some old family photos. Choose some of the pictures that have the best stories, a family vacation, or the one that did *not* get away. Write a brief story about each of several pictures and gather them into a book of family stories.

For more information on telling family stories, please visit my Website: **www.foxtalesint.com**

From *Content Area Reading, Writing, and Storytelling: A Dynamic Tool for Improving Reading and Writing Across the Curriculum through Oral Language Development* by Brian "Fox" Ellis. Westport, CT: Teacher Ideas Press. Copyright © 2008.

HOSTING THE ULTIMATE STORYTELLER-IN-RESIDENCE PROGRAM

An artist-in-residence program is a dynamic way to involve students, parents, teachers, and administrators in a program that enriches everyone's love of storytelling. After creating the yearlong storyteller-in-residence program for the Charlotte-Mecklenburg Schools as outlined in the introduction to this book, every year I present several weeklong residencies at schools across the country.

In the next few pages, I would like to share the lesson plans that are the ideal embodiment of a dynamic, interdisciplinary approach. This program gives the entire community "hands-on" opportunities to improve communication skills with measurable goals in language development along with intergenerational involvement—parents and grandparents, too.

The goal here is to help you to develop a residency program tailored to your community limits and needs, with an emphasis on parental and community involvement.

To begin with, it is important that everyone is on board with an appreciation of the educational impact of storytelling in the classroom. If you think it would be helpful, copy the preface to this book, "Why Tell Stories," and distribute copies to the teachers, PTA, parents, and administrators who will be on the team organizing the residency.

As a team, discuss some of your goals and expected outcomes in light of your school improvement plan. If you decide to hire a professional storyteller as an artist-in-residence—and I encourage you to consider doing so—make sure it is someone who specializes in the types of stories that will meet your goals, and make sure the storyteller is aware of your expected outcomes. Most storytellers are flexible, but some storytellers are better at personal narratives and oral history, whereas others excel in integrating science and social studies. Find a storyteller with a specialty that matches your goals.

I highly encourage you to consider a local storyteller who can more easily provide follow-up visits. If a local storyteller is not handy, you could invite me to present the residency and I would be happy to do so. (Please visit my Web site for more information www.foxtalesint.com.)

Before the visit, communicate with the storyteller concerning scheduling, the content areas you wish to cover, and what each class or grade level has been studying. Storytellers who have done extensive residency work probably have a clear idea of how the process works best for them, but as the client, you have a voice in this matter; feel confident in asking for adaptations to fit your needs. Work with the storyteller to create the best schedule. Share with them the following outline of lesson plans for "A Weeklong Storytelling Residency." Insist on a family night later in the week and schedule a teacher meeting/workshop early in the week. The clearer you are up front, the more likely you will achieve your goals.

One small caveat to watch for: Most artists in residence are not accustomed to working a full day or serving every student in the building. For example, the Illinois Arts Council strongly urges schools to pick one class or grade level as a focus group, providing little if any instruction for the other classes, which means most of the school gets to watch but not participate. With careful scheduling, it is not only possible but necessary that every student receives instruction from the guest artist. (See the sample schedule that follows.)

A WEEKLONG STORYTELLING RESIDENCY (Grades 3–12)

The following lesson plans are an overview of the activities for a storyteller-in-residency program. I have included suggestions for follow-up activities after each hour of instruction. It is vitally important that teachers schedule time after each classroom visit to do this follow-up work so they are ready for the next session.

The Performance

On the first day of the residency, schedule one or two large auditorium performances to build excitement, model effective storytelling, and introduce several key concepts that will be developed through the week.

Story Writing

The first classroom workshop is spent teaching creative writing in the content area, helping students get a solid start on their story.

1. Review the writing process—prewriting, free-writing, and rewriting, editing, and publishing. Discuss the ingredients of an exciting tale—character, setting, and plot.

2. Guide the class through the writing process, allowing time to daydream possibilities, discuss ideas with a partner, and create a rough draft of their story. With younger students, I use the lesson plan on page 24, "The Stone Cutter." For older students, almost any of the writing exercises in this book will work well here.

3. Coach them toward the rewriting process by asking them to make a second draft of the same story. Emphasize adding new ideas or subtracting things that would make it a better story. The rough draft needs to be finished before the third workshop session.

4. As an optional follow-up activity, ask the students to illustrate their stories. These can then easily be put together into a book format.

Storytelling

1. In this second classroom session, begin by telling a short, funny story that exemplifies a variety of storytelling techniques and invites the audience to participate.

2. Lead the students through several exercises that teach various skills to improve their ability to dramatically interpret a tale. These include voice and mime exercises, theater games, and guided imagery, with each isolated skill integrated into the art of telling a story.

3. Tell a short, easily remembered story that exemplifies (exaggerates) these same techniques. Ask the students to pay attention to how the voice changes and how the body, hands, and imagination are used to tell the story. (See "I Tell, We Tell, You Tell," page 3).

4. Retell the same story, inviting the students to stand up and tell the story simultaneously. Everyone is speaking and acting out the story at the same time following the storyteller's lead.

5. Ask the students to choose a partner and take turns telling the same story to each other. The student telling the story should be standing, and the listener should be sitting to facilitate classroom monitoring.

6. If time permits, or as a follow-up activity, allow a few students to take turns telling this folktale to the entire class. Emphasize the use of body language and voice inflection, while encouraging individuality of expression.

Telling Our Story—Storytelling as a Rewriting Tool

1. Begin the third workshop by reviewing the performance given early in the week, with special emphasis on how the stories were told. The key question is: How do you use your hands, body, voice, and imagination to tell a story? Also, review rewriting strategies and challenge students to perpetually ask themselves, "How can I make this a better story?" or "How can storytelling inform the rewriting process?"

2. Pass out the stories the students wrote in the first session. Give the students three opportunities to practice their story before they tell it to the class using the lessons from Retelling Is Rewriting in Chapter 2.

   A. First, students will tell the story to themselves with an emphasis on their voice: character voices, sound effects, inflection, pacing, and volume. (Allow time for rewriting and editing, emphasizing the voice of the author.)

   B. They tell it to themselves again, but this time they will stand up and act it out, emphasizing gesture, body language, and facial expression. (Allow time for rewriting and editing, emphasizing action words, verbs, and adverbs.)

   C. Finally, students choose a partner and take turns telling their story to each other; the one who is telling the story is standing, and the listener is seated to facilitate classroom monitoring. (Allow time for rewriting and editing, emphasizing constructive feedback from their partner.)

3. As time allows, give several students the opportunity to entertain the class with their original tales. Students may be allowed to compliment their peers, but no criticism is permitted. Over the next few days, every student should be given the opportunity to perform before the entire class.

The Storytelling Festival

The residency will culminate in a storytelling festival in which the students will perform before their peers. Each teacher is asked to choose one student who is loud, entertaining, and uses good gestures and a clear voice. Send them to a special coaching session the morning of the festival. In this coaching session, I also teach students how to use the microphone effectively.

The students and teachers gather in the multipurpose room to be delightfully entertained by these aspiring storytellers.

I usually begin with a pantomime piece so that the students are quiet for their peers who may not have a booming voice. I then pump the audience up as M.C. and let five or six students tell a story. No matter how good the student storytellers are, it is hard to listen to too many storytellers in a row, so I break it up with a rowdy sing-a-long song or audience participation story, so they can shake the wiggles out, like a sorbet to cleanse the palette, so students are ready for five or six more storytellers. It is also important for students to see other adults telling stories; integrated into this performance is an opportunity for a teacher, the principal, janitor, or secretary to tell a tale and build rapport with the students.

THE NATIONAL YOUTH STORYTELLING SHOWCASE

The National Youth Storytelling Showcase is a wonderful organization dedicated to encouraging every classroom in America to discover—or rediscover—the beauty and value of storytelling and story performance. They hold an annual contest in the Smoky Mountains in February in which students get to participate in a festival with several of the nation's better storytellers.

The process of auditioning via video tape or DVD is ongoing. Visit their web page for the application process and rules, **www.nationalyouthstorytellingshowcase.org/home/**.

Please help us recruit youth storytellers from your summer camp experiences, your school residencies, your classrooms, and your libraries! Here are some of the logistics.

All selected storytellers from your local storytelling event must mail videotapes or DVDs to your state liaison before the specified due date. (I am the state representative for Illinois.) State representatives will review all tapes and select the five state finalists and send those five videotapes to the Pigeon Forge Office of Special Events.

Videotapes must be accompanied by the required and completed entry forms or they will be disqualified. (*This is crucial!* We have had a few excellent tapes without proper paperwork, which I jumped through hurdles to get, and alas, it wasn't enough.) Finalists will be notified either by telephone or e-mail from Pigeon Forge. Finalists will receive an invitation to present their story during the Smoky Mountains Storytelling Festival during the National Youth Storytelling Showcase in early February in Pigeon Forge, TN. The "Grand Torchbearer" will be selected from among the performing finalists.

Thanks in advance for spreading the word, encouraging youth storytellers, and doing your part to give a leg up to the next generation of storytellers!

APPENDIX A

STORY SOURCES—AN ANNOTATED BIBLIOGRAPHY OF TRULY USEFUL BOOKS

TEN BOOKS OR AUTHORS EVERY STORYTELLER SHOULD KNOW

Courlander, H. *The Tiger's Whisker*. New York: Henry Holt, 1966. ISBN 0-8050-3512-5. (Asian Folklore)

Courlander, H., & Hertzog, G. *The Cow-Tail Switch and Other West African Stories*. New York: Henry Holt, 1974. ISBN 0-395-55176-5.

    Courlander and Hertzog continued the tradition begun by the Grimms, expanding their work to collect folktales from around the world. These books are rich collections of stories that do an unusual and difficult thing: they maintain cultural integrity while translating the stories into tellable English. Both his Asian and African collections include popular stories as well as several wonderful surprises.

DeSpain, P. *Thirty-Three Multicultural Tales to Tell*. Little Rock, AR: August House, 1993. ISBN 0-87483-266-7.

DeSpain, P. *The Emerald Lizard, Fifteen Latin American Tales to Tell*. Little Rock, AR: August House, 1999. ISBN 0-87483-552-6.

    Another modern folklorist and storyteller whose books need to be in every storyteller's library, DeSpain creates literate, highly readable collections of stories in which the simplicity of text masks the depth of understanding and cultural authenticity underlying every story. An early mentor for this author, all of his books include funny, entertaining, and poignant tales.

Hamilton, E. *Mythology*. Boston, MA: Little, Brown, 1942. ISBN 0-316-34151-7.

Readily available in most libraries, this older book is still one of the best collections of the classics. Greek mythology is the soap opera of the ancient world that affirms the idea that myth means higher truth.

Haviland, V. *Favorite Fairy Tales Told in Denmark*. New York: Beech Tree Books, 1971. ISBN 0-688-12594-8.

A librarian with the New York Public Libraries for more years than one can count, Haviland did us all a favor in collecting favorite folktales from many lands. Look for the complete series of sixteen books, *Favorite Fairy Tales Told in (name a country)*.

MacDonald, M. R. *The Storytellers Start-Up Book*. Little Rock, AR: August House, 1993. ISBN 0-87483-305-1.

If you ever see a book by MacDonald, buy it! She is an amazingly prolific author, collector, and editor of folklore who has published excellent how-to books, collections of folktales, and children's picture books, all rooted in the oral tradition. Her stories are guaranteed to bring delight to listeners of all ages. The *Start-Up Book* includes lots of practical tips and some great stories. All of it is grounded in her ample experience as a children's librarian and well-respected elder in the current revival of storytelling. Seriously, do a book search and purchase her entire catalogue.

Phelps, E. J. *The Maid of the North, Feminist Folktales from Around the World*. New York: Holt, Rinehart and Winston, 1981. ISBN 0-03-062374-X.

Usually, if a book contains one story worth telling, it is a worthwhile investment. Almost every story in this book is worth the investment of learning and telling, especially if you will ever have a girl in your audience who needs a role model.

Schwartz, A. *Scary Stories to Tell in the Dark; & More Scary Stories* (boxed set). New York: HarperCollins, 1981. ISBN 0-06-440170-7.

Alvin Schwartz's collections of scary stories are fun to tell, guaranteed crowd pleasers, and every teller of tales needs a few of these short, simple scary stories up their sleeve.

Winter, M., Illus. *The Aesop for Children*. New York: Scholastic, 1994. ISBN 0-590-47977-6.

To be a storyteller in the modern world, one must first have a working repertoire firmly rooted in the classics. Aesop's fables are short, simple stories that are easy to tell and vital to an understanding of what it means to be human.

Yolen, J. *Favorite Folktales from Around the World*. New York: Pantheon Books, 1986. ISBN 398-286-4264-4.

If you buy just one collection of stories this year, this should be the book. Jane Yolen is an award-winning author of fantasy and modern fairy tales. She is also an exceptional folklorist who not only did the scholarly library research but also attended storytelling festivals, collected oral histories, and worked with living, breathing performers to collect very tellable tales.

Zipes, J. *The Complete Fairy Tales of the Brothers Grimm*. New York: Bantam Books, 1987. ISBN 0-553-37101-0.

    The Brothers Grimm are the great-grandfathers of folklore. They collected more than 250 classic stories from their neighbors, stories every storyteller should know, from *Little Red Riding Hood* to *Cinderella*. Jack Zipes has done a great job of going back to the original versions and creating highly readable translations that highlight the depth often missing in the Disney versions.

OTHER RECOMMENDED BOOKS—WORLD FOLKLORE

Brody, E., Goldspinner, J., Green, K., Leventhal, R., & Porcino, J. *Spinning Tales Weaving Hope*. Philadelphia: New Society, 1992. ISBN 0-86571-229-8.

    Recently republished, this is one of the first collections of folklore put together by a collection of working storytellers. Great stories and great lesson plans make this book infinitely useful.

Forest, H. *Wisdom Tales From Around the World*. Little Rock, AR: August House, 1996. ISBN 0-87483-479-1.

    This is another of those rare collections that demonstrates both great scholarship and a working knowledge of the oral tradition. These are short, simple stories—easy to tell, yet filled with a subtle depth of wisdom.

Goss, L. & Barnes, M. E. *Talk That Talk, an Anthology of African American Storytelling*. New York: Simon & Schuster, 1989. ISBN 0-671-67167-7.

    From ancient African roots to modern rap rhythms, this collection of African American folklore is one of the best immersive overviews of the vast diversity within the culture.

Jaffe, N., & Zeitlin, S. *While Standing on One Foot*. New York: Henry Holt, 1996. ISBN 0-8050-2594-4.

    These Jewish tales were one of the first collections to promote the idea of pausing in the middle of the story to allow students to solve the problem, put themselves in the shoes of the main character, and figure out the dilemma.

Martin, R. *The Hungry Tigress, Buddhist Legends & Jataka Tales*. Berkeley, CA: Parallax Press, 1990. ISBN 0-938077-25-2.

    As a working storyteller and practicing Buddhist, Martin is infinitely qualified to collect and edit these illuminating tales.

Starr, J. *Tales from the Cherokee Hills*. Chelsea, MI: BookCrafters, 1988. ISBN 0-89587-062-2.

    These poetic transcriptions of Cherokee folklore are a great model for students to rewrite traditional stories using modern language. It is especially useful to compare and contrast this book with the versions of many of the same stories found in this other highly recommended collection by George F. Sheer, *Cherokee Animal Tales* (New York: Holiday House, 1968).

HISTORICAL NARRATIVES

Blockson, C. L. *The Underground Railroad.* New York: Prentice Hall Press, 1987. ISBN 0-13-935743-2.
> Based on extensive research and oral histories from actual runaways, this is a rich collection of the raw material for creating historical stories.

Botkin, B. A. *A Treasury of American Folklore.* New York: Crown Publishers, 1944.
> This older collection is easy to find in libraries and worth the search. It includes tall tales, folktales, folk songs, and lots of diary entries, news clippings, and primary source material from sea to shining sea.

Chase, R. *Grandfather Tales.* Boston: Houghton Mifflin, 1948. ISBN 0-395-06692-1.
> A perennial favorite, this collection of Appalachian folktales makes a successful effort to put the stories into a sense of the cultural milieu they came from, and the stories are great fodder for "taking an old story and making it new."

Colbert, D. *Eyewitness to America.* New York: Pantheon Books, 1997. ISBN 0-679-44224-3.
> Primary source documents from the first explorers to soldiers' accounts of both World Wars, you will not find a more complete collection of stories from American history. No filters, no bias; these are the raw materials from which great stories are made.

Hamilton, V. *The People Could Fly, American Black Folktales.* New York: Alfred A. Knopf, 1985. ISBN 0-394-86925-7.
> More folktale than history, this book is a wonderful glimpse into the historical mind of black America. Hamilton, an award-winning author of original fiction, demonstrates a rich knowledge of folklore and history. *The People Could Fly* is a deep root into that past.

Keen, S., & Valley-Fox, A. *Your Mythic Journey, Finding Meaning in Your Life Through Writing and Storytelling.* New York: G.P. Putnam's Sons, 1973. ISBN 0-87477-543-4.
> Although written as more of a self-help book than a collection of lesson plans, most of the activities can easily be adapted to the classroom to help students research stories from their culture of origin.

SCIENCE STORIES

Caduto, M. J., & Bruchac, J. *Keepers of the Earth: Native American Stories and Environmental Activities for Children.* Golden, CO: Fulcrum, 1988. ISBN 1-55591-027-0.
> This book is the first of a successful series of books that pairs Native American folktales with hands-on science activities. The stories are written to be told and the lessons include clear step-by-step instructions.

Ellis, B. F. *Learning from the Land: Teaching Ecology Through Stories and Hands-on Activities.* Englewood, CO: Teacher Ideas Press, 1998. ISBN 1-56308-563-1.
> This is a creative nonfiction work that uses a personal narrative as a bridge into the big concepts of ecology, the food web, water cycle, predator-prey relations, and the mineral cycles. Every story comes with hands-on science lessons and creative-writing ideas to help students learn their own stories from their local landscape.

Gail, J., & Houlding, L. A. *Day of the Moon Shadow*. Englewood, CO: Libraries Unlimited, 1995. ISBN 1-56308-248-5.

    Great stories and easy-to-follow lesson plans.

Livo, L. J., M. C. Glathery, G., & Livo, N. *Of Bugs and Beasts*. Englewood, CO: Teacher Ideas Press, 1995. ISBN 1-56308-179-2.

    Zoology comes to life in this great collection of stories.

Strauss, S. *The Passionate Fact*. Golden, CO: North American Press, 1996. ISBN 1-55591-925-1.

    This is one of the more practical how-to books, full of insight and inspiration for bringing science, natural history, and history to life through storytelling.

CLASSROOM COLLECTIONS OF STORYTELLING LESSON PLANS

Livo, N. J., & Rietz, S. A. *Storytelling Activities*. Littleton, CO: Libraries Unlimited, 1987. ISBN: 0-87287-566-0.

    This is a pioneering book that includes lots of fun games for teaching storytelling and stretching stories into teachable moments.

Norfolk, S., Stenson, J., & Williams, D. *The Storytelling Classroom*. Westport, CT: Libraries Unlimited, 2006. ISBN: 1-59158-305-5.

    With more than two dozen contributors, this is a diverse collection of lesson plans for all grade levels and most subjects.

APPENDIX B

STORIES AND LESSON PLANS LISTED BY NATIONAL STANDARDS IN ENGLISH, SOCIAL STUDIES, SCIENCE, AND MATH

Note: Consult the Index to this book to locate the recommended stories for each standard.

National Council of Teachers of English——NCTE

The truth is that every single lesson plan reinforces most of the national standards in English, so it is not necessary to break them down into lists, but it is important that teachers are familiar with the standards:

NCTE 1. Students read a wide range of print and non-print texts to build an understanding of texts, of themselves, and of the cultures of the United States and the world; to acquire new information; to respond to the needs and demands of society and the workplace; and for personal fulfillment. Among these texts are fiction and nonfiction, classic and contemporary works.

NCTE 2. Students read a wide range of literature from many periods in many genres to build an understanding of the many dimensions (e.g., philosophical, ethical, aesthetic) of human experience.

NCTE 3. Students apply a wide range of strategies to comprehend, interpret, evaluate, and appreciate texts. They draw on their prior experience, their interactions with other readers and writers, their knowledge of word meaning and of other texts, their word identification strategies, and their understanding of textual features (e.g., sound-letter correspondence, sentence structure, context, graphics).

NCTE 4. Students adjust their use of spoken, written, and visual language (e.g., conventions, style, vocabulary) to communicate effectively with a variety of audiences and for different purposes.

NCTE 5. Students employ a wide range of strategies as they write and use different writing process elements appropriately to communicate with different audiences for a variety of purposes.

NCTE 6. Students apply knowledge of language structure, language conventions (e.g., spelling and punctuation), media techniques, figurative language, and genre to create, critique, and discuss print and non-print texts.

NCTE 7. Students conduct research on issues and interests by generating ideas and questions, and by posing problems. They gather, evaluate, and synthesize data from a variety of sources (e.g., print and non-print texts, artifacts, people) to communicate their discoveries in ways that suit their purpose and audience.

NCTE 8. Students use a variety of technological and information resources (e.g., libraries, databases, computer networks, video) to gather and synthesize information and to create and communicate knowledge.

NCTE 9. Students develop an understanding of and respect for diversity in language use, patterns, and dialects across cultures, ethnic groups, geographic regions, and social roles.

NCTE 10. Students whose first language is not English make use of their first language to develop competency in the English language arts and to develop understanding of content across the curriculum.

NCTE 11. Students participate as knowledgeable, reflective, creative, and critical members of a variety of literacy communities.

NCTE 12. Students use spoken, written, and visual language to accomplish their own purposes (e.g., for learning, enjoyment, persuasion, and the exchange of information).

National Council for the Social Studies—NCSS

Here is the list of national standards in Social Studies with a detailed explanation of each goal and story titles of the lesson plans that match an important aspect of the standard.

NCSS 1. CULTURE—The study of culture prepares students to answer questions such as: What are the common characteristics of different cultures? How do belief systems, such as religion or political ideals, influence other parts of the culture? How does the culture change to accommodate different ideas and beliefs? What does language tell us about the culture? In schools, this theme typically appears in units and courses dealing with geography, history, sociology, and anthropology, as well as multicultural topics across the curriculum.

The Stone Cutter

Buffalo Brothers

Fun with Fables

Eternal Love

The Great Race

Prairie Fire!

Rowing the Ohio

Watkawes

The Talking Yam

NCSS 2. TIME, CONTINUITY, AND CHANGE—Human beings seek to understand their historical roots and to locate themselves in time. Knowing how to read and reconstruct the past allows one to develop a historical perspective and to answer questions such as: Who am I? What happened in the past? How am I connected to those in the past? How has the world changed and how might it change in the future? Why does our personal sense of relatedness to the past change? This theme typically appears in courses in history and others that draw upon historical knowledge and habits.

Eternal Love

Prairie Fire!

Rowing the Ohio

George Rogers Clark

A Flint Arrowhead

Watkawes

NCSS 3. PEOPLE, PLACES, AND ENVIRONMENTS—The study of people, places, and human-environment interactions assists students as they create their spatial views and geographic perspectives of the world beyond their personal locations. Students need the knowledge, skills, and understanding to answer questions such as: Where are things located? Why are they located where they are? What do we mean by" "region"? How do landforms change? What implications do these changes have for people? In schools, this theme typically appears in units and courses dealing with area studies and geography.

The Stonec utter

Buffalo Brothers

George Rogers Clark

A Flint Arrowhead

Twin Sisters

The Talking Yam

NCSS 4. INDIVIDUAL DEVELOPMENT AND IDENTITY—Personal identity is shaped by one's culture, by groups, and by institutional influences. Students should consider such questions as: How do people learn? Why do people behave as they do? What influences how people learn, perceive, and grow? How do people meet their basic needs in a variety of contexts? How do individuals develop from youth to adulthood? In schools, this theme typically appears in units and courses dealing with psychology and anthropology.

Buzzard Baked Beans

Prairie Fire!

NCSS 5. INDIVIDUALS, GROUPS AND INSTITUTIONS—Institutions such as schools, churches, families, government agencies, and the courts play an integral role in people's lives. It is important that students learn how institutions are formed, what controls and influences them, how they influence individuals and culture, and how they are maintained or changed. Students may address questions such as: What is the role of institutions in this and other societies? How am I influenced by institutions? How do institutions change? What is my role in institutional change? In schools this theme typically appears in units and courses dealing with sociology, anthropology, psychology, political science, and history.

Watkawes

NCSS 6. POWER, AUTHORITY AND GOVERNANCE—Understanding the historical development of structures of power, authority, and governance and their evolving functions in contemporary U.S. society and other parts of the world is essential for developing civic competence. In exploring this theme, students confront questions such as: What is power? What forms does it take? Who holds it? How is it gained, used, and justified? What is legitimate authority? How are governments created, structured, maintained, and changed? How can individual rights be protected within the context of majority rule? In schools, this theme typically appears in units and courses dealing with government, politics, political science, history, law, and other social sciences.

Watkawes

The Talking Yam

NCSS 7. PRODUCTION, DISTRIBUTION, AND CONSUMPTION—Because people have wants that often exceed the resources available to them, a variety of ways have evolved to answer such questions as: What is to be produced? How is production to be organized? How are goods and services to be distributed? What is the most effective allocation of the factors of production (land, labor, capital, and management)? In schools, this theme typically appears in units and courses dealing with economic concepts and issues.

A Flint Arrowhead

A Father's Gift of Camels

The Talking Yam

NCSS 8. SCIENCE, TECHNOLOGY AND SOCIETY—Modern life as we know it would be impossible without technology and the science that supports it. But technology brings with it many questions: Is new technology always better than old? What can we learn from the past about how new technologies result in broader social change, some of which is unanticipated? How can we cope with the ever-increasing pace of change? How can we manage technology so that the greatest number of people benefit from it? How can we preserve our fundamental values and beliefs in the midst of technological change? This theme draws upon the natural and physical sciences, social sciences, and the humanities, and appears in a variety of social studies courses, including history, geography, economics, civics, and government.

   A Flint Arrowhead

NCSS 9. GLOBAL CONNECTIONS—The realities of global interdependence require understanding the increasingly important and diverse global connections among world societies and the frequent tension between national interests and global priorities. Students will need to be able to address such international issues as health care, the environment, human rights, economic competition and interdependence, age-old ethnic enmities, and political and military alliances. This theme typically appears in units or courses dealing with geography, culture, and economics, but may also draw upon the natural and physical sciences and the humanities.

   Fun with Fables

   The Great Race

   Walter the Water Molecule

   The Talking Yam

NCSS 10. CIVIC IDEALS AND PRACTICES—An understanding of civic ideals and practices of citizenship is critical to full participation in society and is a central purpose of the social studies. Students confront such questions as: What is civic participation and how can I be involved? How has the meaning of citizenship evolved? What is the balance between rights and responsibilities? What is the role of the citizen in the community and the nation, and as a member of the world community? How can I make a positive difference? In schools, this theme typically appears in units or courses dealing with history, political science, cultural anthropology, and fields such as global studies, law-related education, and the humanities.

National Academy of Sciences—NAS

NAS 1. Science as Inquiry: Abilities necessary to do scientific inquiry; Understandings about scientific inquiry.

   Twin Sisters

   The Cottonwood

   Whooping Crane's Migration

Ruby-Throated Hummingbird

Mon-Daw-Min

NAS 2. Physical Science: Properties and changes of properties in matter; Motions and forces; Transfer of energy

Walter the Water Molecule

Postcards from Mars

NAS 3. Life Science: Structure and function in living systems; Reproduction and heredity; Regulation and behavior; Populations and ecosystems; Diversity and adaptations of organisms.

A Day at the Zoo

The Great Race

Prairie Fire!

The Cottonwood

Walter the Water Molecule

Whooping Crane's Migration

The Ruby-Throated Hummingbird

Mon-Daw-Min

The Talking Yam

NAS 4. Earth and Space Science: Structure of the earth system; Earth's history; Earth in the solar system

Twin Sisters

Postcards from Mars

The Talking Yam

NAS 5. Science and Technology: Abilities of technological design; Understanding about science and technology; Abilities to distinguish between natural objects and objects made by humans

Postcards from Mars

NAS 6. Science in Personal and Social Perspectives: Personal health; Populations, resources, and environments; Natural hazards; Risks and benefits; Science and technology in society

A Day at the Zoo

Prairie Fire!

The Cottonwood

Walter the Water Molecule

NAS 7. History and Nature of Science: Science as a human endeavor; Nature of science; History of science

National Council of Teachers of Mathematics—NCTM

NCTM 1. Numbers and Operations—Instructional programs from prekindergarten through grade 12 should enable all students to: understand numbers, ways of representing numbers, relationships among numbers, and number systems; understand meanings of operations and how they relate to one another; compute fluently and make reasonable estimates.

    The End of the World

    Dividing the Goose

    A Father's Gift of Camels

    The Talking Yam

NCTM 2. Algebra—Instructional programs from prekindergarten through grade 12 should enable all students to: understand patterns, relations, and functions; represent and analyze mathematical situations and structures using algebraic symbols; use mathematical models to represent and understand quantitative relationships; analyze change in various contexts.

    Dividing the Goose

    A Father's Gift of Camels

NCTM 3. Geometry—Instructional programs from prekindergarten through grade 12 should enable all students to: analyze characteristics and properties of two- and three-dimensional geometric shapes and develop mathematical arguments about geometric relationships; specify locations and describe spatial relationships using coordinate geometry and other representational systems; apply transformations and use symmetry to analyze mathematical situations; use visualization, spatial reasoning, and geometric modeling to solve problems.

NCTM 4. Measurement—Instructional programs from prekindergarten through grade 12 should enable all students to: understand measurable attributes of objects and the units, systems, and processes of measurement; apply appropriate techniques, tools, and formulas to determine measurements.

    Dividing the Goose

NCTM 5. Data Analysis and Probability—Instructional programs from prekindergarten through grade 12 should enable all students to: formulate questions that can be addressed with data and collect, organize, and display relevant data to answer them; select and use appropriate statistical methods to analyze data; develop and evaluate inferences and predictions that are based on data; understand and apply basic concepts of probability.

NCTM 6. Problem Solving—Instructional programs from prekindergarten through grade 12 should enable all students to: build new mathematical knowledge through problem solving; solve problems that arise in mathematics and in other contexts; apply and adapt a variety of appropriate strategies to solve problems; monitor and reflect on the process of mathematical problem solving.

Postcards from Mars

Dividing the Goose

A Father's Gift of Camels

The Talking Yam

NCTM 7. Reasoning and Proof—Instructional programs from prekindergarten through grade 12 should enable all students to: recognize reasoning and proof as fundamental aspects of mathematics; make and investigate mathematical conjectures; develop and evaluate mathematical arguments and proofs; select and use various types of reasoning and methods of proof.

Dividing the Goose

NCTM 8. Communication—Instructional programs from prekindergarten through grade 12 should enable all students to: organize and consolidate their mathematical thinking though communication; communicate their mathematical thinking coherently and clearly to peers, teachers, and others; analyze and evaluate the mathematical thinking and strategies of others; use the language of mathematics to express mathematical ideas precisely.

The End of the World

Dividing the Goose

The Talking Yam

NCTM 9. Connections—Instructional programs from prekindergarten through grade 12 should enable all students to: recognize and use connections among mathematical ideas; understand how mathematical ideas interconnect and build on one another to produce a coherent whole; recognize and apply mathematics in contexts outside of mathematics.

The End of the World

Dividing the Goose

The Talking Yam

NCTM 10. Representation—Instructional programs from prekindergarten through grade 12 should enable all students to: create and use representations to organize, record, and communicate mathematical ideas; select, apply, and translate among mathematical representations to solve problems; use representations to model and interpret physical, social, and mathematical phenomena.

Postcards from Mars

Index

About the Author

Brian "Fox" Ellis

Since 1980, Brian "Fox" Ellis, storyteller, author, and educator, has been touring the world collecting and telling stories. He has been a keynote speaker and featured workshop presenter at hundreds of conferences ranging from the International Wetlands Conservation Conference to the National Association of Gifted Educators Conference. His presentations are always custom-tailored with a mix of pedagogy and practice, humor and inspiration. From the New Mexico Academy of Science to the Michigan Reading Teachers Conference many of the state educational conferences invite him back on a regular basis! He has also published ten books, including the award winning children's picture book, *The Web at Dragonfly Pond*. His DVDs are

some of the most award-winning children's storytelling DVDs ever produced. He has written 20 musical theatre productions as the artistic director of Prairie Folklore Theatre. Fox is a frequent contributor to a wide range of magazines including trade journals, parenting, academic, and general interest magazines. Fox works extensively as a museum consultant with centers large and small, ranging from the Field Museum and Abraham Lincoln Presidential Library to the Macon County Historical Society and Mary Gray Bird Sanctuary in Indiana. His artist-in-residency programs have won honors from the North Carolina PTA where he created a year-long position as the Storyteller in Residence for the Charlotte-Mecklenburg School District.

Please visit his Web page for more information about booking a program: **www. foxtalesint.com.**